RISEN INDEED

A Historical Investigation into the
Resurrection of Jesus

RISEN INDEED

A Historical Investigation into the
Resurrection of Jesus

Gary R. Habermas

Risen Indeed: A Historical Investigation into the Resurrection of Jesus

Copyright 2021 Gary R. Habermas

Originally published as *The Resurrection of Jesus: A Rational Inquiry* (Ann Arbor, MI: University Microfilms, 1976).

Lexham Academic, an imprint of Lexham Press
1313 Commercial St., Bellingham, WA 98225
LexhamPress.com

Print ISBN 9781683595496
Digital ISBN 9781683595502
Library of Congress Control Number 2021939394

Lexham Editorial: David Bomar, Jesse Myers, Jenny-Lyn de Klerk, Abigail Stocker, Danielle Thevenaz
Cover Design: Joshua Hunt, Brittany Schrock
Typesetting: ProjectLuz.com

To DEBBIE
My love, my closest earthly friend and my wife,
whose own love for me was revealed even more by
her diligence in typing this dissertation.

CONTENTS

PART 3

AN EVALUATION OF THE SOLUTIONS TO
THE QUESTION OF THE RESURRECTION OF JESUS

Acknowledgments

S pecial thanks to my PhD students Scott Steven Hyland and Stephen Scott Jordan for their work on the index for this new edition.

Introduction

My PhD dissertation on the resurrection of Jesus was completed while I was a student at Michigan State University. It was published soon afterward, in 1976, by University Microfilms.[1] I will begin here with some autobiographical comments that provide background to my dissertation. Since then, a remarkable number of volumes, essays, articles, and reviews have appeared addressing the many aspects of the crucially important topic of Jesus' resurrection. The majority of this introduction consists of extended comments on the recent state of resurrection research, chiefly since 1976.

MY RELIGIOUS DOUBTS

Having published and lectured on my story on perhaps hundreds of occasions, I will write a brief account here. Though I was raised in a Christian home and attended a German Baptist church in the Detroit area, my young faith took a real hit when the closest person in my life, my great-grandmother, died when I was a child. I was plunged into fears and doubts that I did not know existed in the world. What happens to our loved ones when they die? What about us? Years later, I started down the path of rather dogged religious doubt, which did not abate during ten straight years of ardent questioning, followed by another ten years of intermittent uncertainty, lasting even beyond the completion of my dissertation.

Friends came alongside me during the early years to share what they thought were surefire ways to know that Christianity was true. However, after listening to them and then studying each of these suggested options, I concluded that while some of these evidential trails were potentially

---

1. University Microfilms has since changed its name to ProQuest.

1

worthwhile in one way or another, some more than others, it was still the case that none of these paths could bear the promised weight of the Christian faith.

During this time, I visited other religious sites and places of worship in my area and across the country. Countless hours were spent in public and university libraries, acquiring and studying sources that favored the opposing viewpoints. Throughout this process I debated all sorts of religious ideas and persons, Christian and non-Christian alike, in a constant search for any particular religious system that could be acknowledged as being largely true.

For instance, I specifically recall marching into a Christian professor's office one day and challenging his arguments for the inspiration of Scripture. After disputing at length each of his ideas, probably doing so a little too stridently, I walked out, absolutely convinced that I had easily gotten the best of the argument. A fellow skeptic who had accompanied me into the office readily agreed that there had been no contest. Actually, I was quite bothered that an exceptionally well-trained theologian would have no better basis for his beliefs in the truth of Christianity than what he had presented. After hearing that I had rejected the inspiration of Scripture, another student confronted me in the hallway and told me rather forcefully that I was possessed by seven demons, turned abruptly, and walked away.

At that time, my life consisted largely of sports and incessant personal study related to my doubts. One day while reading, it occurred to me that *if* Jesus had been raised from the dead—especially based on what even critical scholars acknowledged were the accredited facts—and *if* a pared down list of Jesus' central teachings could be established similarly, then this combination could possibly ground the truth of the central teachings of Christianity. But I had no idea if the resurrection could stand the test of potential skeptical assaults. These questions marked the beginning stages of the issues that I later pursued in detail in my dissertation.

At this point, the reader could be forgiven for concluding that this insight on my part regarding the potential for such a resurrection study probably provided the light I needed at the end of the tunnel—and that after I worked out the details concerning the evidence for the resurrection of Jesus, all would be right in the world once again! But that would be far from the case. Actually, the mere recognition of such a possible path for the resurrection case did not lead to the final resolution of my resurrection doubts until many years afterward. They were not fully resolved until long after my initial 1,600 note cards on the subject and, later, the dissertation itself!

After much of my initial study, prior to doing my PhD, I concluded that one of the naturalistic theories stubbornly refused to be discarded. While the resurrection could be accepted by faith, it could not be known to be true historically. That halted my resurrection research for the time being. During this interlude, I considered whether there might not be an afterlife. Many years later, a professional Christian philosopher commented to me, somewhat disapprovingly, that he could tell David Hume had made a big impression on me during my studies. I could have added the names of David Strauss and especially Rudolf Bultmann, my constant reading and dialogue partners.

Still, my worst two episodes with doubt were still ahead of me and actually came long after my PhD had been completed. It is the second of these that I have spoken of often: I thought I was close to walking away from Christianity altogether and embracing a scientific version of Buddhism.

Over the years since that time, there was something I wished for more than anything else. I often hoped that someone would come along beside me and explain that not all doubt is created equal. There are definitely different species of uncertainty, and studies indicate that the most common variety is not factual doubt but emotional doubt. The latter is also the most painful kind.[2] To be sure, the vast majority of my doubt at that time was factual, but emotional elements had begun to creep into the picture. Yet there were few publications on these topics to which I could turn, so I felt as if I would simply have to keep working at it on my own.

Fast forward to years later, after my first book on the subject of doubt had been published, when my wife became ill. The diagnosis changed from the flu to the much-dreaded verdict of stomach cancer. Just a few

---

2. Years later, I began lecturing and publishing about these types of doubt: Habermas, *Dealing with Doubt* (Chicago: Moody, 1990); *The Thomas Factor: Using Your Doubts to Grow Closer to God* (Nashville: Broadman & Holman, 1999); and *Why is God Ignoring Me? What to Do When It Feels Like He's Giving You the Silent Treatment* (Carol Stream, IL: Tyndale, 2010). The first two of these volumes are freely available on my website, www.garyhabermas.com, under the books tab.

short months later, in August 1995, my wife—the mother of our four children, and my very best friend in the world—died. At that time, I told my closest friends that the worst possible suffering I could ever imagine had indeed come upon me. Having struggled years before past the long time of doubt, I feared that, on top of everything else, her sickness and death would reawaken those issues. That's a story in itself.[3] Thankfully, the doubts never returned after my wife's death. It was as if the deaths of the two people who were the closest to me—my great-grandmother and my wife—at those junctions in my early and later life served as bookends to my doubt.

THE MINIMAL FACTS METHODOLOGY
IN RESURRECTION RESEARCH

Chiefly due to my previous doubts surrounding the subject of Jesus' resurrection and my search for a foundation for religious belief, I had learned to depend less on responses that were based chiefly on conservative apologetic answers, since these were frequently unacceptable to more critical researchers. For example, conservatives and some moderates tended to rely much more on eyewitness testimony of the sources and the authors of the Gospels, whereas more skeptical researchers usually would not grant such conclusions. The latter preferred what were judged to be the highly attested epistles of Paul.[4]

Of course, I realized that it did not follow that these skeptical objections were themselves true simply because they were frequently expressed in a negative, challenging manner. These critical positions also had to be established by solid arguments and could likewise be mistaken. But I still sided with the skeptical responses, to the extent that above all I was interested in discovering whether any positive answers could address even such skeptical doubts.

---

3. Gary R. Habermas, *Forever Loved: A Personal Account of Grief and Resurrection* (Joplin, MO: College Press, 1997).

4. The vast majority of more critical scholars agree in identifying the authentic epistles of Paul as these seven: Romans, 1 and 2 Corinthians, Galatians, Philippians, 1 Thessalonians, and Philemon. Bart Ehrman refers to these seven texts as "undisputed" (Ehrman, *The New Testament: A Historical Introduction to the Early Christian Writings*, 2nd ed. [Oxford: Oxford University Press, 2000], 262, 290).

Therefore, early in my doubting I determined that, as much as possible, it would be better to base the most crucial responses on the very strongest critical data. Although fewer total arguments were addressed in that manner, the results were grounded by stronger reasons. This approach attained both a more solid basis for my own personal knowledge and achieved a greater impact in discussions with others. Moreover, all sides recognized this core, critical material. It was the way critical scholars argued, and while conservatives would posit a greater amount of data, the former researchers also recognized and accepted what was arrived at by more stringent methods.

In arguing for the resurrection, then, the strongest constructed case would rely much more on the short list of undisputed Pauline epistles than on the Gospels. And during the times when the Gospels were employed, it was best done by utilizing the more carefully established information from those volumes.

During one of my more advanced research sessions, while studying the particular naturalistic hypothesis that Jesus' resurrection could be accounted for by pre-Christian dying and rising tales or by other versions of legendary accretions, I compiled a list of the very surest refutations. Each of these responses was based on the minimal data accepted by virtually all researchers, due to the strength of the accompanying reasons in its favor. The hard-hitting and establishable nature of these data was precisely why the majority of scholars were on board with the refutations. Hence, the case was at least potentially established via the sturdiest arguments. However, strictly due to the strength of the arguments, scholars across the spectrum would also more or less agree with the reasons listed for rejecting this alternative hypothesis, such as the strict absence of such pre-Christian accounts, the pre-Pauline New Testament creeds, the relevant language being that of persons who actually saw the appearances, the empty tomb, transformed lives, and so on. And in a side comment in the notes for this research session, I remarked that even when addressing the most skeptical commentators of all, a truncated list of these facts could be constructed to refute the alternative view![5]

---

5. This list of minimal refutations remains in my files to this day and is dated just a few years prior to the completion of my dissertation.

Again, it could be thought that this realization might have catapulted me into the final phase of my doubts. But that was once more not the case. My doubts remained for years, continuing even past this time. However, this was the beginning of utilizing the methodological standards that would become my "minimal facts" approach.

After my wife died and my doubts had subsided significantly, I published more on the resurrection of Jesus, moving toward employing almost exclusively the basic, underlying data. I began referring to this move as utilizing the historical "core" or the "minimal facts." The more crucial the subject being discussed, the more I preferred this succinct and technical approach. This methodology was developed in my PhD dissertation, where it was applied specifically to studies of Jesus' resurrection.

To be sure, arguments from the Gospels were also used in the dissertation, but this was done more selectively—particularly when there were more reasons to be careful. But never was an argument based on the assumption that such-and-such must be true solely because it is found in the New Testament ("Because the Bible tells me so!"), as if that alone were a sufficient basis to verify the assumption, for that would be circular reasoning and thus insufficient. But the approach in the dissertation was also layered: the data gleaned from the Gospels could come into greater use in order to appeal to more moderate or conservative scholars. But to repeat, the most powerful facts in an argument were quite often those that were drawn from the Pauline corpus and other, very select, sources.[6] The minimal facts resurrection argument had been born.

THE THIRD QUEST FOR THE
HISTORICAL JESUS

About the same time as my PhD dissertation was being completed, a new trend in contemporary theology was being born. Dubbed by N. T. Wright

---

6. A couple of items need to be carefully noted here. These last comments, just like many in this introduction, are not to deny that any number of considerations from the Gospels or elsewhere could turn out to be stronger than the more narrowly established arguments. I imagine that many critical scholars would agree with this comment. But again, virtually all sides recognize the narrower, critically-derived research. Further, much of what I am describing throughout this introduction reflects where I was *at that specific time* in my thoughts and in my research, along with my doubts. So that is not to say that I would reiterate all of these opinions now, as already stated elsewhere in this introduction. These are crucial distinctions to be made.

as the "Third Quest for the Historical Jesus,"[7] this movement has dominated much of recent New Testament thought ever since. The famous German liberal "First Quest for the Historical Jesus" of the nineteenth and early twentieth centuries lasted over a century, as summarized admirably by Albert Schweitzer.[8] Afterward came a hiatus that is often referred to as the "No Quest" reign of Karl Barth and Rudolf Bultmann, among others, when the role of historical research was downplayed even among scholars who generally held quite different views. This time was followed, in turn, by the "Second Quest for the Historical Jesus," a much more limited, relatively short-lived movement that was birthed by several of Bultmann's own students.[9]

Unlike the earlier explorations, the overall thrust of the Third Quest participants has been anchored firmly and centrally in interpreting Jesus and his teachings against the Jewish milieu of the time just prior to and current with Jesus. There were still different interpretations of Jesus within this framework, as pointed out in detail by many researchers, including Ben Witherington III.[10] As Witherington states concerning the Third Quest, "One thing is clear—a non-Jewish Jesus is a non-sequitur. Jesus must make sense within his historical context ... studying the life of Jesus in his first-century setting."[11]

This reliance on a strong Jewish background and flavor is apparent in all of Witherington's scholarly categories except that of Jesus actually being a Hellenistic cynic sage, a thesis that is held by a number of members of the Jesus Seminar. The majority of historical Jesus researchers, liberal

7. N. T. Wright, "Towards a Third 'Quest'? Jesus Then and Now," ARC 10, no. 1 (1982): 20–27. Wright makes a later reference to this article in "Jesus, Israel and the Cross," in SBL 1985 Seminar Papers, edited by K. H. Richards (Chico, CA: Scholars Press), 75–95. Wright also discussed at an early date a number of pertinent details regarding the Third Quest; see Stephen Neill and Tom Wright, The Interpretation of the New Testament: 1861–1986, 2nd ed. (Oxford: Oxford University Press, 1988), 288n1, 379–403.

8. Albert Schweitzer, The Quest of the Historical Jesus: A Critical Study of Its Progress from Reimarus to Wrede, trans. W. Montgomery (1906; repr., New York: Macmillan, 1968).

9. James M. Robinson, A New Quest of the Historical Jesus, Studies in Biblical Theology 25 (London: SCM, 1959).

10. Many of these examples are summarized by Ben Witherington, with supporting scholars listed in each category, concluding that Jesus was exemplified best as a cynic philosopher, a man of the Spirit, an eschatological prophet, a prophet of social change, the wisdom of God, or as a Jewish messianic figure. See Ben Witherington III, The Jesus Quest: The Third Search for the Jew of Nazareth (Downers Grove, IL: InterVarsity Press, 1995), with a summarized listing, closing words, and critique in chapter 9.

11. Witherington III, The Jesus Quest, 41.

or conservative, would reject such a notion out of hand. But the Jesus Seminar is a radical group of scholars that differs quite drastically from other Third Questers in many of its methods and conclusions. Similarly, and among the most noticeable items, the Seminar deals more with non-Jewish categories for Jesus—distinct from virtually all of the other Third Questers. As a result, many scholars, including a number of Third Questers, criticize the Seminar quite severely, both on these more general matters as well as because their overall approach places their ideas outside the realm of the Third Quest altogether. Wright is not alone in thinking that the Jesus Seminar is better characterized as a holdover position from the Second Quest that separated from Bultmann rather than as part of the Third Quest.[12] The point of this brief critique of the Jesus Seminar will be more obvious below.

None of the earlier groups identified above—the First, Second, and No Quest adherents—concentrated primarily on the Jewishness of Jesus and his ideas. Rather, each of these movements largely reflected the philosophical milieus of their day: German idealism plus the advent of more sophisticated biblical criticism in the case of German liberalism, followed by historical skepticism and existentialist theory in at least the earlier forms of both the No Quest and Second Quest periods. The Third Quest movement is perhaps best known today for the world-class scholars involved and their unequalled literary output, especially as viewed from the angle of their major sets of tomes and other massive studies devoted to the Jewishness of Jesus and related areas.[13] The sheer quantity of information being communicated in recent years could take a lifetime of study to digest! This emphasis on a specific Jewish starting point has taken many

---

12. For various critiques of the Jesus Seminar, especially Wright's, see *Jesus and the Victory of God*, vol. 2 of *Christian Origins and the Question of God* (Minneapolis: Fortress, 1996), 29–45, 78–82; also Neill and Wright, *The Interpretation of the New Testament*, 288, 379, 397–98; Ehrman, *The New Testament*, 236; Luke Timothy Johnson, *The Real Jesus: The Misguided Quest for the Historical Jesus and the Truth of the Traditional Gospels* (New York: HarperSanFrancisco, 1996), see chapter 1, especially pages 1, 5, 8, 25, 95–101; James D. G. Dunn, "Remembering Jesus: How the Quest of Jesus Lost its Way," in *The Historical Jesus: Five Views*, eds. James K. Beilby and Paul R. Eddy (Downers Grove, IL: IVP Academic, 2009), 221–23.

13. A few examples of these huge sets of research include John P. Meier's five volume study, *A Marginal Jew: Rethinking the Historical Jesus* (New Haven, CT: Yale University Press, 1991–2016), James D. G. Dunn's three large texts, *Christianity in the Making* (Eerdmans, 2003–2015), as well as N. T. Wright's four volume investigation, *Christian Origins and the Question of God* (Fortress, 1992–2013).

researchers into studies of the New Testament writers and their works, the earliest church and what was taught by its leaders, and whether there is any factual confirmation of their primary teachings and claims.

By the very nature of studying Jesus' contemporary Jewish environment in relation to his life and teachings, the research produced by the Third Quest over the past forty-five years or so has tended to be generally more moderate or even conservative in many of its responses and outcomes, especially compared to its predecessors in the earlier movements.[14] As will be pointed out below, even the most critical scholars in the Third Quest are milder than the more critical members of the older movements!

A comparison and contrast on a crucial subject may be helpful in demarcating these differences between the earlier scholars and the more recent ones. Rudolf Bultmann freely recognized the presence of dozens of very early creedal teachings, both in the form of key phrases as well as longer statements, drawn from a variety of New Testament authors and writings.[15] These originally oral statements clearly predated the New Testament writings in which they were embedded, as even Bultmann allowed without question. He referred to many of these early traditions as pre-Pauline liturgical formulas and traditions, identifying them with adjectives such as "old," "quite early," "crystalized," and "highly schematic"—with at least some of them even going back geographically to Jerusalem, and with their very origination being the "earliest church."[16]

However, though Bultmann recognized the presence of these data, his theoretical allegiance largely favored the remnants of the First Quest's *religionsgeschichtliche Schule*—with its reliance on non-Jewish, largely Hellenistic influences on Christianity—in addition to sporting

---

14. This depends in part on which camp the Jesus Seminar was thought to belong. But even if grouped with the Third Quest scholars, the basic conclusion above regarding the at least somewhat more conservative trajectory would still hold true, if to a lesser degree, both because of the strong criticisms of the Seminar made by the other Third Quest scholars, as well as the fact that some members of the Jesus Seminar themselves weighed in separately on these research areas, as will be seen below.

15. Even as a partial list of the large numbers of these early traditions, Bultmann cites the following two dozen passages, among many others that are also found in his works: John 12:32; Acts 1:22; 2:33; 3:15; 5:30; 9:14; 10:40–41; 13:34; 22:16; Rom 1:3–4; 3:24; 4:25; 10:9; 1 Cor 11:23–26; 12:3; 15:3f.; 16:22b; Phil 2:6–11; 2 Tim 2:8; 2:22; 4:18; Jas 2:7; Rev 5:9–10, 12; 22:20 (Rudolf Bultmann, *Theology of the New Testament*, vol. 1, trans. Kendrick Grobel [New York: Charles Scribner's Sons, 1951, 1955], 46–47, 82–83, 125–26, 293–94, 312).

16. Bultmann, *Theology of the New Testament*, vol. 1, 46–52, 80–83, 294–96.

a prior rejection of supernatural events.[17] Therefore, in spite of arguing that these creedal traditions indeed emanated from the earliest Jewish church, Bultmann decided that they were largely derived from Hellenistic thought—borrowed from notions of the gnostic redeemer myth![18]

How did these foreign myths and other ideas infiltrate the earliest church, overpowering the apostolic memories of Jesus' teachings and, most of all, doing so from the very beginning of New Testament history? This seems to be especially difficult to entertain when Jewish views would be in much closer geographical proximity and drawn from a stronger religious context. Further, the latter is particularly the case in the detailed defenses of these creedal traditions that had already appeared from major researchers during Bultmann's career and that were strongly opposed to his ideas on this subject.[19]

The Third Quest scholars readily agreed with Bultmann and similar researchers that the nature of the data indicated that these numerous creedal texts were indeed present in the writings of several New Testament authors and did originate in the earliest church. However, they disagreed with the ideas of Bultmann and other scholars in related camps that these traditions were Hellenistic in nature. Since at least some of these creeds were traceable to Jerusalem in the earliest times after Jesus, many of the Third Quest scholars concluded that the clearest and most direct route of origination would entail that, rather than having been imported from Hellenistic sources, such early information in Jerusalem would have emanated from and been chiefly concerned with more general Jewish roots plus Jesus' teachings. This realization amounted to discovering a veritable

---

17. The latter point of Bultmann's rejection of any actual supernatural or miraculous events are found throughout his many works, including *Theology of the New Testament*, vol. 1, 45, 83, 295; "New Testament and Mythology," in *Kerygma and Myth: A Theological Debate*, ed. Hans Werner Bartsch, rev. trans. Reginald H. Fuller (New York: Harper & Row, 1961), 4–5, 34–35, 38–43; *Jesus Christ and Mythology* (New York: Charles Scribner's Sons, 1958), 61–62, 71–72, 80, 84.

18. Bultmann, *Theology of the New Testament*, vol. 1, 51–52, 295, 298–99, 302, 345–46; also, Bultmann, *Jesus Christ and Mythology*, especially 16–17.

19. These volumes included Oscar Cullmann, *The Earliest Christian Confessions*, ed. Gary R. Habermas and Benjamin Charles Shaw (London: Lutterworth, 1949; repr., Eugene, OR: Wipf and Stock, 2018), especially 13, 16, 49–50, 53, 56–58; C. H. Dodd, *The Apostolic Preaching and its Developments* (London: Hodder and Stoughton, 1936; repr., Grand Rapids, MI: Baker, 1980), 11, 15–34; Vernon H. Neufeld, *The Earliest Christian Confessions*, ed. Bruce M. Metzger, New Testament Tools and Studies (Grand Rapids, MI: Eerdmans, 1963), especially 8–12, 140–46; Max Wilcox, *The Semitisms in Acts* (Oxford: Oxford University Press, 1965), particularly 79–80, 163–67, 171–79.

historical gold mine, clearly indicating that these texts provided useful data concerning the events and teachings that formed the basis of Christian beliefs.

Further, these Third Quest researchers rejected almost uniformly the various strands of the larger *religionsgeschichtliche Schule* movement and similar Hellenistic or other pagan conclusions that went back to the late nineteenth-century German studies. After Bultmann's death in 1976, these older interpretations took a rather precipitous plummet, especially after the realization that there was actually an incredible dearth of material to support the argument that there never was a pre-Christian gnostic redeemer myth in the first place.[20] James D. G. Dunn sums up the matter thusly: "The problem with all this has been that the full-blown Gnostic redeemer myth here inferred is nowhere clearly attested before the Second Century CE." Then Dunn adds that "the first redeemer figures as such do not appear till the second century—probably Christianity's contribution to syncretistic Gnosticism!"[21]

So, as Dunn hints, could Christianity have not only pre-dated these gnostic redeemer stories but even encouraged their rise? Because of the failure to engage this crucial data—among many other issues—the pendulum of research swung far away from the Hellenistic views of the older *religionsgeschichtliche Schule*, Bultmann, and others.[22]

---

20. Some researchers even asserted that the critics who were losing their influence either had not studied the contrary literature in the first place or were simply unwilling to engage it. See Edwin M. Yamauchi, *Pre-Christian Gnosticism: A Survey of the Proposed Evidences* (Grand Rapids, MI: Baker, 1983; repr., Eugene, OR: Wipf and Stock, 2003), 163–249 in particular; E. P. Sanders, *Jesus and Judaism* (Philadelphia: Fortress, 1985), 29; Larry W. Hurtado, *How on Earth Did Jesus Become a God?* (Grand Rapids, MI: Eerdmans, 2005), particularly 18.

21. James D. G. Dunn, *Beginning from Jerusalem*, vol. 2 (Grand Rapids, MI: Eerdmans, 2009), 41.

22. As expressed so well by Carl H. Holladay, *Theios Aner in Hellenistic Judaism: A Critique of the Use of the Category in New Testament Christology*, Society of Biblical Literature Dissertation Series 40, ed. Howard C. Kee and Douglas A. Knight (Missoula, MT: Scholars Press for The Society of Biblical Literature, 1977), especially 1–14, 44, 235–42; Larry W. Hurtado, "New Testament Christology: A Critique of Bousset's Influence," *Theological Studies* 40 (1979): 306–17; Hurtado, *How on Earth Did Jesus Become a God?*, 16–20, 24, 37, 47–48; Dunn, *Beginning from Jerusalem*, 36–42, 372–73; Neill and Wright, *The Interpretation of the New Testament*, 365, 369–73, 377; W. D. Davies, *Paul and Rabbinic Judaism: Some Rabbinic Elements in Pauline Theology*, 4th ed. (Philadelphia: Fortress, 1980); Sanders, *Jesus and Judaism*, 26–31; David Wenham, *Paul: Follower of Jesus or Founder of Christianity?* (Grand Rapids, MI: Eerdmans, 1995), 2–13, 17–18. Bart Ehrman presents a detailed critique of some of the more fanciful beliefs regarding ancient pagan incursions in *Did Jesus Exist? The Historical Argument for Jesus of Nazareth* (New York: Harper Collins, 2012), 207–30.

The absence of clear Hellenistic roots influencing the Christian gospel message—combined with the realization that the early creedal traditions that originated in Jerusalem and its environs were most obviously Jewish in nature and were very early indeed—resulted in a growing agreement that these sources provided much crucial material upon which to interpret the very center of earliest Christian theology. In a sense, then, the factors just mentioned—Bultmann's death, the gradual demise of the Second Quest and the turn of the evidence against their ideas, plus the rise of the Third Quest with its emphasis on Jewish backgrounds—provided an impetus for the new direction of research. This focus on Jewish foundations, along with Jesus' teachings, brought these ideas together, most of which pointed to the more moderate or conservative leanings mentioned above. Here is a clear indication that methodological starting points can yield absolutely crucial results!

Fast forward briefly to where the Third Quest is presently, a few decades later, regarding studies of the Christian gospel message. The research on Jesus within his Jewish surroundings has continued in largely the same direction as mentioned above, with a diverse scholarly consensus concluding that the earliest message emerged out of Jerusalem very soon after Jesus' crucifixion. In fact, several researchers such as Richard Bauckham have commented that this is the consensus position at present.[23] But we are moving too quickly now: we need to step back and observe how research arrived at this point from the beginning of the Third Quest for the Historical Jesus.

RESURRECTION STUDIES FROM
1975 TO THE PRESENT

How did the critical study of Jesus' resurrection progress after the completion of my dissertation? During the next thirty years and into the twenty-first century, studies related to the Third Quest continued to develop. In

---

23. Richard Bauckham, *Jesus and the Eyewitnesses: The Gospels as Eyewitness Testimony* (Grand Rapids, MI: Eerdmans, 2006), 264–71; James Ware, "The Resurrection of Jesus in the Pre-Pauline Formula of 1 Cor 15.3–5," *New Testament Studies* 60 (October 2014): 475–98, especially 475, 489. Actually, Reginald H. Fuller drew a similar conclusion in 1979 regarding the "remarkable unanimity" of critical scholars even at that time. Reginald H. Fuller, "The Resurrection Narratives in Recent Study," in *Critical History and Biblical Faith: New Testament Perspectives*, ed. Thomas J. Ryan (Villanova: Villanova University Press, 1979), 91–107, particularly 93–94.

a 1994 volume on the state of parallel studies in Christology during the last portion of the twentieth century, Raymond Brown noted that after the influence of Bultmann's "radical" New Testament research diminished, there was a positional shift to a more moderately conservative Christology, which became the most popular position in that field.[24] This was strongly consistent with a large portion of the Third Quest leanings as well.

Beginning about the same time as the publication of Brown's work and extending over a number of years, I initiated a personal effort that began simply as a modest attempt to update my own dissertation research in order to remain informed on resurrection studies. But the project quickly morphed into a huge exploration of its own. For personal use, I detailed the represented positions in an ongoing documentation that expanded to cover thousands of recent resurrection sources that had been published in German, French, and English. The document grew to several hundred pages. A few years later, with the help of my PhD research assistant who could record the data much more quickly than I could, the study expanded to about 1,500 pages in length! It did not contain reactions to the scholarly views, but simply recorded and specified the various contemporary approaches to about 140 separate but related questions regarding the early source data on the death, burial, and resurrection appearances of Jesus, along with various scholars' jabs at their peers on these subjects.

In an attempt to parallel Brown's treatment of Christological views, I defined two approaches to the crucial question concerning the possible resurrection appearances of Jesus. The moderate/conservative approach was a range of positions which held that, after his death by crucifixion, Jesus appeared in some actual sense—either in a real body of some sort or in a more glorified manner that could still be seen and experienced by his followers. The chief point in the moderate/conservative classification was that this change happened to Jesus himself: he was actually alive. On the other hand, the more liberal or skeptical range of views, whatever the species, held that nothing actually occurred to Jesus himself after his death. Physically speaking, Jesus remained dead. Rather, real internal, subjective changes occurred to his followers. The key issue here is whether the

---

24. Raymond E. Brown, *An Introduction to New Testament Christology* (New York: Paulist, 1994), 4–15, 102.

events in question actually happened to a living Jesus, who was seen in some sense, or whether the occurrences happened internally to the disciples alone, bringing them to a new understanding apart from any real appearances. This distinction formed the watershed demarcation.

I checked my repository of resurrection sources and—after doing a representative survey of scholarly works on the appearances of Jesus published approximately during the same time frame as Brown's Christological study and extended about ten years afterward—published the early results in 2005. According to my classifications above, the indication was that the overall majority position was a general approximation of what Brown had described as a moderate/conservative position.[25]

By way of scholarly differentiation, the German sources tended more toward theological emphases, critiques, and problem-solving discussions, exhibiting a greater variety of both moderate/conservative as well as skeptical approaches. The French writings tended to be less numerous overall, were frequently more exegetical in nature and leaned slightly to the moderate/conservative side. The British publications seemed to entail a larger mixture of views across the entire board; some were fairly conservative while others were quite skeptical. The North American works were the most numerous and encompassed the widest range of positions and nuances, extending from outright skeptical, dismissive views and denials all the way to moderate and conservative positions.[26]

Without any attempts beforehand to arrange the results of the data in any particular manner, a rough estimate from 1975 to 2005 (the date of the article) shows that the combined European sources (German, French, and British) and the North American sources both came to approximately a 3:1 ratio of moderate/conservative to liberal/skeptical publications. Needless to mention, such headcounts at best indicate the scholarly lay of the land; they don't demonstrate anything concerning what may actually have occurred on the occasions of the resurrection appearances.

---

25. Habermas, "Resurrection Research from 1975 to the Present: What are Critical Scholars Saying?," *Journal for the Study of the Historical Jesus*, vol. 3 (2005), 136.

26. Habermas, "Resurrection Research from 1975 to the Present," 136–39.

MAJOR RESURRECTION TRENDS IN
THE EARLY TWENTIETH CENTURY

In the 2005 study on these contemporary resurrection inclinations, I noted six important research trends that had either already emerged or appeared to have developed significantly since 1975. Each of these trends had captured a good portion of the researchers at that time, often across the liberal/conservative divide.[27] These six trends were:

(1) Naturalistic theories seemed to be at least somewhat on the rise. They also were manifest in a considerable amount of variety.[28] The vast majority of scholars opposed these theories and frequently engaged in offering their own comebacks. The combination of these clashes amounted to quite a flurry of debates.

(2) The facticity of the empty tomb was supported by approximately 75 percent of the scholars writing at that time, with a surprising number of arguments—almost two dozen— in favor of this event and with a little over a dozen opposing arguments.

(3) The apostle Paul was accepted across the board by skeptical, moderate, and conservative scholars alike as the strongest witness in favor of the resurrection appearances. Further, the pre-Pauline creedal statement in 1 Corinthians 15:3–7 was viewed by virtually all researchers as the strongest and earliest witness to the resurrection appearances of Jesus. Paul probably received this material when he visited Jerusalem in 35–36 CE to stay with Peter and James, the brother of Jesus, as recorded in Galatians 1:18–20.

(4) The significance of the dozens of early Christian creedal traditions and sermon summaries in Acts, which had already been singled out by Bultmann, had attained a place of growing historical importance. Many more works had appeared on these subjects since Bultmann's time, and the results had bolstered the understanding of the historicity of the earliest Christian beliefs and the growth of the young movement. Bultmann's view that these confessions had emerged from Hellenistic origins had been dispatched by the emerging data.

---

27. Habermas, "Resurrection Research from 1975 to the Present," 140–45.

28. A few years earlier I had also published on this naturalistic development: Habermas, "The Late Twentieth-Century Resurgence of Naturalistic Responses to Jesus' Resurrection," *Trinity Journal* 22 (Fall 2001): 179–96.

(5) A major move among the Third Quest for the Historical Jesus scholars was to acknowledge that, at least among the New Testament's authors, Jesus' resurrection appearances were understood to have been bodily in nature. Thus, even a number of skeptical scholars who rejected the resurrection event still recognized that bodily appearances of some sort were originally taught in the canonical sources.

(6) Virtually all scholars across the theological spectrum held to the application of the resurrection teaching, whether or not such an event actually occurred. The resurrection was interpreted as the primary force that grounded Christian ethics, hope, and belief, either metaphorically or literally. This was a foundational teaching point for Bultmann decades beforehand, including his famous dictum that Jesus was risen in the proclamation of the church. Likewise, it was a central emphasis made enthusiastically in the works of scholars such as John Dominic Crossan, Willi Marxsen, and Marcus Borg, as cited in the 2005 article above.[29]

ONGOING RESURRECTION TRENDS

Since the early twentieth century, some changes have occurred in these six resurrection areas and beyond. The earlier conclusion that the predominant theological ethos of the Third Quest was moderately conservative has arguably been borne out in many studies. That approach has also been increasingly manifested in many resurrection studies.

In the first trend I identified in my initial research observations in 2005, I noted that during the past quarter-century there was an increase in the amount of naturalistic resurrection appearance theories, with a subtle shift that began to transpire during the last couple of decades. The number of scholars who choose a particular alternative thesis at least seems to have been reduced among younger skeptical researchers. When such natural theses are still held strongly by some observers, these theories appear to be held mostly by older skeptics, whereas in the most recent research, fewer of the newer generation of trained skeptics seem to be willing to pick a single natural thesis. This could be due in part to the diminishing

---

29. Habermas, "Resurrection Research from 1975 to the Present," 144–45, 147–48.

influence of Bultmann's ideas.[30] But this intriguing development also could have emerged due to the recognized historical data being so well-established and honed during recent years, even by critical scholars, so that skeptics were not so quick to get roped into a corner on a single hypothesis in case they have to backtrack!

This was pointed out to a certain extent by Bart Ehrman himself while speaking of his early days as a believer. Conservatives often seem to enjoy encouraging skeptics to choose their favorite naturalistic view, only to present the unbeliever with a cascade of challenges, one after another. In this regard, Ehrman noted that believers "typically have a field day with such explanations." This is particularly the case when so many scholars today—liberals as well as conservatives—begin their studies of the historical Jesus by providing their lists of accredited, well-established historical facts.[31] It just may be the case that being aware of this established and broadly accepted information is at least one of the reasons why fewer younger scholars willingly choose specific naturalistic theses. Such a procedure on the part of a young skeptic might be likened to driving a vehicle through a difficult obstacle course: while some may enjoy the challenge, others may wonder why they should volunteer and take such a risk. Similarly, why choose a particular naturalistic alternative route to the resurrection appearances if there is even a chance that believers could "have a field day" at their expense?[32]

In 2005, the same year that my article was published, John Dominic Crossan and N. T. Wright held one of their public discussions on the

---

30. In his famous 1941 essay, "New Testament and Mythology," Bultmann remarks that the historian might "reduce the resurrection appearances to a series of subjective visions," without doing so himself (page 42). Though Bultmann is critical of the *religionsgeschichtliche Schule* of Bousset, Pfleiderer, and others (pages 14–15), he still drinks fairly deeply from their conclusions; and this, too, could retain naturalistic theories as viable options in the first half of the twentieth century. Thus Bultmann's death in 1976 would very possibly have signaled a decline of these options, especially in the face of the new historical searches that were beginning.

31. In a recent, unpublished PhD dissertation, my research assistant Benjamin Shaw summarized the research of almost two dozen of the scholars who provided various listings of accepted historical data pertaining to aspects of Jesus' life. It is noteworthy that of the lists pertaining more generally to Jesus' life as a whole, more than half of the examples are from liberal scholars. Benjamin C. F. Shaw, "Philosophy of History, Historical Jesus Studies, and Miracles: Three Roadblocks to Resurrection Research" (PhD diss., Liberty University, 2020), Appendix, 153–68.

32. Bart D. Ehrman, *How Jesus Became God: The Exaltation of a Jewish Preacher from Galilee* (New York: Harper Collins, 2014), 164, also 164–65, 173, 186–87.

subject of Jesus' resurrection. As a respondent to that dialogue, I contributed a tally of many naturalistic theories held by recent scholars. In my published count of those researchers, less than one-quarter of all the critical scholars chose naturalistic theories. By far the majority of the remainder chose either the bodily appearances or glorious resurrection views.[33] Intriguingly, once again, this is approximately a 3:1 result in favor of the present ethos that we have identified as the moderate/conservative position.

The second research area in my 2005 article concerned the empty tomb. During the earlier influence of the No Quest and Second Quest periods, fewer scholars accepted the details in the Gospels, and fewer still thought there were strong historical reasons for embracing the empty tomb. It was often rejected by large margins, except by conservative researchers. After the beginning of the Third Quest movement, however, things began to change. I commented that the number of scholars who accepted the historicity of the empty tomb had grown incredibly from where it had been decades before to approximately 75 percent.[34] The next year I commented that the percentage may have dropped somewhat.[35] But with additional indications, both positive and negative, the overall research still indicates that the clear majority, perhaps in the vicinity of two-thirds of researchers, affirms the empty tomb. In a doctoral dissertation devoted to this subject, Mark Waterman also concluded that a majority of recent scholars held that, at the very least, the empty tomb tradition contained a kernel of historicity.[36]

The third area has only grown stronger in the last dozen or so years. It remains the case that Paul is accepted by virtually all commentators across the spectrum, from the theological left to the right, to be the best witness to the resurrection appearances of Jesus, with the pre-Pauline creedal tradition in 1 Corinthians 15:3–7 being the strongest textual argument in

33. Habermas, "Mapping the Recent Trend toward the Bodily Resurrection Appearances of Jesus in Light of Other Prominent Critical Positions," in *The Resurrection of Jesus: John Dominic Crossan and N. T. Wright in Dialogue*, ed. Robert B. Stewart (Minneapolis: Fortress, 2006), 91.

34. Habermas, "Resurrection Research from 1975 to the Present," 141.

35. Gary R. Habermas, Theological Update, "Experiences of the Risen Jesus: The Foundational Issue in the Early Proclamation of the Resurrection," *Dialog: A Journal of Theology* 45 (Fall 2006): 292.

36. Mark M. W. Waterman, *The Empty Tomb Tradition of Mark: Text, History, and Theological Struggles* (Los Angeles: Agathos, 2006), 192–93.

favor of these events. Moreover, the argument that Paul received these data no later than 35–36 CE, upon his first visit to Jerusalem to visit Peter and James, the brother of Jesus, has been strengthened considerably. Extending beyond this consideration, yet aligned with it, the fourth area—the study of the many other early Christian creeds—has also grown significantly. But we will return to these two points below for more discussion and additional comments concerning the earliest traditions.

The fifth area mentioned in the 2005 article capitalized on what, at that time, may have been the beginning of a trend that was just starting to be recognized. Decades of critical interpretation going back to the nineteenth century had argued the dominant view that Paul (and hence the other apostles) had witnessed disembodied, glorified appearances of Jesus similar to Paul's encounter on the way to Damascus. But during the Third Quest for the Historical Jesus and the predominant influence of the Jewish background on Christian origins, the tables began to turn. During this time it was increasingly being recognized—even by a number of scholars who rejected the resurrection—that Paul, at least, held to some species of *bodily* appearances of the resurrected Jesus, in keeping with the predominant Jewish views of the time. For example, in the Crossan-Wright dialogue mentioned above, Crossan noted more than once that he agreed with Wright on this subject of Paul's view of the bodily resurrection appearances of Jesus.[37]

Wright's huge study *The Resurrection of the Son of God* added much of the impetus here, to be sure, with almost four hundred pages devoted chiefly to this issue of the bodily nature of the resurrection appearances.[38] Then just seven years later, Michael Licona's equally enormous text, *The Resurrection of Jesus*, added other arguments from a slightly different angle, further ensuring that the influence of the bodily resurrection appearance position was moving forward.[39] Even prior to these two studies, Robert

---

37. Crossan, "Opening Statement," 24–25; also, Crossan, "Appendix: Bodily-Resurrection Faith," 175–76, both in Stewart, ed., *The Resurrection of Jesus*. See also this agreement spelled out in Habermas, "Resurrection Research from 1975 to the Present," 147.

38. N. T. Wright, *The Resurrection of the Son of God*, vol. 3 of Christian Origins and the Question of God (Minneapolis: Fortress, 2003), 85–479.

39. Michael R. Licona, *The Resurrection of Jesus: A New Historiographical Approach* (Downers Grove, IL: IVP Academic, 2010), especially 400–37, 469.

Gundry had released a landmark work on the same subject, *Sōma in Biblical Theology*, which was largely a critique of Bultmann's anthropology.[40]

In my response to the Crossan-Wright dialogue above, I also mentioned another count: the predominant New Testament views on the nature of the resurrection appearances to the apostles (including to Paul). Again, even counting those researchers who themselves doubted or rejected these appearances, three-quarters of the scholars still chose some form of bodily appearance as being the position held by the New Testament authors. Less than a quarter of these researchers chose the recently more prominent view that Jesus appeared in a glorious, non-bodily manner.[41] The approximate 75-percent-to-25-percent margin held, yielding a 3:1 ratio in support of the moderate/conservative position.

The sixth and last research trend mentioned in the 2005 article was the exceptionally strong impetus across the entire theological landscape, from liberal and conservative commentators alike, that in various ways the resurrection of Jesus grounds many areas of theology and practice, both in the New Testament and in the church today. For some scholars, this event actually evidences particular doctrines, such as salvation and eternal life. Even when other researchers reject the resurrection event, they still emphasize, often metaphorically, the implications for various ethical, political, and other truths that proceed from this event. My 2005 article provided detailed examples from Willi Marxsen and Marcus Borg, and an entire host of other examples could easily be added here.

During the more recent Crossan-Wright dialogue cited above, the two scholars insisted that the resurrection should lead believers to transform the world in which they live. Wright's characteristic line was: "God's new creation has begun and we've got a job to do."[42] Crossan is clear that his vision "applies to both the literal and the metaphorical" realms. With his characteristically verbal artwork, Crossan states that what we need is a

---

40. Robert H. Gundry, *Sōma in Biblical Theology: With Emphasis on Pauline Anthropology* (Grand Rapids, MI: Zondervan Academic, 1987), particularly chapter 13: "The sōma in death and resurrection," 159–83.

41. Habermas, "Mapping the Recent Trend toward the Bodily Resurrection Appearances of Jesus in Light of Other Prominent Critical Positions," 91.

42. Wright, "Opening Statement," in *The Resurrection of Jesus*, ed. Stewart, 21.

"Great Divine Clean-Up," because "I want really to know how we are going to take back God's world from the thugs."[43]

Concerning this matter of world clean-up, Crossan suggested the words "*collaborative eschaton.*"[44] Then Wright borrowed those words and declared, "I love the phrase, *collaborative eschatology*" regarding the idea that, due to believers being raised bodily in God's new, future, renovated cosmos, they need in the present to offer "justice and mercy and grace and forgiveness and healing and liberation and all the rest of it, all that is done in the name of Christ and in the power of the Spirit."[45] These provide examples of how the resurrection of Jesus can be applied in both literal and metaphorical approaches.

Somewhat remarkably, these six resurrection research trends that were relevant in 2005 remain so today, including additional developments. In their own regard, these areas of disagreement and agreement cover wide and diverse areas of application, both theoretically as well as pastorally.

THE MINIMAL FACTS ARGUMENT: SPOTLIGHTING THE BEST DATA

As the central methodological concept throughout my resurrection research, the minimal facts argument deserves a brief word.[46] Many (though not all) of the initial ideas that developed into this method are found in my 1976 dissertation. Admittedly, the ideas were in their infancy; they were just beginning to bloom.[47] But the kernel of the concept is recognizable in several places.[48]

This approach features two major steps, and it has been pointed out at length that the initial stage is easily the most crucial. (1) No historical or

---

43. Crossan, "Opening Statement," in *The Resurrection of Jesus*, ed. Stewart, 24, 25, 29.

44. Crossan, "Opening Statement," in *The Resurrection of Jesus*, ed. Stewart, 26. Crossan's emphasis.

45. Wright, "Dialogue," in Stewart, ed., *The Resurrection of Jesus*, 42–43 (Wright's emphasis).

46. Many details can be found elsewhere, such as Habermas, "The Minimal Facts Approach to the Resurrection of Jesus: The Role of Methodology as a Crucial Component in Establishing Historicity," *Southeastern Theological Review* 3 (Summer 2012): 15–26.

47. Were I to rewrite my thesis today, I would not say some of the things that are contained in the original; others I would keep but nuance and hone differently. But that is to be expected with the growth of ideas over the intervening decades!

48. A few of the applicable page numbers from the dissertation will be listed parenthetically throughout the introduction, and in this section particularly.

other fact will be employed unless it can be established by multiple lines of evidence, each being derived by critical means. Because of this initial underpinning, (2) virtually all recent critical scholars, including atheists, agnostics, and other skeptical specialists in relevant fields, accept these facts. Hints of these two rules can be seen in the dissertation (particularly pages 256–58).

In the vast majority of my publications on the resurrection, the task begins with a list of approximately ten or a few more "known" or "accepted" historical facts.[49] These are in turn pared down to a shorter list of usually four to six facts, which are termed the "minimal facts."[50] It is this smaller list that is conceded by virtually all of the critical scholars mentioned above. The second step is absent from the dissertation; it was developed shortly afterward and published four years later, in 1980.[51]

In recent years, the six minimal facts[52] that are generally used are: (1) Jesus' death by crucifixion (pages 113–21, 256–57 of the dissertation), followed by (2) the disciples' experiences that, they concluded, were appearances of the risen Jesus (pages 122–34, 256–57). (3) These data from the Gospels began to be taught exceptionally early, sometime between the initial year of the crucifixion itself and the next year or two (pages 129, 140–42, 257, 260). (4) The disciples were transformed by these events, even to the point of being willing to die for the resurrection message (pages 144–45, 256–57). Lastly, two former unbelievers, (5) James,

---

49. See pages 256, 257–58 of my dissertation.

50. Earlier in my process, they were also termed the "Core Events."

51. In the dissertation, I do begin with ten initial "known historical facts" (pages 256–58) and then reduce these to a list of seven (pages 258–60), but these later seven facts highlight the evidential considerations from the longer list rather than providing "minimal" data. Hence, these seven are not called minimal facts and do not correspond to any of the data on the minimal facts list that was published initially in 1980 and again afterward. For example, the empty tomb is present in the longer list in the dissertation, as it usually is, but the empty tomb never appears in the minimal facts listings, for reasons that I have explained repeatedly elsewhere. The initial appearance of the minimal facts (referred to here as both core and minimal data) is found in Habermas, *The Resurrection of Jesus: An Apologetic* (Grand Rapids, MI: Baker, 1980), 38, 40.

52. It should be noted that throughout these methodological considerations, the minimal facts are never explicitly stated as simply true apart from the recognition that many facts stand behind each of them, establishing their credibility in the first place. This well-evidenced quality is precisely what accounts for the initial scholarly assent. The same is the case with the almost two dozen liberal, moderate, and conservative scholars referred to in footnote 31 who likewise provide their own lists of historical data, which generally contain much in common. They all likewise employ accredited reasons behind each of these data points that allow their facts to be stated usually without challenge.

the brother of Jesus (cf. pages 141–42), and (6) the church persecutor, Saul of Tarsus (pages 140–41, 256–57, 258, 259), both became believers because they concluded that they, too, had witnessed appearances of the risen Jesus.[53]

Of crucial note regarding these minimal facts is that the naturalistic hypotheses that are frequently proposed in order to account for these data have failed. One critical indication that this is the case is the diminishing use of these natural views even among skeptical specialists, as already noted above. In the refutations of these objections, one of the major considerations is that even the briefest statements supporting these basic facts are often enough to provide the foremost critiques. The treatment of the alternative views was the longest single topic in the dissertation, occupying more than one hundred pages in length (pages 89–151, 235–44).[54]

In addition to refutations of the natural views, decisive evidential topics within the minimal facts also should be emphasized when discussing the recent trends in resurrection research. The single most crucial portion of the entire resurrection discussion concerns Jesus' appearances. They are both the best-attested of the evidential considerations and the most important. In a 2006 journal article, I listed eight major considerations specifically in favor of these appearances, each accompanied in turn by their own attesting critical data.[55] These can only be outlined here. The first four are drawn from the undisputed epistles of Paul, as identified above, along with other Pauline considerations. The second four are derived from other well-attested research. Virtually all eight of these

---

53. In the dissertation, several of the seven evidences (pages 258–60) are certainly thoughtful and have their place, but I would no longer use them today in the first tier of defense—not because they have been weakened, but because there are so many stronger points to make. These include the responses of the Jewish leaders, the birth of the Christian church, and Sunday worship.

54. For just a few of the equally in-depth critiques of naturalistic options, see Gary R. Habermas and Michael R. Licona, *The Case for the Resurrection of Jesus* (Grand Rapids, MI: Kregel, 2004), 81–150, 290–318; Licona, *The Resurrection of Jesus*, 465–610, 618–20; Wright, *The Resurrection of the Son of God*, 27–28, 77, 80–81, 318, 550, 638–39, 686, 689–91, 697–706, 709–10; William Lane Craig, *Assessing the New Testament Evidence for the Historicity of the Resurrection of Jesus* (Lewiston, NY: Edwin Mellen, 1989), 374–79, 397–404, 412–18.

55. Habermas, "Experiences of the Risen Jesus: The Foundational Issue in the Early Proclamation of the Resurrection," 289–93. Many accompanying reasons are provided in this article in favor of these eight indications that all point to the appearances of the risen Jesus. Similarly, though configured differently, see also Habermas, "The Resurrection Appearances of Jesus," in *In Defense of Miracles: A Comprehensive Case for God's Action in History*, ed. Gary R. Habermas and R. Douglas Geivett (Downers Grove, IL: InterVarsity Academic, 1997), especially 265–70.

considerations are taken from the information contained in the minimal facts, and most of these eight topics were addressed at least briefly in my 1976 dissertation.

The first four Pauline considerations include:

(1) Paul being an eyewitness and the most respected overall resurrection observer according to critical scholars (pages 256–58, 259), especially given his seven undisputed epistles.

(2) An incredible amount of critically recognized data from the 1 Corinthians 15:3–7 creedal tradition includes its being a pre-Pauline report that lists five appearances, three of which occurred in groups. Moreover, Paul probably received the report when he visited Jerusalem to converse with Peter and James, the brother of Jesus, in Galatians 1:18–20—a meeting that is dated at 35–36 CE (pages 129, 139–42, 260).

(3) Paul's second trip to Jerusalem in Galatians 2:1–10 was likewise to specifically examine the nature of the gospel message with Peter, James, and the apostle John, as well. The result was that the other three major apostles approved Paul's gospel teaching (especially Gal 2:6b, 9), which certainly included Jesus' resurrection (as per creeds like 1 Cor 15:3–5, Rom 1:3–4, and 10:9).

(4) Paul knew personally at least the three other most influential apostles (just mentioned) and confirmed that they were teaching the very same message of Jesus' resurrection appearances that he was (1 Cor 15:11, also 12, 15). From this critically accepted Pauline text, the other key eyewitnesses all taught the same resurrection truth (pages 140–42).

The additional four strong arguments include:

(5) The witness of James, the brother of Jesus and a former unbeliever, who saw the risen Jesus (1 Cor 15:7) (pages 140–41).

(6) Many very early and critically recognized creedal traditions and the Acts sermon summaries[56] also mention the resurrection testimony (page 359).

(7) The disciples' total transformations, including even being willing to die for their resurrection beliefs, were the very center of their teaching and preaching (pages 144–45; 257–58).

---

56. The latter list alone includes Acts 1:21–22; 2:22–36; 3:13–16; 4:8–10; 5.29–32; 10:39–42; 13:28–31; cf. 17:1–3, 30–31.

(8) The strong critical testimony that favors the historicity of the empty tomb (pages 257, 258–59).[57]

In the overall discussions of the historical Jesus that most occupy the studies of the Third Quest, these creedal traditions account for perhaps the strongest data in favor of the exceptionally early date for the historical facts involved in the gospel proclamation. That these teachings were not simply hearsay, idle rumors, or legends and myths is accounted for by noting the sources of these teachings. That this material occupies the centermost proclamations of Jesus' apostles themselves is indicated, for example, by the content of the Acts creedal summaries mentioned both earlier and also below.[58] Even more directly, Paul's two trips to Jerusalem to discuss these gospel essentials in Galatians 1:18–20 and 2:1–10 served to verify that it was the eyewitnesses themselves—Paul, Peter, James the brother of Jesus, and John—who were making these proclamations regarding the gospel content. Further still, Paul's comment in 1 Corinthians 15:11 specifically notes that the other apostles had both witnessed the risen Jesus and were declaring these observations, both singly and in groups. In other words, the earliest eyewitnesses themselves were the sources, rather than tall tales.

Due to the strength and clarity of these arguments, it is no wonder that even atheist New Testament scholars such as Bart Ehrman acknowledge freely and often that these creedal traditions dated very early, beginning within just one to two years after the crucifixion, and thus even predated Paul's conversion.[59] Further, the exceptionally early creeds that Paul recorded in his epistles may all have originated in Jerusalem, and could well have come from the original apostles themselves.[60] Ehrman even

---

57. As mentioned above and everywhere else in this research, the argument for the empty tomb is taken from the longer list of known facts in my dissertation rather than from the more recent, briefer minimal facts.

58. See especially Dodd, *The Apostolic Preaching and its Developments*, 11, 15–34; Max Wilcox, *The Semitisms in Acts*, particularly 79–80, 163–67, 171–79.

59. Ehrman, *Did Jesus Exist?* 22, 27, 92–93, 97, 111–12, 131–32, 141, 144–45, 155–58, 163–64, 170–73, 251, 254, 260–63. Some of the primitive traditions in the sermon summaries of Acts came from this same time, as well (see pages 108–11, 131, 158, 194, 216–17 of the dissertation).

60. Ehrman, *Did Jesus Exist?* 131, 144–45, 261; Ehrman, *How Jesus Became God*, 138.

goes as far as to attest that the resulting testimony gets us the closest to the original eyewitness teaching.[61]

Though the equally skeptical New Testament scholar Gerd Lüdemann also rejected traditional Christianity, he still made very similar comments to Ehrman's in regard to the early creed in 1 Corinthians 15:3–7: "All the elements in the tradition are to be dated to the first two years after the crucifixion of Jesus." Further, "we may reckon that appearances of Jesus were talked about *immediately* after they happened."[62]

The resurrection argument developed in my PhD dissertation has moved much further since 1976, progressing quickly onward to the minimal facts argument for the resurrection, which has been constantly honed and nuanced since that time. In fact, in a recent volume Lydia McGrew, a scholar who does not disparage the argument but thinks it needs to be developed more broadly, stated that the minimal facts argument has had "widespread use [that] may be in part a result of the fact that it provides a straightforward template for a debate format." She then mentions its "near-exclusive use in Christian apologetic circles"[63] before moving on to discuss her own strategy. Even with the differences she sees between our approaches, her kind comments are welcomed.

A LAST MAJOR AREA OF STUDY

In addition to the early creedal traditions, another influential area that has been quite common in recent decades is the application of the historical criteria of authenticity that indicate the likelihood that individual New Testament passages are historical. Robert Stein lists almost a dozen of these tests, including examples such as multiple independent attestation of sources, multiple forms of tradition, the presence of Aramaisms in the text, dissimilarity with Jewish or New Testament sources, and coherence.[64] Other such tests have also been used regularly, such as embarrassment,

---

61. Ehrman, *Did Jesus Exist?* 144–46, 148.

62. Gerd Lüdemann, *The Resurrection of Jesus: History, Experience, Theology*, trans. John Bowden (Minneapolis: Fortress, 1994), 38 (Lüdemann's emphasis); see also 181–84, where his rejection of Christianity is mentioned.

63. Lydia McGrew, *Hidden in Plain View: Undesigned Coincidences in the Gospels and Acts* (Chillicothe, OH: DeWard, 2017), 220–21.

64. Robert H. Stein, *Gospels and Tradition: Studies on Redaction Criticism of the Synoptic Gospels* (Grand Rapids: Baker, 1991), 158–85.

enemy attestation, and of course, eyewitness and early reports. Though often qualified and even doubted in some cases, these criteria are still generally used quite widely in biblical studies among critical scholars in historical Jesus scholarship.[65]

These various tests can be of great value in assisting to establish the historicity of many circumstances that are relevant to our present study of the death and resurrection of Jesus. Ehrman has one of the best examples: he identified at least fifteen independent sources for Jesus' crucifixion, a number of which are not located in the New Testament.[66] That Jesus was a miracle worker and exorcist is attested in all five of the major underlying gospel sources, as is Jesus referring to himself as the Son of Man. Jesus' Son of Man teachings are also dissimilar from both prior Jewish thought as well as the early Christian epistles. We have already discussed at length the multiple examples of what is probably the strongest evidence of all: the very early sources were derived from the eyewitnesses.

There are many embarrassing details in the New Testament, too, such as the prior unbelief of James the brother of Jesus, who later became the leader of the Jerusalem church; the apostle Peter's denials of Jesus; the unanimous reports in each of the Gospels that the women were the chief witnesses (the most popular argument for the historicity of the empty tomb); or that Paul was the best-known persecutor of Christians in the early church. Enemy attestation can be observed in the case of the Jewish priests who became believers in the very early church (Acts 6:7b), along with the many examples of the early believers' stalwart faith in the presence of challenge and strong persecution, sometimes even to the death of the witnesses.

The strengths of these authenticity criteria were that they zeroed in on the historicity of individual New Testament passages, had been used by ancient historians in their own research, and, while there were questions and nuancing to be worked out, were widely recognized and employed by

---

65. Stein, *Gospels and Tradition*, raises a large number of important questions concerning the criteria (160–61, 163, 166, 168, 170–71, 174–75, 178–79, 181–83) while still defending their use at each of these points, usually in a narrower form (159, 161–62, 166, 168, 171, 176, 179, 181, 183–84); also, Norman Perrin, *Rediscovering the Teaching of Jesus* (New York: Harper & Row, 1967), 20–22, 29, 37–47; Ehrman, *Did Jesus Exist?* 262, 271, 288–93; Licona, *The Resurrection of Jesus*, 101.

66. Ehrman, *Did Jesus Exist?* 74, 156–58, 163–64, 173, 290–92, 327–31.

critical New Testament scholars. Thus, one more set of validating tools was introduced to strengthen the historical process relative to studies pertaining to the death and resurrection of Jesus.

CONCLUSION

The case for the historicity of Jesus' resurrection and his appearances was already strong in 1976. It is significantly more robust today. Critical scholars readily allow that something strange and unique may have happened, while sometimes inquiring as to how such an event could be connected to the supernatural world of God and eternal life. That is a topic for another day, but it has been treated regularly by resurrection researchers, including myself and others.[67]

---

67. Gary R. Habermas, *The Risen Jesus and Future Hope* (Lanham, MD: Rowman and Littlefield, 2003), chapters 2–6; Habermas, *The Resurrection of Jesus*, chapters 2–5 and Appendix 3; Habermas and Licona, *The Case for the Resurrection of Jesus*, chapter 11; Wright, *The Resurrection of the Son of God*, chapters 12, 19; Wright, *Surprised by Hope: Rethinking Heaven, the Resurrection, and the Mission of the Church* (New York: Harper Collins, 2008), chapters 10–12.

PART 1

Approaching the Question of the Resurrection of Jesus

CHAPTER I

The Present State of the Question

T he belief in the resurrection of Jesus has raised many questions and provoked much thought throughout the history of the Christian church. Is such an event possible and in what sense, if any? Can it still be believed in today or not? This "question of the resurrection" has received an increased amount of attention, especially in recent years. One quite surprising fact is that the discussion surrounding this topic is no longer relegated just to the field of religion alone, as various scholars from other disciplines have also shown some interest.

No one doubts that such inquiry falls primarily into the field of theology. Therefore we will turn here first in order to view generally the present state of the question of Jesus' resurrection. Later we will also deal briefly with the interest in this topic shown in two other areas—history and philosophy. The purpose of this chapter is primarily to note some present trends related to this question, *keying* on its importance for the Christian faith.

For the purposes of this paper, the resurrection will initially and briefly be defined in the terms of the New Testament concept. This event thus refers to the Christian belief that Jesus was actually dead but later was literally raised to life by God. Jesus was believed to have appeared afterward to his followers in a *spiritual body*, which was neither an unchanged physical body or a spirit. Rather, there were both objective and subjective qualities in this spiritual body. The Christian concept of resurrection therefore differs from other ideas concerning immortality in that Jesus was not reincarnated, neither did he simply experience the continuance of his personality beyond the grave, nor was his soul absorbed into some type of universal soul. To the contrary, Jesus was believed to have literally been raised from the dead, as he appeared to his followers before his return to heaven. It is this Christian belief in Jesus' resurrection which must be investigated here. This definition will continue to broaden as this work expands.

Just before we turn to our first section certain cautions are in order. Because we are endeavoring to look at both sides of the argument and consider views that are "pro" and "con," we must take as little as possible for granted at the outset. For this reason we will refrain in almost all instances from capitalizing pronouns for Jesus, lest we begin to decide the question in advance. Concerning the use of such words as "this event" or "this occurrence" when referring to the resurrection, we do not mean to imply that we have already decided that it has happened. Rather, these words refer to what the New Testament *claims* has happened. Whether it actually did or not must yet be determined. Indeed, many theologians also refer to the resurrection as an event and still mean that it happened in other than a literal way. These words, then, must not always refer to something literal and often do not, as we shall see. In these ways the issue will hopefully not be prejudiced ahead of time.

A. THEOLOGY AND THE RESURRECTION

1. THE IMPORTANCE OF THE RESURRECTION

Many theologians today consider the resurrection of Jesus to be the central claim of Christianity, whether they interpret this event literally or not. Such was often true of past theologians as well. In other words, even those who do not affirm the post-mortem bodily appearances but sometimes stress instead the "spiritual presence" or "continuing influence" of Jesus often feel that the resurrection is still the basis of the Christian faith.

For instance, German redaction critic Willi Marxsen believes that Jesus' resurrection plays the most decisive part of theological discussion today. This scholar feels that its importance was precisely stated by the Apostle Paul in the first century AD when he wrote "if Christ has not been raised, then our preaching is in vain and your faith is in vain" (1 Cor 15:14, RSV). For Marxsen this event is therefore linked with the very faith of the church. An uncertainty about questions such as those raised above might cause a corresponding uncertainty in our faith today.[1]

Another German theologian, Günther Bornkamm, agrees with the ultimate importance of the resurrection, even if it may be impossible to grasp exactly what took place. He remarks that

> there would be no gospel, not one account, no letter in the New Testament, no faith, no Church, no worship, no prayer in Christendom to this day without the message of the resurrection of Christ.[2]

Thus we see that for these two critical scholars, theological discussion and even theology itself finds its central aspect in the resurrection. This of course does not solve the problem of whether this event occurred or not and in what sense, as this must be given future consideration. Indeed, both Marxsen and Bornkamm do not believe we can prove it, but only affirm it by faith.[3] However, such statements do help serve to demonstrate how important a place in the Christian faith it is given by many, and that is the primary object of this chapter.

Other scholars also verify these convictions. For instance, Laurence Miller likewise believes that the resurrection of Jesus is the very heart of New Testament theology. Like Marxsen, he finds the definitive statement of this belief in Paul (1 Cor 15:12–22).[4] Merrill Tenney prefers to use the resurrection as a framework for all of Christian theology, even dealing with some of the doctrines that can be integrated under this theme.[5] Charles Anderson, in a section devoted entirely to the impor-

---

1. Willi Marxsen, *The Resurrection of Jesus of Nazareth*, translated by Margaret Kohl (Philadelphia: Fortress Press, 1970), p. 12. This quote from 1 Corinthians 15:14 and other Biblical quotes in this work are from the *Revised Standard Version* of the Bible (New York: Thomas Nelson & Sons, 1946, 1952).

2. Günther Bornkamm, *Jesus of Nazareth*, translated by Irene and Fraser McLuskey (New York: Harper & Row, 1960), p. 181.

3. Marxsen believes that it is now impossible to prove the resurrection event (*op. cit.*, pp. 112–13, 119, 122), but we can still accept the offer of faith in Jesus even if he is dead (*Ibid.*, pp. 128, 147). Bornkamm agrees that the resurrection cannot be demonstrated or proven to have occurred (*op. cit.*, pp. 180–186; especially pp. 180, 184). But we can still exercise faith in Jesus apart from any such proof (*Ibid.*, pp. 183, 184). More will be said about the logic of this type of reasoning later—how it can be held by some that one can have faith in Jesus whether or not he has risen (and even if he is still dead!).

4. Laurence Miller, *Jesus Christ Is Alive* (Boston: W. A. Wilde, 1949), p. 9.

5. Merrill C. Tenney, *The Reality of the Resurrection* (New York: Harper & Row, 1963), pp. 7–8.

tance of the resurrection, also speaks of some of the Christian doctrines that are explained in the New Testament on the basis of this event. Again 1 Corinthians 15:14 is used as a key.[6]

Closely related views are held by other theologians as well. The former Anglican Archbishop of Canterbury, A. M. Ramsey, believes that the resurrection is not only the center of theology, but that it is also the starting place for studies revolving around the New Testament and its meaning.[7] For Daniel Fuller the resurrection is the basis of redemptive history. Events such as the cross receive much of their redemptive meaning because they are closely associated with the belief in a risen Jesus.[8] C. C. Dobson asserts that even those who oppose all accounts of the resurrection still admit its importance as the keystone of Christianity.[9]

Every once in a while a thesis such as the importance of the resurrection for the Christian faith will receive a new "twist," further demonstrating its relevance. This was achieved in recent years by Markus Barth and Verne H. Fletcher, who postulated that Jesus' resurrection was also the basis for Christian ethics. This event was perceived to have definite implications as a foundation for human virtue and justice. In spite of its being a little-recognized theme, the authors believe that it is as relevant for us today in these matters as it is in a strictly theological context.[10]

Even though many of the theologians above differ in other aspects of Christian belief, they all perceive that the resurrection is the center of theology even today. To be sure, they come from differing backgrounds, but they are all in agreement with Paul that if this event was to be completely abrogated, the Christian faith would be in jeopardy. As Marxsen states, if there is uncertainty or obscurity in the matter of belief in the

---

6. Charles C. Anderson, *The Historical Jesus: A Continuing Quest* (Grand Rapids: William B. Eerdman's Publishing Company, 1972), pp. 157–59.

7. A. M. Ramsey, *The Resurrection of Christ*, 2nd ed. (London and Glascow: Collins, 1965), pp. 9–11.

8. Daniel P. Fuller, *Easter Faith and History* (Grand Rapids: William Eerdman's Publishing Company, 1965), pp. 18, 19.

9. C. C. Dobson, *The Empty Tomb and the Risen Lord*, 2nd ed. (London and Edinburgh: Marshall, Morgan and Scott, n.d.), pp. 24–25.

10. Markus Barth and Verne H. Fletcher, *Acquittal by Resurrection* (New York: Holt, Rinehart and Winston, 1964), Foreward, pp. v–viii, cf. p. 3.

resurrection, then Christianity becomes endangered. This demonstrates its importance as the center of theology today.[11]

Before leaving the subject of the importance of Jesus' resurrection, it should be mentioned that it is not only an integral part of today's theology. In New Testament times it was also the doctrine upon which the Christian faith was built. We have already discussed Paul's statement to this effect above, where he states "if Christ has not been raised, then our preaching is in vain and your faith is in vain" (1 Cor 15:14, RSV; cf. verses 12–20). It was Paul's opinion that the resurrection of Jesus and the Christian faith stood or fell together. A stronger statement establishing the priority and importance of this occurrence for first-century Christianity could hardly be established.

Recent theological studies have recognized this importance for the early church. Eminent New Testament scholar Rudolf Bultmann, while not personally accepting any sort of literal resurrection of Jesus, still states that for the earliest Christians this event served the purpose of proving that God had substantiated the claims of Jesus by raising him from the dead.[12] The early Christians also believed that the resurrection proved Jesus' Lordship,[13] his Messiahship,[14] and even that he was the Son of God.[15] According to the New Testament the resurrection also establishes the Christian doctrines of repentance,[16] salvation and justification by faith,[17] and judgment.[18] James McLeman has pointed out that early Christianity

---

11. Marxsen, *op. cit.*, p. 12.

12. Rudolf Bultmann, "New Testament and Mythology," in *Kerygma and Myth*, edited by Hans Werner Bartsch, translated by Reginald H. Fuller (New York: Harper & Row, 1961), p. 39 referring to Acts 17:31.

13. Marxsen, *op. cit.*, p. 169, referring to Acts 17:30f.; Fuller, *op. cit.*, pp. 14–15, referring to Romans 10:9.

14. Rudolf Bultmann, *Theology of the New Testament*, translated by Kendrick Grobel (New York: Charles Scribner's Sons, n.d.), Part I, p. 27, referring to Acts 2:36 and Romans 1:4. Cf. also Fuller, *op. cit.*, p. 15, referring to Acts 2:22–36.

15. Fuller, *op. cit.*, pp. 15–16, referring to Romans 1:4.

16. Marxsen, *op. cit.*, p. 169, referring to Acts 16:30f.

17. Anderson, *op. cit.*, pp. 158–59, referring to Romans 4:25, 10:9; cf. also Barth and Fletcher, *op. cit.*, p. 4 and Tenney, *op. cit.*, p.8.

18. Marxsen, *op. cit.*, p. 169.

also witnesses to the belief that God began new dealings with mankind through the risen Jesus.[19]

Now we must be quick to point out once again that these beliefs by no means establish the fact of the resurrection. All we have demonstrated is that it is the center of Christian theology both in New Testament times and today. But this does not make it a proven fact. The importance of an event does not, of course, establish whether it has actually occurred or not.

2. THE CONTEMPORARY THEOLOGICAL APPROACH TO THE RESURRECTION

Perhaps the primary approach to the theological study of the resurrection today from a critical viewpoint is the application of the literary methods of form criticism and the related discipline, redaction criticism, to the New Testament texts.[20] Two key works done on the resurrection from this standpoint are those by Willi Marxsen[21] and Reginald H. Fuller.[22]

According to Norman Perrin, the theological application of form critical literary techniques was insinuated in the work of Julius Wellhausen (1844–1918) and an early form of redaction criticism was first applied to theology in the writings of Wilhelm Wrede (1859–1906). After the First World War these studies were rejuvenated. Instead of a few theologians simply suggesting the form critical literary approach to Scripture studies, it became the common interest and a major emphasis of such scholars as K.L. Schmidt (1891–1956), Martin Dibelius (1883–1947) and Rudolf Bultmann (born 1884).[23] Bultmann is probably the one who is best known

---

19. James McLeman, *Resurrection Then and Now* (New York: J. B. Lippincott Company, 1967), p. 92; cf. 87 also.

20. It should be noted that neither form or redaction criticism is actually theology. Rather, these are literary methods that have been used in diverse endeavors, such as in studying classical literature. They are therefore utilized here as literary approaches which are presently being applied to the New Testament. These methods are thus referred to as the current theological approach to the resurrection because they are employed by theologians and not because these disciplines are mistakenly being referred as theology themselves. For the relationship between form and redaction criticism, see Norman Perrin's *What is Redaction Criticism?*, edited by Dan O. Via (Philadelphia: Fortress Press, 1971), p. 13 for instance.

21. The aforementioned *The Resurrection of Jesus of Nazareth* by Marxsen.

22. Reginald H. Fuller, *The Formation of the Resurrection Narratives* (New York: The Macmillan Company, 1971).

23. Perrin, *op. cit.*, pp. 13–15. Some of Bultmann's conclusions on the importance of the resurrection in the early church have already been noted above.

for popularizing form criticism, applying it especially to the synoptic gospels and publishing the results in such essays as "The Study of the Synoptic Gospels."[24]

Briefly, according to this theory of interpretation, the synoptic gospels were the products of the faith of the earliest first-century Christian church. In other words, after years of orally spreading the gospel of Jesus Christ (and perhaps also by some written records which we no longer have, such as the Quelle document), the earliest church decided to write down what it could recall of the life of Jesus. But since the first Christians were not given a complete historical narrative of his life, their recollections could only be of *independent occurrences*. The gospels, then, can be broken down into these separate occurrences which in turn correspond to certain forms. When all of these occurrences are divided up into these forms, Bultmann notes that we have several classifications such as miracle stories, parables, and apocalyptic words.[25]

Since the church was interested in a complete biography, however, these events had to be connected into a day-by-day account of Jesus' life. One can find a good many of these editorial links that tie one story to another. This is how the likeness to "beads on a string" has come to be used for the form critical approach. A main object for theologians who employ this approach is to ascertain which of the accounts (or parts of accounts) in the gospels are actually historical stories and which were "constructed" by the faith of the early church.[26]

Redaction criticism relies heavily on the procedures of form criticism and builds upon its premises. In fact, Perrin notes that these may be seen as being two stages of the same discipline.[27]

Redaction criticism has developed significantly since the work done by Wilhelm Wrede at the end of the nineteenth and beginning of the twentieth centuries. Today more positive attention is given to the gospel authors, as they are seen as having more of an integral and original role to play in the choosing of material and in the written portrayal of it. Critics today

---

24. Rudolf Bultmann, "The Study of the Synoptic Gospels," in *Form Criticism*, translated by Frederick C. Grant (New York: Harper & Row, 1962), pp. 11–76.

25. Bultmann, *Ibid.*, pp. 36–63.

26. *Ibid.*, p. 25.

27. Perrin, *op. cit.*, pp. 1–3, 13.

also feel that a primary goal is to be able to trace the material through the various phrases of influence, through the various additions by redactors and then as closely as possible to the source(s). This will enable them to determine, among other things, where the facts originated and what is at the basis of the reports. The object is, of course, to ascertain the reliability of the data as much as possible, to see what is historical and what has been added to the original facts.[28]

Three of the leading redaction critics today, at least in a chronological sense, are Günther Bornkamm,[29] Hans Conzelmann, and Willi Marxsen.[30] They worked independently on the synoptic gospels of Matthew, Luke and Mark, respectively. In a sense they have paved the way for similar studies today.[31]

We have briefly investigated form and redaction criticism for two main reasons. First, its importance as the currently accepted literary approach to Biblical studies should not be underrated. We have noted above that some entire works and portions of others have been devoted to studies on the resurrection by scholars who favor these two disciplines.[32] Thus form and redaction criticism will provide a basis for much of what will be said hereafter. Second, although this writer does not embrace many of the facets and conclusions of either form criticism or redaction criticism, we will adopt many of its procedures here as the most commonly accepted "rules of the trade." With this background and theological foundation, it is advantageous to proceed now to two other fields of study which have also given recent attention to the subject of the resurrection.

---

28. *Ibid.*, pp. 3, 12–13.

29. Bornkamm's belief in the importance of the resurrection for Christian theology has been noted above.

30. Some of Marxsen's contributions to the current study of the resurrection have also been noted above.

31. Perrin, *op. cit.*, pp. 25–39.

32. See, for instance, Marxsen's and R. Fuller's work above, footnotes 21 and 22 respectively, which are entirely devoted to the resurrection. Portions of many works have also dealt with this subject, like those of Bultmann and Bornkamm cited above, footnotes 12 and 2, respectively.

B. HISTORY, PHILOSOPHY, AND
THE RESURRECTION

We have already stated that one interesting aspect of current study on the resurrection of Jesus is that several scholars in other fields of study besides religion have also become interested in this question. These men have applied their various interdisciplinary backgrounds and educations to the problem and have understandably come to various conclusions. Although these trends are probably most observable in the disciplines of history and philosophy, they are by no means confined to these two areas. Other scholars (and their fields) who have shown as interest in this event include C. S. Lewis, the late Cambridge University professor of English literature,[33] J. N. D. Anderson, a lawyer and the University of London's director of Advanced Legal Studies,[34] Peter L. Berger, professor of Sociology at Rutgers University,[35] Louis Cassels, journalist and late columnist for United Press International,[36] and scientist Henry Morris.[37] Let us turn now specifically to the fields of history and philosophy to observe some of the current interest in the question of the resurrection.

1. HISTORY AND THE RESURRECTION

It is true that most modern historians do not show an extraordinary amount of interest in the resurrection. Neither are they usually concerned over whether it was a historical event or not. Generally the attitude taken in historical works toward this occurrence is one either of skepticism[38] or one that relates the Biblical accounts of the death and resurrection of

---

33. C. S. Lewis' work *Miracles* (New York: The Macmillan Company, 1965) deals with the resurrection on pp. 148–55.

34. J. N. D. Anderson has at least two writings dealing with the resurrection. See *Christianity: The Witness of History* (London: Tyndale Press, 1969), pp. 84–108 and the booklet *The Evidence for the Resurrection* (Downers Grove: InterVarsity Press, 1966).

35. Berger's work, *A Rumor of Angels* (New York: Doubleday Publishing Company, 1970) does not deal directly with the resurrection, but rather with the possibility of miracles and Supernatural events occuring.

36. Cassels has written at least two books which deal with the question of the resurrection. See *This Fellow Jesus* (New York: Pyramid Publications, 1973), pp. 84–90 and *Christian Primer* (New York: Doubleday and Company, 1967), pp. 23–26.

37. One of Morris' books *Many Infallible Proofs* (San Diego: Creation-Life Publishers, 1974), devotes a chapter to the resurrection, pp. 88–97.

38. H. G. Wells, *The Outline of History*, 2 vols. (Garden City: Garden City Books, 1949), vol. 1, pp. 539–40.

Jesus only after a short preface which states "the Bible *claims*," or "early Christians *believed* that," or another similar expression.[39] This general non-interest in the resurrection by historians is understandable in view of the fact that many feel that this event is an item of faith, even if they believe that it actually occurred.

Yet there are some historians who have investigated this event to some extent. It is not our purpose here in this chapter to cover all areas of historical inquiry, but rather to briefly survey a sample of a few historians who have shown interest in the subject of the resurrection. Later the position of historian David Hume will be discussed in much more detail, as his views were extremely influential on the question of miracles.

Ancient historian Paul Maier has recently published a book entitled *First Easter*.[40] This work is concerned to a large extent with the first Easter Sunday and the question *"What did happen at dawn* on Sunday morning?"[41] His purpose is to try and ascertain if *history* can tell us what really happened that day.[42] His method is first to investigate the original sources, comparing the various accounts of the early church which claim that Jesus rose from the dead. Alternate theories are then proposed and examined. Lastly, some interesting but seldom mentioned historical evidence that bears directly on this issue is studied.[43]

Maier has also contributed other scholarly articles concerning the death and resurrection of Jesus.[44] One, entitled "The Empty Tomb as History," further examines the historical facts surrounding this event.[45] The conclusion to the article is concerned with whether or not the resurrection can be said to be an actual datum of history.[46] We will return to some of Maier's conclusions later.

---

39. Shepard B. Clough, Nina G. Garsoian and David L. Hicks, *A History of the Ancient World*, 3 vols. (Boston: D. C. Heath and Company, 1967), vol. 1, *Ancient and Medieval*, p. 127.

40. Paul L. Maier, *First Easter* (New Yorks: Harper & Row, 1973).

41. *Ibid.*, p. 93. The italics are Maier's.

42. "Can history tell us what *actually* happened on that crucial dawn?" (*Ibid.*, p. 114. The italics are Maier's).

43. *Ibid.*, cf. especially pp. 93–122.

44. See, for instance, Paul L. Maier, "Who Was Responsible for the Trial and Death of Jesus?" *Christianity Today* 18, no. 14 (April 12, 1974): 8–11.

45. Paul L. Maier, "The Empty Tomb as History," *Christianity Today* 19, no. 13 (March 28, 1975): 4–6.

46. *Ibid.*

Another ancient historian, Edwin Yamauchi, has also written of the resurrection. His investigation is found in the two-part article entitled "Easter—Myth, Hallucination or History?"[47] He explores carefully each of the possibilities named in the title—the resurrection seen as an ancient myth, as a hallucination, and as actual history. Yamauchi concludes first that the Christian concept of Jesus' resurrection could not have been derived from the myths in ancient cultures such as those of the Sumerians, Babylonians, or Egyptians, which appear to espouse a belief in dying and rising vegetation gods. These latter myths reveal both far too superficial resemblances and even very questionable evidence concerning this belief in a "resurrection" to have been the basis of belief for Jesus' rising.[48]

Yamauchi's second conclusion is that the hypothesis of hallucination is likewise not a strong enough impetus for belief in the resurrection of Jesus. None of the needed psychological prerequisites for visions are found in the New Testament accounts. For instance, the disciples were very despondent at the death of Jesus and failed to believe even after perceiving that he had risen, whereas hallucinations occur when individuals *imagine beforehand* that a certain thing has, in fact, happened. Visions are produced when people think so *positively* that they actually visualize what they desire and the disciples were certainly not in this frame of mind after Jesus' death. The facts simply do not provide support for this theory at all. The conditions needed for hallucinations were plainly lacking.[49]

The final conclusion reached by Yamauchi is that the resurrection of Jesus is a historical event and must be dealt with as such. It simply cannot be termed as an existential occurrence and neither can it be forgotten about as a simple myth or delusion.[50]

We will at this point just quickly mention two other scholars in this field who also have dealt with the resurrection in their works. Historian and theologian John Warwick Montgomery has dealt with this question

---

47. Edwin M. Yamauchi, "Easter—Myth, Hallucination or History?," *Christianity Today* 18, no. 12 (March 15, 1975): 4–7; and 18, no. 2 (March 29, 1975): 12–16 (two parts).

48. *Ibid.*, March 15, 1974, pp. 4–6.

49. *Ibid.*, pp. 6–7. We will turn to this theory in greater depth later in this paper.

50. *Ibid.*, p. 7 and March 29, pp. 12–16.

in several works which are directly concerned with historical methodology.[51] Church historian William Wand has also fit the resurrection into an explicit historical framework.[52] Rather than explore the views of these two men at this point, we will return to them much more fully in the chapter on history and miracles. Suffice it to say at this time that while historians as a whole have not been overly concerned with Jesus' resurrection, it has been dealt with by several in this field. Thus it is the opinion of these scholars (and others) that this question is a historical one, to be decided by historical inquiry. Maier,[53] Yamauchi,[54] Montgomery,[55] and Wand[56] all agree that the question of the occurrence of the resurrection should be decided by the historical process of carefully weighing the evidence both for and against this event before a decision is made.

2. PHILOSOPHY AND THE RESURRECTION

As with most of the historians, so we also find that most contemporary philosophers are not often concerned with the question of Jesus' resurrection. But we find that several of these scholars have also dealt with it as a part of their system of thought. As with the theologians, these philosophers offer a variety of approaches and answers to this event. Similar to the preceding short section on history, it is not our object in this chapter to treat every field of philosophy. To the contrary, the purpose here is simply to present a sample of a few philosophers who have dealt with the resurrection in their works. Later the positions of David Hume and Søren Kierkegaard will be examined in depth. Hume especially is recognized even by conservative theologians as offering a challenge to the belief in a literal resurrection and Kierkegaard also develops a popular philosophical view of this event. But at present it is our desire only to state the interest shown by a few philosophers of various intellectual inclinations.

---

51. For instance, see John Warwick Montgomery's, *The Shape of the Past: An Introduction to Philosophical Historiography* (Ann Arbor: Edwards Brothers, 1962) and *Where Is History Going?* (Grand Rapids: Zondervan, 1969).

52. William Wand, *Christianity: A Historical Religion?* (Valley Forge: Judson Press, 1972).

53. Maier, "The Empty Tomb as History," *op. cit.*, p. 6.

54. Yamauchi, *op. cit.*, March 29, 1974, p. 16.

55. Montgomery, *Where Is History Going?, op. cit.*, pp. 71, 93.

56. Wand, *op. cit.*, pp. 93–94; cf. also pp. 51–52, 70–71.

Probably the best known philosopher who has investigated this occurrence is John Hick. In his essay "Theology and Verification"[57] he approaches the ancient topic of the possibility of verifying the existence of God. This is done in an interesting and novel (if somewhat questionable) manner.

For Hick, one cannot prove God's existence beyond any doubt. However, the author believes that one can reason logically to the *probability* of God's existence by the use of what he terms "eschatological" (or future) verification.[58]

The Christian faith (and various others as well) teach the reality of life after death. For Hick this concept of continued survival is one which will ultimately be verified after death. In other words, the future resurrection of mankind can be verified experientially by each individual after his own personal death. The post-mortem knowledge one gains would prove that life does survive death.[59]

Concerning this odd-sounding apologetic for life after death, Hick attempts to explain how this is possible by the introduction of several interesting illustrations.[60] He feels that ultimately the question of immortality may be likened to two men walking down the road of life. One says that there is life after death at the end of the road, the other disagrees. But for them it is an experiential question. Sooner or later they will each turn the last bend in life and die. Then one will have been proven right and one wrong. This is eschatological verification of immortality.[61]

Even verification of the existence of God is to be found by the same future experience. Here Hick appropriates the role that Jesus plays. As we experience the risen Jesus and his reign in the Kingdom of God, and finally receive eschatological corroboration for this, we then also receive indirect verification of God. Thus the individual's own resurrection is the ultimate, experiential proof both of life after death and of God's existence.

---

57. John Hick, "Theology and Verification," in *Religious Language and the Problem of Religious Knowledge*, edited by Ronald E. Santoni (Bloomington: Indiana University Press, 1968). This article first appeared in *Theology Today*, vol. 17, 1960, pp. 12–31.

58. *Ibid.*, pp. 367, 376.

59. *Ibid.*, p. 375.

60. *Ibid.*, pp. 371–75.

61. *Ibid.*, pp. 368–69.

These truths are thus perceived as realities. Everyone will eventually prove the validity of these facts for themselves, however, because all will achieve this salvation and subsequent state of verification.[62]

Unfortunately, Hick's perception of the ability of one's own resurrection to verify such key tenets of theology raises more questions than it answers. It is interesting, to say the least, but it fails to logically reason out (and even presupposes) too many beliefs such as life after death and the ability to verify something such as God's existence even if the first was proven to be true.[63] Hick realizes that his hypotheses and those of Ian Crombie, who also accepts eschatological verification, have both been met by disapproval from other philosophers and from theologians, but still feels that this is the best alternative in establishing the truth of theism.[64] Thus, while we must conclude that none of these doctrines can really be proven in this way, it does show the interest of a certain segment of philosophy in the question of the resurrection.

But it is not only in the writings of Hick (and those who agree with him) that we find an interest in the subject of the resurrection. The recent popularity of process thought has apparently opened up a new area of interest in the formulating of, among other things, a Christology based on process philosophy. For instance, Schubert Ogden's prospects for the development of a new theism have led him to a reinterpretation of the resurrection based on the love of God.[65] Another example is Bernard Loomer's attempt to explain the Christian faith, including the resurrection, in terms of process philosophy.[66]

In the work *Process Philosophy and Christian Thought*, Peter Hamilton proposes a modern Christology with a special emphasis upon the resurrection. For Hamilton, process philosophy offers the proper framework

---

62. *Ibid.*, pp. 376–81.

63. Cf. *Ibid.*, pp. 375–76 for instance, where Hick admits that it would be easy to conceive of after-life experiences that would *not* at all verify theism, but he does not entertain the objections.

64. *Ibid.*, pp. 367–68.

65. Schubert M. Ogden, "Toward a New Theism," in *Process Philosophy and Christian Thought*, edited by Delwin Brown, Ralph E. James, Jr. and Gene Reeves (Indianapolis: The Bobbs-Merrill Company, 1971), p. 183. Cf. also Ogden's examination of a modern approach to the resurrection in his work *The Reality of God and Other Essays* (New York: Harper & Row, 1966). pp. 215–20.

66. Bernard M. Loomer, "Christian Faith and Process Philosophy," in *Process Philosophy and Christian Thought, Ibid.*, pp. 91, 95 for his treatment of the resurrection.

within which one can more properly view and formulate theology. This philosophy is perceived to be especially helpful in dealing with the resurrection.[67]

The key term that Hamilton adopts from process philosophy here is "immanence," which refers to the possibility of one reality being immanent or indwelt by another. This is illustrated by the way we often refer to the experiences of one individual "living on" in another's memory.[68]

When applied to the relationship between God and the world, immanence is a reference both to God's indwelling mankind and mankind's indwelling God. As Hamilton applies this concept to Christology, we may now speak of the chief example of God's indwelling mankind as having occurred in the incarnation. Here God indwelt Jesus. We can also perceive that the primary example of mankind's indwelling God is to be found in the resurrection. Here Jesus is said to "live on" in God.[69] By "live on" it is meant that it is Jesus' experiences, ideas, and actions that were raised into God. We are therefore to understand that his resurrection is the most outstanding instance of God's desire and purpose to raise into Himself everything else that compliments His own character as well.[70]

It is obvious here that the resurrection is not interpreted literally. For Hamilton, the disciples had a God-given awareness (*not* self-generated, it is emphasized) that Jesus was somehow still both alive and present with them. This was the beginning of the Easter experience. But they did not have an actual encounter with the risen Lord as portrayed in the New Testament gospels.[71]

Hamilton realizes, however, that there are some serious criticisms regarding his views. One is that the uniqueness of Jesus' resurrection has not been properly maintained. Rather, this occurrence is only a model for other such actions of God.[72]

---

67. Peter N. Hamilton, "Some Proposals for a Modern Christology," in *Process Philosophy and Christian Thought, Ibid.*, pp. 371, 376, 379, 381.

68. *Ibid.*, p. 379.

69. *Ibid.*, pp.379–80.

70. *Ibid.*, pp. 378, 381.

71. *Ibid.*, pp. 371, 375, 380.

72. *Ibid.*, pp. 377–78.

Another criticism (which is admitted by Hamilton to be a stronger one) is that, according to this interpretation, the "risen" Jesus is not really alive although the disciples believed that he was because of the afore-mentioned God-given awareness of this fact. In other words, the New Testament writers witness to a risen Jesus who was *really* alive and the author agrees with this conviction as well. Otherwise there would be no origin for the Easter faith. Yet, this thesis does not allow for the type of resurrection that would give rise to such a belief. Hamilton admits that this criticism is a valid one to a certain extent.[73]

The last scholar to be dealt with briefly at this time is Swiss philoso-pher Francis Schaeffer. Formerly an agnostic, Schaeffer became convinced through personal research that belief in God was rational.[74] Afterward he became concerned to a large extent that rationality must be kept in religious belief and that knowledge must precede faith (but certainly not to the exclusion of faith).[75]

Exploring this concept of rationality in Christian belief, Schaeffer came to espouse the view that God's revelation occurred in history and is thus open to verification.[76] An event which is reported to have happened can be examined and found to be either a valid claim or to be some sort of falsehood. This is the nature of historical revelation. For Schaeffer, the death and resurrection of Jesus are both verifiable in this way. They are referred to as actual historical facts which literally occurred in our space-time world.[77]

We have in this chapter investigated both the importance of the res-urrection of Jesus and the current theological approach to it as a religious occurrence. In addition, we have examined the views of several scholars from various other fields (especially history and philosophy) who have also shown varying degrees of interest in this event.

---

73. *Ibid.*, p. 378.

74. Francis Schaeffer, *Escape from Reason* (Downers Grove: InterVarsity Press, 1968), see pp. 84–85 for instance.

75. Francis Schaeffer, *The God Who Is There* (Downers Grove: InterVarsity Press, 1968), pp. 112, 142.

76. Schaeffer, *The God Who Is There, Ibid.*, p. 92; see also Schaeffer's *Escape from Reason, op. cit.*, p. 77.

77. Schaeffer, *Escape from Reason, Ibid.*, pp. 79, 90 and Schaeffer's *The Church Before the Watching World* (Downer's Groves: InterVarsity Press, 1971), pp. 98–99.

We have found that the resurrection is the central event in the Christian faith and thus of central importance in theology. Therefore the questions raised here concerning its character are both valid and consequential ones.

The contemporary theological approach to the resurrection was found to be one that utilizes the literary methodology inherent in form and redaction criticism. Hopefully through a study of this event, making use of these disciplines, we will be able to make a judgment as to its credibility.

We have also seen that there appears to be a surprising interest in the resurrection by scholars in other fields besides religion. This especially appears to be the case in history and philosophy. The purpose for our investigation of several views in these two specific fields is threefold. First, it enables us to understand that this question is not one that is isolated to the field of religion and theology alone. Second, it serves to familiarize us with some views of the resurrection that are surprisingly close to those proposed by some theologians which will be referred to constantly. Third, this previous discussion prepares the way for our later investigation of three scholars (one theologian, one historian, and one philosopher) who deal with these questions concerning the resurrection in much more depth, thus relating all three fields together in a "search for the truth" on this issue.

CHAPTER II

The Possibility of Miracles Today

The question of whether or not miracles have occurred in the past (or whether they are possible today) is one that has far-reaching consequences much beyond the field of theology. We will turn now to an examination of some major possibilities.

A. MIRACLE AND MYTH

1. A DEFINITION OF MIRACLE

In searching for a possible definition for "miracle," one encounters many approaches and conclusions. However, there are several similarities and points concerning which most appear to be in agreement. We must realize, though, that the definition we arrive at actually has nothing to do with the problem of whether the events that are defined thusly really do occur. For example, many scholars who do not believe that miracles happen at all still define them as occurrences which are not caused by nature and which must be performed by God. They simply believe that no such events ever take place. Therefore we see that the definition does not mean that a certain type of phenomenon has happened.

Bultmann is just such a scholar who believes that our modern world is enough to make us reject all miracles. The ancient view of the world is obsolete and we no longer rely on its cosmology or mythological language.[1] Even so, it is recognized that at least the New Testament defines miracles

---

1. Bultmann, "New Testament and Mythology," in *Kerygma and Myth, op. cit.*, pp. 1–5.

as events which occur due to the Supernatural intervention of God rather than by the power of nature. For Bultmann, the purpose of miracles is to express spiritual truths that may otherwise be unexplainable.[2]

Historian and philosopher David Hume, who also rejects the miraculous, relates that

a miracle may be accurately defined, *a transgression of a law of nature by a particular volition of the Deity, or by the interposition of some invisible agent.*[3]

Once again we find that while Hume clearly rejects the miraculous (as we shall perceive in more detail later), he defines these occurrences as the intervention of God or of another invisible agent. Philosopher Richard Swinburne accepts essentially the same definition, realizing that in so doing he is close to Hume's view.[4]

English scholar C. S. Lewis defines miracles as follows:

I use the word *Miracle* to mean an interference with Nature by supernatural power. Unless there exists, in addition to Nature, something else which we may call the supernatural, there can be no miracles. (The italics are Lewis'.)[5]

Like the other definitions, here Lewis also conceives of miracles as having a direct effect on nature. But the miracles are seen as being brought less forcefully into the world. Lewis perceives of nature as an entity which can *receive* such extraordinary occurrences into its own pattern of events when they are caused by Supernatural power. Thus they do interfere with the laws of nature, but do not break them.[6] These miracles are not taken for granted by the author, however, but are investigated to ascertain if they actually did occur.[7]

---

2. *Ibid.*, pp. 34–35, 39.

3. David Hume, *Essential Works of David Hume*, edited by Ralph Cohen (New York: Bantam Books, 1965), p. 128n3. The italics are Hume's.

4. Richard Swinburne, *The Concept of Miracle* (London: Macmillan and St. Martin's Press, 1970), p. 11.

5. Lewis, *op. cit.*, p. 10.

6. *Ibid.*, pp. 47, 60.

7. *Ibid.*, pp. 148–69 for instance.

The last definition of miracles which we will state is that of theologian John McNaugher, who agrees with Lewis in asserting that these occurrences are out of the normal sequence of events in nature. They cannot be explained by natural processes, but are due to the agency of God. They are obvious to the senses and designed for the purpose of authenticating a message.[8]

In these five definitions of miracles there are obviously several similarities (as well as some differences). For instance, all five scholars are agreed (to varying extents) that real miracles require Supernatural intervention and are not to be explained naturally.[9] All five also believe that these occurrences have a direct relation to the laws of nature, requiring some sort of interference. Some think that miracles have a purpose. But all are not agreed, for instance, as to whether these miracles actually occur or not. In other words, it is possible in this case to describe what an occurrence would entail *if* it were to happen, while not actually believing that there are such events. Nevertheless, there is a surprising amount of similarity in these definitions for scholars who disagree on this last point.

In this paper, the writer will refer to a miracle as an event which interferes with the laws of nature, but does not violate them. They cannot be explained by any natural causes (including man's power) and thus must be accomplished by some type of Supernatural activity. They are effected for a purpose and may be perceived by man's senses. The question now is to ascertain if there really are such events.

2. A DEFINITION OF MYTH

A discussion of miracles should ideally also include an inquiry into the meaning of myth. We will attempt to explore a couple of earlier meanings of the word and some modern definitions of it. We would thus endeavor to discover what myth is and what function it plays in society.

---

8. John McNaugher, *Jesus Christ the Same Yesterday, Today and Forever* (New York: Fleming H. Revell Company, 1947), pp. 91–92.

9. In the case of Bultmann we are referring to this scholar's references to what "miracle" meant in the New Testament, as mentioned above. Like Hume he does not believe they occur, but grants that this was still believed to be the definition of the word in first-century Christian thought.

Originally,[10] myths were generally defined by scholars as fictitious narratives containing very little or no factual content. They were mainly concerned with stories of gods, goddesses, and questions about the cosmos.[11] Because of such content, myths were judged to be simply fiction. The definition was one which implied the essential contradiction between myth and history.[12]

Later, the word also came to mean a fictitious story revolving around a historical personage, circumstance, or event, but one which was not really factual.[13] Perhaps an example of this type of popular myth would be the narrative of how George Washington chopped down a cherry tree and chose the subsequent punishment rather than tell a lie concerning his actions.

There is much disagreement as to a suitable definition of myth today.[14] This is made even more difficult by the variations in the definition utilized by scholars from different disciplines.[15] One popular practice is to define myth as being the opposite of history, thereby signifying that it is almost completely untrue in a factual sense.[16]

As used by most contemporary theologians and religious scholars, myth is not usually taken to be so unrealistic. The emphasis is clearly placed most often on the function of the myth and on what such a concept

---

10. For a very brief introduction to the question of some older theories concerning the origins of myth, see Daniel Dodson's introductory essay "What is 'Myth'?" in Thomas Bulfinch's *The Age of Fable* (Greenwich: Fawcett Publications, 1961), pp. 6, 9. For an examination of the origins of myth according to many historians of religion, see Burton H. Throckmorton's *The New Testament and Mythology* (Philadelphia: The Westminster Press, 1959), pp. 81–85.

11. Wand, *op. cit.*, p. 40; see also James K. Feibleman's article "Myth" in the *Dictionary of Philosophy*, edited by Dagobert Runes (Totowa: Littlefield, Adams and Company, 1967), p. 203.

12. Wand, *Ibid.*

13. Runes, *op. cit.*, p. 203.

14. For instance, see Mircea Eliade, *The Quest: History and Meaning in Religion* (Chicago: The University of Chicago Press, 1969), p. 72f. See also Throckmorton, *op. cit.*, p. 80.

15. See Victor Turner's article "Myth and Symbol," in the *International Encyclopedia of the Social Sciences*, edited by David L. Sills (no city: The Macmillan Company and The Free Press, 1968), vol. 10, pp. 576–82. For the definition of "myth" employed in literature, see for example James F. Knapp, "Myth in the Powerhouse of Change," *The Centennial Review* 20, no. 1 (Winter 1976): 56–74. Cf. Wesley Barnes, *The Philosophy and Literature of Existentialism* (Woodbury: Barron's Educational Series, 1968), pp. 34–40.

16. See S. H. Hooke, *Middle Eastern Mythology* (Baltimore: Penguin Books, 1966), who lists this view as one which is still employed in current treatments of this subject (p. 11). See also Wand, *op. cit.*, p. 40.

is supposed to accomplish in society. Thus, theologians are more interested in studying the message which the myth is meant to convey.

For nineteenth-century theologian David Strauss, myth is the clothing
for the expression of religious truths. For this reason, one must endeavor
to ascertain the societal function and meaning given to a myth, trying
to understand the religious message being communicated by means of
this imagery. The importance of Strauss' view of myth is that before his
time this concept was either not completely recognized or not applied
consistently.[17]

Rudolf Bultmann believes that New Testament myth is essentially
unhistorical, but that its primary purpose is to express existential truths
about man.[18] Thus, this scholar also agrees that this question of the myth's
purpose is the key one.[19] Bultmann freely admits that the actual imagery of the myth is not the most important part of mythology. Rather,
the recovery of its message about human existence is the most essential thing.[20] The stress here is also on understanding what the myth was
intended to accomplish.

Few scholars have done more research on the idea of myth than has
Mircea Eliade. For Eliade, myths are accounts of deeds which are always
acts of creation, in that they speak of some reality coming into existence.
Myths are very complex cultural factors whose main function is to serve
as models for the rites and other important activities of humans. Thus
myths present religious explanations for what is believed to have occurred.
For this reason, a myth is perceived to be an actual reality in that it always
depicts something that has happened, such as the beginning of the world
or the fact of death.[21]

---

17. See Albert Schweitzer, *The Quest of the Historical Jesus*, translated by W. Montgomery (New
York: The Macmillan Company, 1968), pp. 78–79; cf. David Strauss' work *The Old Faith and the New*,
translated from the sixth edition by Mathilde Blind (New York: Henry Holt and Company, 1874),
pp. 56–59 for instance.

18. Bultmann, "New Testament and Mythology," in *Kerygma and Myth op. cit.*, especially pp. 1–11.
Cf. Schubert Ogden, *Christ Without Myth* (New York: Harper & Row, 1961), pp. 39–40.

19. Throckmorton, *op. cit.*, p. 23; cf. John Macquarrie, *An Existentialist Theology* (New York:
Harper & Row, 1965), pp. 172–73.

20. Bultmann, "New Testament and Mythology," in *Kerygma and Myth, op. cit.*, pp. 10–11.

21. Mircea Eliade, *Myth and Reality*, translated by William R. Task (New York: Harper & Row,
1963), pp. 5–14.

Eliade stresses the symbolic character of such myths. They are capable of revealing something which is deeper than known reality. Such symbols point to various facets of human existence. Perhaps the most important aspect of mythical symbolism is that truths can be expressed by this mode which can be expressed coherently in no other way. It is therefore very important to study the message of the myth. Scholars who do not discover this function of myth fail in their endeavor to understand this concept.[22]

For S. H. Hooke, myth is still viewed as being essentially nonhistorical, but it nevertheless is a result of a particular circumstance and therefore it does have a purpose. Thus the proper approach is not to try to determine how much actual truth it contains, but rather to determine what the real function of the myth is—what it is supposed to accomplish. As with Eliade, Hooke stresses that the function of a myth is to use imagery to express truths that otherwise could not be explained.[23]

These definitions of myth have pointed to at least a few general conclusions with which many theologians seem to be in agreement, at least to a certain extent. Myths can be identified as the use of various types of imagery to portray different aspects of life (real or imaginary), including one's beliefs, customs, or folklore. Myths are essentially nonhistorical, but they may reflect actual occurrences and teach religious or moral truths. Myths do have a societal function.[24] They are often the devices by which one can express what otherwise would be inexpressible, whether it concerns cosmology, man's existence, the Divine, or one's religious and moral beliefs. In other words, myths serve the function of allowing various societies to speak of treasured beliefs, mysteries, and customs in a way that ordinary language might not quite be able to duplicate. This could be either because of a lack of proper words or a lack of the necessary knowledge needed to explain these things. For instance, mythical imagery could easily have been employed to explain certain cosmic events such as eclipses. In this way societies could pass on verbal or written accounts of their experiences.

---

22. Mircea Eliade, *Mephistopheles and the Androgyne: Studies in Religious Myth and Symbol*, translated by J. M. Cohen (New York: Sheed and Ward, 1965), pp. 201–8.

23. Hooke, *op. cit.*, pp. 11, 16.

24. For Paul Ricoeur's understanding of the intermingling of theology and culture, see his work *History and Truth*, translated by Charles A. Kelbley (Evanston: Northwestern University Press, 1965), pp. 177–79 for example.

That this was an important function of myth is witnessed by the discoveries throughout various parts of the world pointing to this usage.[25]

These general conclusions will be the basis for the definition of myth that will be used in this paper. Briefly, myth will mainly be utilized to refer to the essentially nonhistorical use of imagery by societies in order to express certain beliefs, customs, or events. They allow people to speak of realities that might be much harder to express apart from the use of this imagery.

The distinction between miracle and myth is an important one. It will be the purpose of the remainder of this paper to investigate the resurrection of Jesus in light of these definitions. Was this occurrence a myth voicing the beliefs of early Christendom, or was it a literal event requiring Supernatural action? Our investigation will thus view the evidence of each possibility in order to ascertain where it points in regard to this question. We agree with Wand in the assertion that it is very important to distinguish myth from history. The purpose of the myth must be determined and real history must not be confused with the myth.[26] Therefore, each has its own purpose and it will be our task not to let the two become indiscriminately mixed.

B. TWENTIETH-CENTURY
SCIENCE AND MIRACLES

1. INTRODUCTION

It is a common practice today to conceive of science and the miraculous as being totally opposed. Bultmann, for instance, rejects early Christian cosmology on the grounds that it is opposed to modern science. All of our contemporary knowledge is based on science and this includes an application of its laws to the study of the New Testament.[27] Thus Bultmann speaks of the relationship between science and miracles:

> It is impossible to use electric light and the wireless and to avail ourselves of modern medical and surgical discoveries, and at the

---

25. Hooke, *op. cit.*, pp. 19–32.

26. Wand, *op. cit.*, p. 42.

27. Bultmann, "New Testament and Mythology," in *Kerygma and Myth, op. cit.*, pp. 1–10.

same time to believe in the New Testament world of spirits and miracles.[28]

Thus this scholar believes that we live in too modern an age to believe in miracles. The world is closed to such occurrences.[29] The Supernatural simply does not occur and is therefore quickly dismissed, often arbitrarily.[30] Others also agree with Bultmann's approach.[31]

This line of reasoning is not very recent, however. For a couple of hundred years prior to the twentieth century many have also held that science ruled miracles out. The universe was usually seen as being a closed system, meaning, among other things, that it could not be interfered with by the Supernatural. James Jauncey defines it this way:

> The standpoint of science was that nature was a 'closed universe.' This meant that everything within the universe was governed by an unvarying sequence of cause and effect. The universe was closed to any occurrences which deviated from this pattern. ... Whenever you had a certain combination of factors operating, the result was always the same and could not be different. Miracles, on the other hand, could not be fitted into this framework of cause and effect.[32]

This view of miracles is actually found very early in critical thought. We need not wait until the eighteenth and nineteenth centuries to find this opinion expressed against the possibility of miracles. For instance, seventeenth-century philosopher Benedict Spinoza (1632–1677) also opposed miraculous events which were said to break the laws of nature.[33]

---

28. *Ibid.*, p. 5.

29. *Ibid.*, pp. 4–5; cf. Montgomery, *Where Is History Going?*, *op. cit.*, p. 194, especially footnote number 37.

30. Bultmann, *Ibid.*, p. 38; cf. Macquarrie, *op. cit.*, pp. 185–86.

31. Cf. for example John A. T. Robinson's *Honest to God* (Philadelphia: The Westminster Press, 1963). pp. 13–18.

32. James H. Jauncey, *Science Returns to God* (Grand Rapids: Zondervan, 1966), p. 37. Cf. also philosopher Gordon Clark's statements about the mechanism of the nineteenth century in his essay "Bultmann's Three-Storied Universe," in *Christianity Today*, edited by Frank E. Gaebelein (Westwood: Fleming H. Revell Company, 1968), pp. 218–19.

33. Benedict Spinoza, *The Chief Works of Benedict De Spinoza*, translated by R. E. M. Elwes, 2 vols. (New York: Dover Publications, 1951), vol. 1, p. 87.

Since the beginning of the twentieth century, however, science has begun to change these former conceptions about the workings of nature. In man's past history there have been many scientific revolutions.[34] In the opinion of most, we are living today in the midst of just such a revolution. Jauncy states in his Introduction titled "The Scientific Revolution":

> The evidence is piling up that we are in the midst of the greatest evolution in human living since the Renaissance. This is due to the tremendous explosion in scientific knowledge which has been occurring within the last few years. Even for those of us who have been close to the frontiers of science all of our lives, it is hard to believe what is happening.[35]

What are the results of these changes and how do they affect the possibility of miracles? Jauncy relates that one result of this scientific revolution is that today the idea of a closed universe is rejected. Scientific research has replaced this other view with a new understanding of nature.[36] Clark also notes that the idea of causality was dropped by science about one hundred years ago and the belief in a mechanistic universe has also come under attack.[37] The resulting new view of nature is sometimes referred to by such titles as the "Einsteinian-relativistic interpretation of 'natural law' " and perceived as being essentially opposed to "the world of Newtonian absolutes."[38] Thomas S. Kuhn also believes that the theories of Einstein are incompatible with the older ones formulated by Newton. In fact, we can only accept this Einsteinian system after recognizing that the theories of Newton were incorrect.[39]

A recent work by eminent German physicist Werner Schaaffs has succeeded both in describing these comparatively recent trends in physics and in dealing with the resultant influence on the possibility of miracles.

---

34. See Thomas S. Kuhn, *The Structure of Scientific Revolutions*, vol. 2, no. 2 of the *International Encyclopedia of Unified Science*, edited by Otto Neurath, Rudolf Carnap and Charles Morris (Chicago: University of Chicago Press, 1971).

35. Jauncey, *op. cit.*, p. 3.

36. *Ibid.*, pp. 37–38.

37. Clark, "Bultmann's Three-Storied Universe," in Gaebelein, *op. cit.*, pp. 218–19.

38. John Warwick Montgomery, *The Suicide of Christian Theology* (Minneapolis: Bethany Fellowship, 1970), pp. 263, 320.

39. Kuhn, *op. cit.*, pp. 98ff.

Schaaffs informs us that the rejection of a closed universe by modern science took place about the turn of the century. In fact, the year 1900 is seen as being the turning point for modern physics.[40] Therefore we can no longer scientifically hold to the belief in a closed universe as was the case in the nineteenth century.[41]

Schaaffs refers to the replacing of the closed universe view with the present view of physics as "double negation." This is because older opinions which were once used to negate all miracles are, in turn, negated themselves.[42] The old law of causation has been replaced by statistical description and thus the law of probability.[43] To this we will turn directly. But we must first remark that new theories in physics usually build upon older ideas and thus appear at least somewhat to be a process of development (rather than a case of total displacement). The old views are thus expanded and corrected by the modern ones.[44] We will now take a closer look at some important developments in physics that have led to these conclusions.

2. SOME PRINCIPLES OF PHYSICS

We have been speaking of the modern view of physics and its negation of the eighteenth- and nineteenth-century belief in a closed universe where no outside intervention was believed to be possible. It should be mentioned in all fairness that not all scholars in these two centuries accepted this view of cause and effect in a mechanistic world[45] although it was very popular.[46] Therefore, before the twentieth century the world was, for the most part, conceived to be one of mechanical cause and effect. Any events which did not fit into this pattern, such as miracles, were often rejected

---

40. Werner Schaaffs, *Theology, Physics and Miracles*, translated by Richard L. Renfield (Washington, DC: Canon Press, 1974) pp. 26, 31, 37–38. Cf. Jauncey, *op. cit.*, p. 37.

41. *Ibid.*, cf. pp. 25–26.

42. *Ibid.*, pp. 24–26.

43. *Ibid.*, pp. 63–64; cf. pp. 44–45.

44. Kuhn, *op. cit.*, pp. 67, 149; cf. Schaaffs, *Ibid.*, p. 64.

45. For instance, David Hume firmly rejected cause and effect. See O. W. Heick, *History of Protestant Theology*, vol. 2 of *A History of Christian Thought* by J. L. Neve, 2 vols. (Philadelphia: The Muhlenberg Press, 1946), p. 65 and also J. Bronowski and Bruce Mazlish, *The Western Intellectual Tradition* (New York: Harper & Row, 1962), p. 474.

46. Schaaffs, *op. cit.*, pp. 63–64 and Clark, "Bultmann's Three-Storied Universe," in Gaebelein, *op. cit.*, p. 218.

immediately. It was the "reign of 'unalterable law'" in which it was imag-
ined that one could be sure of events and in which miracles were simply
not possibilities.[47]

With the emergence of the twentieth century experimentation in
physics it was found that, contrary to the then accepted scientific belief,
there was much *uncertainty* in our universe. It could not be predicted
with complete accuracy how a particular event would occur. There were
found variations and differences in principles that were once thought to
be invariable. It was beginning to be apparent that the universe could not
be expected to behave any one certain way all of the time.[48]

Even though we have been discussing the field of physics, it should
be pointed out that this information definitely has had an affect on other
fields of knowledge as well. This was obvious because, if these facts were
true, then other studies also had to adjust to them. Later, for example,
the affect of these discoveries on the discipline of history will be shown.
Schaaffs notes, for instance, that few actually understand that the significance of these findings extends far beyond the field of physics.[49]

Some may object that these principles affect only questions which
deal with the microcosm and therefore have no bearing on the topic of
miracles. Schaaffs deals with this very problem, concluding that one can
work from any of three directions[50] to demonstrate that occurrences in
the microcosm have a great bearing on events in the macrocosm. These
reasons show that chain reactions can be caused by deviations in individual atoms which eventually have macroscopic results. Thus, minute
and unpredictable changes in atomic processes cause major events to also
become somewhat indeterminate and unpredictable. In fact, the uncer-
tain pairing of microscopic transactions can either cause a macroscopic

---

47. Jauncey, *op. cit.*, pp. 37–38.

48. *Ibid.*, p. 38; for this principle as it is applied to physics, see Schaaffs, *op. cit.*, pp. 57–61 and
Otto Blüh and Joseph Denison Elder *Principles and Applications of Physics* (New York: Interscience
Publishers, 1955), pp. 760ff.

49. Schaaffs, *Ibid.*, p. 61.

50. Schaaffs mentions three approaches in noting the affect of the microcosm on the macrocosm. One way would be to work from the microscopic elements to the macroscopic ones, noting
the affect single atoms can have on whole processes or events. Or one might work in the opposite
direction, beginning with the macrocosm and endeavoring to find the minute particles that affect it.
Lastly, Schaaffs has experimented with de Broglie's equation of the matter wave demonstrating that
it can also be applied to the macrocosm, just as it can be applied to the microcosm (*Ibid.*, pp. 80–81).

event to occur or keep it from occurring. Thus the macroscopic event itself becomes unpredictable and it is not within the reach of science to control it.[51]

It is true that microscopic events are more unpredictable than macroscopic ones, but both are often found to be unexplainable.[52] For these reasons, *both* microscopic and macroscopic events "can be interpreted only as a law of probability."[53] This means that a "statement in science is seldom now considered true in itself, but only within a certain limit of probability."[54] In other words, we can no longer consider a scientific statement as being absolute, but only probable to one extent or another. Statistical probabilities must be given to events according to the degree to which they can be expected to occur and not viewed as being positively certain as might be the case in a closed universe.

One use of statistics that is perhaps not at first obvious is that they "have enabled us to appreciate the extreme cases"[55] because "the rarer an event, the harder it is to determine a precise time for its occurrence. One can only assign a probability to it."[56] Therefore more common events receive a higher probability and rarer ones a lower probability. Unique events are given still lower chances of occurring. But this is intriguing in the case of these very rare events because "even the greatest probability cannot rule out the possibility that the event will occur tomorrow."[57] There is an infinite number of possibilities for such events to occur daily and thus they cannot be thought to be impossible.

Can giving a probability to rare events, as described above, have any relevance to the possibility of miracles occurring? Schaaffs answers in the affirmative:

> Though a miracle is a rare, or perhaps even unique, event or experience, quite out of the ordinary, it can with comparative ease, as our example shows, be placed in a statistical framework. It has no

51. *Ibid.*, pp. 52–53, 71, 79–81. This last point is illustrated by Schaaffs (pp. 52–53).
52. *Ibid.*, pp. 16, 71. Cf. Blüh and Elder, *op. cit.*, pp. 806–7, 803.
53. Schaaffs, *op. cit.*, p. 64.
54. Jauncey, *op. cit.*, p. 38.
55. Schaaffs, *op. cit.*, p. 55.
56. *Ibid.*, p. 56.
57. *Ibid.*

intrinsic peculiarity requiring that it be placed outside that frame-work. Thus, a miracle, though a rarity to be sure, is a phenomenon of natural law, for statistics are the essence of natural law.[58]

Therefore we see that for this German physicist miracles are *possible*. We will also note here that Montgomery, for one, agrees with this above analysis and insists that the only way that an account of a miracle can be verified is by an "unprejudiced confrontation" with the sources which claim that such an event actually occurred. We need not try to ascertain *a priori* what is able to occur today (as was done in a closed universe), since almost anything is possible according to its statistical probability. In other words, the "question is no longer what *can* happen, but what *has* happened" because "the universe since Einstein has opened up to the possibility of *any* event" (the italics are Montgomery's).[59] Therefore, we can only determine what has happened by investigating the sources in order to ascertain which events probably are and which events probably are not a part of history.

3. MIRACLES

Few understand how far-reaching these results in physics are and "how far beyond physics their significance extends."[60] The knowledge thus gained surpasses the bounds of physics and affects other fields such as theolo-gy.[61] We have found that the belief in a mechanistic, closed universe is no longer valid and thus cannot be used to rule out miracles *a priori*, as in the past. We can only find out if an event has occurred or not by inves-tigating the sources thoroughly. This could lead to either a positive or to a negative conclusion.

A key point we want to stress in this chapter is that these former worldviews can no longer be used, as contemporary theology often does,[62] against the occurrence of miracles. We are certainly not saying at this

---

58. *Ibid.*, p. 45.

59. Montgomery, *Where Is History Going?*, *op. cit.*, p. 93; cf. pp. 73, 168–69.

60. Schaaffs, *op. cit.*, p. 61.

61. *Ibid.*, p. 65.

62. Schaaffs directs some of his criticisms against Bultmann (*Ibid.*, pp. 13, 24–25) and other theologians who insist on using these outdated worldviews (*Ibid.*, pp. 8, 15, 31, 60, 64).

point that miracles do occur. But they can only be disbelieved today on the merits of each. Montgomery drives this last point home in the following words, using the resurrection of Jesus as an example of a miracle:

> To oppose the resurrection on the ground that miracles do not occur is, as we have noted earlier, both philosophically and scientifically irresponsible: philosophically, because no one below the status of a god could know the universe so well as to eliminate miracles *a priori*; and scientifically, because in the age of Einsteinian physics (so different from the world of Newtonian absolutes in which Hume formulated his classic anti-miraculous argument) the universe has opened up to all possibilities.[63]

This is surely not to affirm that Einstein said that miracles *would* happen but only that there is always the possibility that they *could*, given our present concept of physics.

Concerning the conception of nature with which we have been working, we must mention that the results described above do not invalidate the idea of essential lawful order in nature. All are agreed that such a general order does exist, even though it must only be described statistically.[64] In addition, as McNaugher explains, where there is no regularity in nature we cannot speak of any departure from it.[65] In other words, if nature were disorderly, it would be impossible to know if something had occurred that could be described as irregular.

Thus, along with all recent studies, we also affirm the belief in the regularity of nature. A true miracle, then (if there is such an occurrence), must interfere with this regularity, according to our definition. Therefore, if miracles are to happen, nature cannot be the cause of them, but can only be open to their occurrence.[66]

Thus we hold that modern scholarship can no longer deny miracles simply by referring to a closed universe and to our civilization as being

---

63. Montgomery, *The Suicide of Christian Theology, op. cit.*, pp. 262–63.

64. See Schaaffs, *op. cit.*, pp. 64, 71; cf. also Swinburne, *op. cit.*, pp. 23–26.

65. McNaugher, *op. cit.*, p. 92; cf. Swinburne, *Ibid.*, pp. 26–29.

66. Note that we are showing the result on nature if miracles were to occur. We have not yet established if they actually do or not.

"too advanced." They can only be denied on the grounds of historical and philosophical (logical) research.

It may appear that there is too much reliance here on a current scientific worldview that may change again in the future to yet another understanding of nature. To this there are at least two valid responses.

First and most important, it must be pointed out that an investigation into the possibility of miracles does not *require* the contemporary relativistic view of nature in order to arrive at valid conclusions. It is true that this modern view of science does help considerably both in negating the old closed universe hypothesis and in allowing for the *possibility* that miracles do occur. However, it must be asserted that the procedure we will deal with later, namely, investigating an event first before any judgment is given concerning the probability of its occurring, does not depend on science. We cannot overstate this enough. If we were to rest upon an existing view of nature we would always be in danger of having our system upset because of new ideas when this need not be the case. Regardless of the contemporary state of physics, we hold that an account of a miracle (as defined above) should be investigated inductively to ascertain if it has occurred *apart* from any other worldview of what can or cannot happen. Such is a much more logical and scholarly approach than beginning with presuppositions as to what is possible. These conclusions could thus be maintained even if physics was not in the state in which we find it.[67] Thus the conclusions to be reached do not depend solely upon our modern understanding of science, but are rather based upon this aforementioned investigation of the reported facts.[68]

Second, Schaaffs answers this very question by asserting that physics is unlike other disciplines in that it does not regress backward: "Accurate knowledge and the results of earlier research are *never* simply discarded;

---

67. We wish to make it plain, however, that our study of contemporary physics is an extremely important one and not simply a "nice addition" to this work. Although this study is based on an investigation of the facts to determine if an event has occurred and not upon a current scientific worldview, this chapter has still provided some insight into the question of what is possible in today's world. Understanding the current scientific outlook has demonstrated at least that our beliefs must not exclude miracles a priori. Also, it makes us realize that there is a scientific basis for our historical approach to investigating a purported event.

68. See Bernhard Ramm, *Protestant Christian Evidences* (Chicago: Moody Press, 1953), pp. 146–49.

rather, they serve as building blocks for further advances."[69] He adds later that "the knowledge discovered in the present century will remain valid within the framework in which it was obtained."[70] Present concepts in physics may even be broadened, but they do not disappear. This is because knowledge in this discipline is not discarded in order to return to older ideas.[71] As mentioned, the truths discovered in physics remain valid. Therefore, even if we did rest our conclusions on the current scientific worldview (although we do not, as stated above), they would still appear safe.

Before proceeding to the next chapter, it must be mentioned in all fairness that most men of science do not hold that this current view of physics gives any preference to miracles.[72] Therefore we will conclude this chapter with the assertion of philosopher Gordon Clark, who is cautious in his evaluation of the relationship between miracles and modern physics. He feels that while some theological conservatives have gone too far in their application of scientific principles to the Supernatural, others have gone too far in the opposite direction by presenting science as being totally opposed to anything which is really miraculous. Clark believes that we can at least minimally conclude that the once-popular theories of a closed and mechanistic universe can no longer be used to invalidate miracles. In addition, neither these older theories or contemporary scientific ones can be used as objections against the Supernatural. While we cannot agree with those who believe that science gives preference to miracles, neither can we agree with those who believe that it forbids them.[73]

In other words, Clark's conclusion is stated in negative terms. Rather than holding that the universe allows for the miraculous, Clark simply states that we can no longer appropriate a scientific worldview that rules out the miraculous. Thus he speaks not about what is *possible* in nature, as do many of the scholars we have dealt with above, but about what we *cannot* say about it. We cannot hold that science gives preferential

---

69. Schaaffs, *op. cit.*, p. 14. The italics are Schaaffs.

70. *Ibid.*, p. 67.

71. *Ibid.*, p. 14.

72. Cf. Ernst Cassirer, *Determinism and Indeterminism in Modern Physics*, translated by O. Theodor Benfrey (New Haven: Yale University Press), p. 193 for instance.

73. Clark, "Bultmann's Three-Storied Universe," in Gaebelein, *op. cit.*, pp. 218–19.

treatment to miracles, but neither can the scientific worldview be used to show that they cannot occur.[74] This, then, is the conclusion we will work with, one which directly favors neither opinion. Therefore we are also left with the conclusion which we reached earlier—that decisions concerning the probability of certain miracles (such as the resurrection of Jesus) must be determined by a thorough investigation of the reported facts in order to ascertain if they actually happened.

---

74. Ibid.

CHAPTER III

History and Miracles

As stated above, this study is not based upon the findings of modern physics, but rather upon the idea that any accounts which claim that a miracle has occurred must be historically investigated in order for its veracity to be determined. Therefore we will look first at the concept of history that will be used in this work and then view the method of this investigation.

A. A CONCEPT OF HISTORY

The term "history" is used in various ways by different scholars. There is no uniform definition which is agreed to by all scholars, as numerous approaches and interpretations are commonly utilized.[1] Therefore it is not our purpose here to give a complete or exhaustive treatment of the contemporary definitions of history. However, it seems that there is at least some general agreement concerning the content of history.

Most historians are agreed that history includes at least two major factors—the actual events in particular and also the recording of these events. Thus this discipline is mainly concerned with what has happened and how these occurrences have been annotated. It is this conception which will form the core understanding of history as it will be used in this work. Other elements are surely involved, as will now be noted. But the inclusion of these

---

1. See Patrick Gardiner's article "The Philosophy of History" in the *International Encyclopedia of the Social Sciences*, edited by David L. Sills, *op. cit.*, vol. 6, pp. 428–33 for some of these interpretations.

two major ideas is essential and are thus the foundation of this concept as it will be used here.[2]

Now we surely do not mean to affirm that the presence of these two elements is all that is involved in a definition of history. Rather, these are the ones which seem to reoccur most often. However, a few other factors that are part of this discussion should also be mentioned quickly.

First, there is always a subjective factor involved in the writing of history. For instance, the historian must select the material which he will (and will not) cover. The historical event is obviously objective. It is the recording of the event that introduces subjective factors. For W. H. Walsh, the subjectivity of the writer is present, but it is not a real serious roadblock to the obtaining of objective history. This subjectivity can be allowed for its efforts can be overcome.[3] Wand agrees with Walsh in asserting that the best approach to take toward history is one of caution,[4] as we should try and recognize this subjective bias and then make the proper allowance for it.[5]

We will also endeavor to allow for this subjective factor in our investigation of the resurrection. This occurrence has been reported as an objective historical event and we must ascertain if it is the best explanation for the known facts.

Second, we find that history cannot reach the point where it is *totally positive* of its findings in all instances. As with physics, so there is also a certain amount of dependence on probability in history as well.[6]

For instance, Ernest Nagel, who accepts a deterministic view of history, admits that he does so in spite of the convictions of contemporary physicists who almost unanimously hold the opposite viewpoint.[7] The

---

2. Most historians also recognize these two factors—the events themselves and the records of these events—as being an essential part of history. For such related views, see Carl L. Becker, *The Heavenly City of Eighteenth-Century Philosophers* (New Haven: Yale University Press, 1969), pp. 17–18; Bronowski and Mazlish, *op. cit.*, pp. xi–xii; Clough, Garsoian, and Hicks, *op. cit.*, vol. 1, p. 1; Runes, *op. cit.*, p. 127; Wand, *op. cit.*, p. 22.

3. W. H. Walsh, *Philosophy of History* (New York: Harper & Brothers, 1960), pp. 101, 103.

4. Wand, *op. cit.*, pp. 29, 42.

5. *Ibid.*, p. 31. See also Patrick Gardiner's article "The Philosophy of History," in Sills, editor, *op. cit.*, pp. 432–33.

6. Wand, *op. cit.*, pp. 51–52.

7. Ernest Nagel, "Determinism in History," in Dray, *op. cit.*, p. 355.

conclusions of these scientists have had an affect on historians, for the accepted scientific view against a deterministic universe has also helped to turn historians against a deterministic view of history.[8]

Nagel lists five main reasons why historical determinism is generally rejected by so many historians today. First is the argument from the absence of any developmental laws or patterns in history. Second is the argument based on the inability to explain and predict events in human history. The third argument concerns the appearance of the novel in historical occurrences. Fourth is the argument from the chance events which are also a part of history. The fifth argument concerns the conflicting results when one attempts to make the concept of a deterministic world compatible with the freedom and moral duty of human beings.[9]

It is because of these and other similar findings that so many historians have rejected the deterministic view of history. Nagel further states (to reiterate the point), that the findings of modern physics, which also oppose determinism, have been a key factor that has exercised a direct influence on a similar rejection of this concept by most historians.[10] Montgomery concurs in this belief that contemporary science has made it impossible for historians to accept a closed system of natural causes.[11]

The appearance of these chance and novel events mentioned above, together with the aforementioned inability to explain or predict many other occurrences, has helped to further the use of probabilities in historical studies (as well as in scientific investigation).[12] Historians both recognize and utilize this concept of probability. For instance, Montgomery observes that historical studies can never reach the one hundred percentile level in certainty.[13] Ronald VanderMolen agrees completely with Montgomery's assessment and thus accepts the belief that historical scholarship is not completely positive of its findings. In fact, historians must not

---

8. *Ibid.*

9. *Ibid.*

10. *Ibid.*

11. Montgomery, *Where Is History Going?*, *op. cit.*, p. 71.

12. See Schaaffs, *op. cit.*, cf. pp. 52–53, 64 for instance.

13. Montgomery, *Where Is History Going?*, *op. cit.*, pp. 168–69.

fail to allow for this amount of uncertainty.[14] For this reason Montgomery opts for a critical investigation of the sources in question, with the decision about the occurrence of any specific event being based upon the probability of the evidence. In fact, probability is referred to as the only sufficient guide for a historian.[15] Wand also notes that we cannot be as sure of historical investigation as was thought possible in the past.[16] However, we must make our judgments as to which facts are most probable according to the historical evidence.[17]

These elements, then, are to be included in a contemporary treatment of history. While it has not been our purpose to deal with this subject exhaustively, we have come to some conclusions on the concept of history as it will be used in this work. We will refer to history as both the occurrence of past events and the recording of them. Realizing that there is always a certain amount of the subjective in this recording, allowance must be made for it as much as is possible in order for objective data to be obtained. Realizing also that in speaking of history we are dealing with probabilities, it will be our desire to ascertain as nearly as is possible which facts best fit the evidence. With these probabilities and uncertainties there is always room for the possibility of any event, however high the probability may be against it.[18] Events can therefore not be ruled out (either scientifically or historically) before they are researched. The only answer is a thorough investigation of the evidence.

B. INVESTIGATING THE HISTORICAL EVENTS

1. HISTORICAL RESEARCH AND INVESTIGATION

It is the opinion of most historians today that the veracity of past events can be discovered (within a certain probability) by a careful investigation of the facts.[19] Walsh notes that since these events have occurred in the past,

---

14. Ronald VanderMolen, " 'Where Is History Going?' and Historical Scholarship: A Response," in *Fides et Historia* 5, nos. 1–2 (1972/1973): 110.

15. Montgomery, *Where Is History Going?, op. cit.*, pp. 71–74.

16. Wand, *op. cit.*, pp. 25–27.

17. *Ibid.*, pp. 30, 51–52, 156, 167.

18. Schaaffs, *op. cit.*, p. 56.

19. Wand, *op. cit.*, p. 5.

they are only accessible by a study of the historical evidence. Although the historian himself will not be able to participate in the event that has already occurred (unless he was originally there), he is able to inspect the relevant data such as written documents and various other records, structures, or archeological finds. Upon such confirmation as this the historian must obtain his evidence. This is what Walsh feels is the working principle of historical research.[20]

Of course, what the existing data and written sources reveal is not usually automatically accepted as being true. It is therefore the job of the historian to critically investigate the available claims in order to ascertain as closely as possible what has happened. This includes the procedure of determining if the sources best support the claims that are made in them. The proper results can be obtained even though there exists this need to determine which facts *best* fit the evidence. Then it is the duty of the historian to formulate the facts based upon this groundwork.[21] One is therefore to decide upon the evidence at hand—that which is shown to be the most probable conclusion.

Even claims of miracles must be investigated in this way, since they cannot be ruled out *a priori*, as noted above. On this subject Montgomery asserts:

> But can the modern man accept a "miracle" such as the resurrection? ... For us, unlike people of the Newtonian epoch, the universe is no longer a tight, safe, predictable playing-field in which we know all the rules. Since Einstein no modern man has had the right to rule out the possibility of events because of prior knowledge of "natural law." ... The problem of "miracle," then, must be solved in the realm of historical investigation.[22]

---

20. Walsh, *op. cit.*, p. 18. For a good example of such an investigation with regard to ancient historical events, see Delbrück's methods of determining how ancient battles had been fought in the times of the Greek and Roman empires. It is fascinating to perceive how this scholar was able to arrive at historical facts concerning how large the opposing armies were, how they maneuvered, and other such facets of specific battles in ancient times by examining the ancient historical records. For instance, see Edward M. Earle, editor, *Makers of Modern Strategy* (Princeton: Princeton University Press, 1943), especially pp. 264–68 with regard to Delbrück's historical method.

21. *Ibid.*, pp. 18–19; cf. Daniel Fuller, *op. cit.*, p. 22 for these same conclusions.

22. John Warwick Montgomery, *History and Christianity* (Downers Grove: InterVarsity Press, 1972), p. 75. Cf. also Montgomery's *Where Is History Going?*, *op. cit.*, p. 71.

As Montgomery concludes, since we cannot decide in advance what *can* happen, we must determine, by historical research, what really *has* happened already.[23]

We must quickly point out here that miracles are not to be believed simply because they are Supernatural. In fact, we would desire to be the more careful before accepting a miracle-claim as a historical event. But, on the other hand, we must also guard against the presupposition that miracles cannot occur at all. There is no real basis, either scientific or historical, for this presupposition.[24] Although many are skeptical about the reality of miracles, it may be that a Supernatural explanation fits the facts best and is the most probable solution.[25]

On this last point of skepticism Wand has made a very pertinent point. His words were specifically directed at the historical skepticism of theologian Van Harvey, but Wand points out that the same can also be applied to others of this persuasion as well. Harvey argued that we cannot accept the New Testament accounts of the empty tomb even though there is much historical evidence in favor of them and no convincing evidence contrary to them. To this Wand responds:

> We may well ask Harvey how a critical historian can do anything else than decide on the evidence before him—unless indeed he already holds some secret which will invalidate in advance any evidence that can be brought in favor of the phenomenon in question? The plain fact is that in this kind of argument the skeptic is not functioning as a historian at all. He starts with the assumption that there could be no corporeal resurrection since that would be against nature. ... That is to say, he rejects the evidence because he does not like a conclusion that it may be used to support.[26]

It appears that Wand's point is well taken here. What else can the historian do except investigate the available evidence and make a decision based on it? Since this is the way that other historical facts must be

---

23. *Ibid.*, cf. also *Where Is History Going*, pp. 168–69.
24. Wand, *op. cit.*, pp. 30, 101.
25. *Ibid.*, pp. 51–52.
26. *Ibid.*, pp. 70–71.

decided (as we have seen above) it seems that we do not have the right
to demand different criteria simply because, as Wand notes, we do not
like or agree with the conclusions. We must therefore approach this subject with an open mind, endeavoring to ascertain which explanation is
the most probable.[27]

Now some may judge that Wand's conclusions are those of the theological "fundamentalist" who endeavors to prove every word of Scripture
as being true. To this it should be remarked that not only does this Oxford
scholar object to such beliefs,[28] he holds to the quite contemporary theological opinion that while some of the New Testament is historical and
trustworthy, some is also simply propaganda which was written without
any claims to being objectively historical. Thus he cannot accept the view
that the Bible itself is the guarantee and proof that all of Christianity was
completely historical.[29] Because of this, Wand believes that we should
inquire into whatever mythical elements could possibly be present in the
texts. But, at the same time, we cannot allow the portions that evidence
indicates are historical to be labelled as myth.[30]

Wand's conclusion in these matters is that we must approach these
ancient documents cautiously. Bias and subjective factors must be allowed
for and dealt with accordingly. But, in spite of all of this, we may find
that the Supernatural explanation is more historically probable than the
natural one. In this case we must be prepared to accept the miraculous
conclusion.[31]

2. THE RESURRECTION AND HISTORICAL INVESTIGATION

According to Wand, the resurrection is the central claim of New Testament
Christianity and as such it cannot simply be ignored.[32] Neither should we
be content to leave the question simply by affirming that the original disciples *believed* that Jesus had risen. Since it is the center of the Christian

---

27. *Ibid.*, pp. 29–31.
28. *Ibid.*, p. 55.
29. *Ibid.*, pp. 17–18.
30. *Ibid.*, p. 42.
31. *Ibid.*, pp. 29–31.
32. *Ibid.*, pp. 80, 114.

faith it should be carefully investigated. We must inquire into this belief in order to ascertain whether or not it is valid.[33]

Other historians also agree to the need for such research. Ancient historian Paul Maier also believes that the historical evidence for the resurrection must be investigated. Then we can better judge whether it can be referred to as an actual part of history.[34] Another ancient historian, Edwin Yamauchi, agrees that we must investigate this occurrence in order to conclude if it is best explained as myth or as history.[35] We have already discussed Montgomery's preference to historically investigate this event as well.[36]

Therefore, after dealing with the problem of faith and reason in the next chapter, we will turn to this investigation.[37] The New Testament authors certainly *claimed* that Jesus rose from the dead, meaning literally that he appeared to many of the early Christians after having actually died. No one doubts that this is what the accounts report. It remains for us to endeavor to determine the facticity of these claims.

We have in this chapter explained the concept of history that is to be used in this work. We have also determined that history, like science, cannot rule out the possibility of miracles *a priori*, that is, without investigating the available evidence and deciding upon it. To this end we have briefly described the approaches taken by several historians as to historical research and investigation. Procedures such as these will be used in our own investigation of the resurrection of Jesus.

---

33. *Ibid.*, pp. 90–94.

34. Maier, *First Easter, op. cit.*, pp. 105–122 and "The Empty Tomb as History," *op. cit.*, pp. 4–6.

35. Yamauchi, *op. cit.*, March 15, 1974 pp. 4–7 and March 29, 1974, pp. 12–16.

36. Montgomery, *Where Is History Going?*, *op. cit.*, pp. 71–73, 93, 168–69 for instance.

37. It is important to note that historical studies have also been made about other miracle-claims in ancient history. M. I. Finley, for instance, investigates Homer and his claims of miraculous intervention into early history, such as with the Trojan war. Or for another example, various scholars have examined claims of tongue-speaking, or glossolalia, in ancient history. For Finley's work, see *The World of Odysseus* (New York: The Viking Press, 1954), especially pp. 10–19. For a historical discussion of speaking in tongues, see George Barton Cutten, *Speaking with Tongues Historically and Psychologically Examined* (New Haven: Yale University Press, 1927), pp. 36–47 for instance. For another example, see Frank Stagg, E. Glenn Hinton, and Wayne E. Oates, *Glossolalia: Tongue Speaking in Biblical, Historical and Psychological Perspective*, (Nashville: Abingdon Press, 1967), pp. 48–57.

CHAPTER IV

Reason and Faith

I t has been said that Christian history and thought is a history of the
opposition between faith and reason. This is a reference to the continual
conflict between these two aspects of the Christian life—the spiritual and the
rational.[1] There has always seemed to be a variety of views on this subject,
often intermingled and overlapping. Historian of philosophy Etienne Gilson
has dealt with several of these opinions in his work *Reason and Revelation in
the Middle Ages*.[2] For instance, early church theologian Tertullian believed
not only that faith was primary, but that all reference to human philosophy
or other teachings should be excluded.[3] Passing to the twelfth century, we
find Saint Bernard voicing a similar opinion in favor of faith alone.[4]

A second view was that of Augustine, who held that one's reason and
understanding do play a part, but a secondary one since faith is to precede
them. Therefore we must exercise faith first before we can understand.[5]
Another exponent of this view was Anselm.[6]

Gilson finds that a third important view was voiced by the twelfth century Arabian philosopher Averroes. Although his was not a Christian system

---

1. See Manfred T. Brauch, "Head and Heart Go to Seminary," *Christianity Today* 19, no. 9 (June
10, 1975): 11–12.

2. Etienne Gilson, *Reason and Revelation in the Middle Ages* (New York: Charles Scribner's Sons, 1966).

3. *Ibid.*, pp. 9–10.

4. *Ibid.*, pp. 12–13.

5. *Ibid.*, pp. 17–19.

6. *Ibid.*, pp. 23–26.

of thought, it did influence Christianity. For Averroes, reason was primary and faith was subordinated to it.[7]

The fourth view was that of Thomas Aquinas, who endeavored to find harmony between faith and reason. He believed that some truths could be known only by revelation while others could be attained by reason.[8]

This is just a sample of some of the possibilities when one views the history of opinions on the relationship between faith and reason. Some favor the use of either faith or reason exclusively. Some give a place to both, while subordinating one to the other. Either reason is seen as being subordinate to faith or vice versa. Others try to find a balance between the two methods. In this work a system will be set forth which is both a workable one and one that is justified by the facts.

A. REASON AND FAITH: DEFINITIONS

In order to lay a groundwork for our discussion on this topic, this study will begin with a look at the dictionary definitions of these two terms.[9] *The American Dictionary of the English Language* defines reason as follows:

> The basis or motive for an action, decision, or conviction. ... A declaration made to explain or justify an action, decision, or conviction. ... The capacity for rational thought, inference or discrimination. ... To ... think logically. ... To talk or argue logically or persuasively. ... To persuade or dissuade (someone) with reasons.[10]

According to this definition, reason includes at least two concepts. First, reason is the *capacity* to infer, discriminate or even to think rationally.

---

7. *Ibid.*, pp. 37–62. See especially pp. 42–48.

8. *Ibid.*, see especially pp. 82–83.

9. This writer realizes that philosophical conclusions such as these cannot be based soley on dictionary definitions. Since dictionaries only show how a word is used by most intelligent people, we would be epistemologically naive if we were to assume that such definitions are capable of settling these philosophical issues. Nevertheless, such an approach can be very valuable as a *groundwork* for later conclusions and this is how these definitions are to be used here. They serve as guidelines for the more sophisticated scholarly views which will be presented afterward to further corroborate these usages. The definitions themselves can *point* to a consensus of opinion as they reveal how these words are often defined. However, this will be corroborated by later references to scholars who verify these statements.

10. William Morris, editor, *The American Heritage Dictionary of the English Language* (New York: American Heritage Publishing Company, 1970), p. 1086.

Second, reason is the *explanation* or outworking of this capacity. This second concept includes (among other things) several component parts. Reason is defined as being the basis or motive for one's decisions or convictions, or a statement explaining or justifying these decisions or convictions. Reason is also the ability to think logically or to argue persuasively, including persuading (or dissuading) someone one way or another.[11]

If this definition was shown to be a valid one, other conclusions could be drawn from these two concepts of reason as well. For instance, reason would be at the very basis of all of our knowledge, for one cannot even have the *capacity* to think apart from reason (by definition). Without reason the *explanation* or outworking of this capacity would also fail to be accounted for because rational thought is defined as being at the basis of all actions, decisions or convictions. In fact, we cannot even formulate these convictions or make these decisions (intellectual or otherwise) except by utilizing reason. Therefore reason is the beginning of knowledge since it becomes obvious that we could not even think in the sense which we are accustomed to, except by reason. Considering the definition, we would have to think without formulating any convictions, making any decisions or coming to any conclusions in order to do so apart from a rational process. Finally, any attempt to counteract these conclusions or argue otherwise is also reason, again by definition.

However, as we have stated above, dictionary definitions cannot in themselves solve philosophical problems such as this one. Therefore, after faith is defined, the views of those who argue in favor of these definitions will later be investigated.

The *American Heritage Dictionary of the English Language* defines faith as:

> A confident belief in the truth, value, or trustworthiness of a person, idea, or thing. ... A system of religious beliefs.[12]

Faith, then, is trust or belief in a person, thing, idea, value or truth. Belief itself is defined as mental *action* centered in a *conviction* that is thought to

---

11. *Ibid.*
12. *Ibid.*, p. 471.

be valid.[13] We have already determined in our previous definition that the basis for such actions and convictions is reason.[14] In addition, belief generally involves thinking of some sort, even if it is only the elemental thought that what one is told to believe is "good."[15] Both of these procedures of thinking about one's faith, along with the convictions and decisions that often accompany them, are grounded in reason, by definition. Even the capacity to understand these beliefs is part of the cognitive process and has its basis in reason.[16]

There are two general reasons why faith is usually exercised. Some believe by intuitive conviction, while others require reasonable persuasion and rational argument (indeed, some claim an interest in both). But the capacity for both is acquired by reason, as defined above. This is because the ability even to hold convictions and the ability to reason concerning them is rational.[17]

Our study has thus far shown that faith must rely upon reason as its basis. However, this discussion has not so far been one of finding which of the two is the most important and it should not be construed as such. Therefore we will look briefly at this question now.

Even though reason composes the groundwork, we still hold that faith is the most important element of religious belief for two main reasons. First, it is not possible to logically and reasonably *prove* everything in the Christian faith. Thus faith extends beyond the reaches of this reason, which is more limited. Since we can only speak of varying degrees of probability, as stated above, any religious system which places such research at the apex of achievement will find that it is very limited

---

13. Cf. *Ibid.*, p. 121.

14. *Ibid.*, p. 1086.

15. One may object that many have exercised religious faith because they were told to do so or for other reasons which require no real contemplation. But we would hold that if one was capable of understanding his faith he would have been required to have thought about it at some time, if only in a naive and simple way. This is because faith would even involve affirmation of what others have dictated. However simple, it would be an acceptance of the existence of God or some such belief. Real faith involves at least some thinking as a part of this conviction or it could not be said to be such. For this reason, if one has never thought about his belief in any way it can only be because real faith was never exercised in the first place.

16. Morris, *op. cit.*, p. 1086.

17. *Ibid.*

in what is presented for belief. The realm of faith and hope would be narrowed considerably.

Second, although reason can yield true data from a logical investigation of the facts, faith is capable of transcending the rational when one puts trust in these facts. Therefore, one exercises faith based on the reasonable probabilities. Without such belief one could not speak of the Christian *faith*. God cannot be known by reasonable processes (beyond the knowledge that He exists), but rather a faith is needed which appropriates and trusts the evidence, with definite ethical implications for one's life. Without this primary importance of faith and these accompanying ethical implications, Christianity would not be a faith system. This is almost the unanimous witness of Christianity through the centuries, and it has a sound basis. While reason and knowledge are very important, especially as a basis for belief, faith is more so.[18] Reason is thus not the ultimate. This position is also accepted in this work. Faith should remain in this pre-eminent position, being careful to note that this is a reasonable faith based on the facts and not a leap in the dark. More will be said in favor of this opinion below.

So we now reach our conclusion pertinent to the results of these definitions and the roles they play in the issue between faith and reason. We have so far concluded that while reason is temporally primary, faith is the most important. Neither should be excluded and both should be used in its proper place. These definitions, however, will not be regarded as the final word in this discussion, nor will it be assumed that they can totally solve the issues. Therefore it is advantageous to turn now to those who also hold to some of the results arrived at here.

B. REASON AND FAITH: SCHOLARLY VIEWS

A study of definitions has revealed that reason must be the basis of all thinking processes, including the mental activity of faith. While reason is thus temporally first, when speaking in the context of Christian theology, faith is the most important.

---

18. Cf. the New Testament's primary emphasis on faith in such verses as John 20:29; Ephesians 2:8; Hebrews 11:1, 6.

Several contemporary scholars have come to similar conclusions based upon personal studies of the evidence. Secular theologian Paul Van Buren believes that faith always requires a thinking process. This is because faith usually includes both logical contemplation and a consideration of historical sources, and these, in turn, involve reasoning. Any type of Christian faith that neglects these processes is quite inadequate.[19]

Theologian John R. Stott also believes that faith is not irrational. It is neither credulity or optimism.[20] Rather, it is a trust based upon reason—a rational belief. As such faith does not contradict or oppose reason, but rather it is essentially complimented by it.[21]

For philosopher Francis Schaeffer, rationality, knowledge, and faith are all related. Rationality is very important, but not to the exclusion of the other elements. A balance must be kept between each. Nevertheless, we cannot expect faith to be exercised prior to a rational investigation of the evidence, or before a proper knowledge and understanding of the truth has first been achieved. These conditions precede faith.[22]

Theologian Wolfhart Pannenberg stresses the need for grounding faith on an objective, rational basis. In two essays entitled "Insight and Faith" and "Faith and Reason" he sets forth his rationale for this belief. Faith cannot stand alone and be its own criteria and proof for belief. This is because the subjective qualities of one's own faith alone provide no solid reasons as to why it is also good for another individual. The original question as to whether the grounds of this faith are solid is never answered. There is no logical reason to accept it. Therefore a knowledge based upon reason must precede faith.[23]

As pointed out earlier, Montgomery also holds that there must be an objective, historical basis for faith. Faith that is not based on some such

---

19. Paul M. Van Buren, *The Secular Meaning of the Gospel* (New York: The Macmillan Company, 1963), pp. 174–175.

20. John R. W. Stott, *Your Mind Matters: The Place of the Mind in the Christian Life* (Downers Grove: InterVarsity Press, 1973), pp. 33–36.

21. *Ibid.*, pp. 34, 36, 49–52.

22. Schaeffer, *The God Who Is There*, *op. cit.*, pp. 112–13, 141–43.

23. These two essays are found in one of Pannenberg's collections of other such works entitled *Basic Questions in Theology*, translated by George H. Kehm, 2 vols. (Philadelphia: Fortress Press, 1972), see vol. 2, pp. 28–35, 53–54 for instance. We will further elaborate on Pannenberg's theories on reason and faith below.

reasonable evidence can give no logical reason as to why it should be accepted over other alternatives. Faith cannot verify itself and neither can an experience demonstrate its own validity in and of itself. Therefore we have no reason to accept any faith as being valid if there are no grounds upon which to base this claim.[24]

We have *briefly* investigated the views of five scholars on the question of the relationship between reason and faith. We will turn now to the rationale behind these views, as to why reason is held to precede faith. The general conviction seems to be, first, that faith must be based upon knowledge and that, second, reason begins the entire process and provides the basis for this knowledge. We will examine these premises more closely.

First, faith must be based upon a knowledge of certain facts which are at least believed to be true. In order for one to have a faith-conviction there must ideally be this basis for belief. At the very least (in the absence of any intellectual or rational investigation), religious faith is trust in the existence of God or a reliance upon certain believed truths.[25] Therefore, religious faith must be grounded on some sort of knowledge, even if it is only the belief that God does (or does not, in the case of atheism) exist.[26] When we perceive that the Christian faith is thus based upon knowledge,

---

24. See the appendix of *History and Christianity, op. cit.*, pp. 99–101, 106–8. Cf. also Montgomery's debate with "God is dead" theologian Thomas Altizer, where Montgomery charges that Altizer's irrational faith provides no reason for others to believe him because it is based on no objective evidence. This debate is recorded in *The Altizer-Montgomery Dialogue* (Chicago: InterVarsity Press, 1967). See pp. 26, 59–60, 72, 76 and others where this charge is made. As with Pannenberg, so we will return to this reasoning below.

25. Even the case of atheism is no exemption here. If one designates atheism as a "religious faith," then it still must be acknowledged that it is also based on the knowledge of certain facts which are believed to be true. In this case, this would be the non-existence of God.

26. Cf. Van Buren, *op. cit.*, op. 174–75; Stott, *op. cit.*, p. 57; Schaeffer, *The God Who Is There, op. cit.*, pp. 143–45; Pannenberg, *op. cit.*, vol. 2, pp. 37, 45; Montgomery, *History and Christianity, op. cit.*, pp. 106–8. It is extremely important to note here, in addition, that the reason or knowledge upon which faith is based is not always a very sophisticated one. As asserted in footnote number 15 above, faith must be based on some knowledge, even if it is an uncomplicated and simple belief in what one is told. But even in this case acceptance of belief in God (or whatever it is that one is told to believe) still involves the acceptance of the knowledge that these beliefs are true. Anything short of this is not real faith. At no point in this work is the assertion ever made that one must be capable of a logical investigation of the facts before one can believe. Such is clearly not the case. A reasonable faith can be shown to be more valuable, but a faith based upon a less sophisticated knowledge is not thereby invalid. If the Christian faith can be shown to be based on a logical investigation of the facts, then faith in these facts is valid even if one is not capable of demonstrating the evidence for oneself.

we can then view this knowledge as preceding the faith.[27] Even some of the end results of faith, such as various kinds of action or ethical involvement, are due at least partially to the attainment of this prior understanding.[28]

Second, reason begins the process and provides the basis for this knowledge. We have seen that faith-conviction relies on knowledge and that this must involve some thinking, if only at the rudimentary level. Indeed, Van Buren states that real faith is only possible when one thinks[29] and Stott asserts that one cannot have faith at all apart from such cogitation.[30] But thinking is a rational process which requires the use of reason.[31] Therefore, reason both begins this process and provides the framework for it.[32]

In addition, faith must have an objective basis. Without such a foundation, one would never know if the grounds for one's belief were solid or not. Apart from a foundation of reasonable knowledge, faith is not capable of substantiating itself. Its subjective qualities provide no rational basis or criteria according to which its trustworthiness may be ascertained. For instance, one cannot appeal to one's personal spiritual experiences for the needed authority factor. Montgomery notes that an appeal to such private experiences is an unconvincing testimony, since it is sometimes hard to tell if the heartfelt experiences of another amount to anything more than heartburn![33] At first this appears to be simply a humorous illustration, but upon closer examination it is found to contain much truth. How can we even hope to differentiate between real experiences or beliefs and false ones if there are no factual criteria which gives us at least some idea as to what may be most trustworthy? A faith which is grounded upon rational facts and which rests upon an objective basis is in a much better position to ascertain its trustworthiness than is a faith which is admittedly irrational and subjective in its approach. It is true that one may prefer the latter,

---

27. Pannenberg, *Ibid.*, p. 32, footnote and also Wolfhart Pannenberg, editor, *Revelation as History*, translated by David Granskou (New York: The Macmillan Company, 1969), pp. 139, 157, note 15. Cf. Schaeffer, *Ibid.*

28. See Stott, *op. cit.*, p. 57.

29. Van Buren, *op. cit.*, p. 174.

30. Stott, *op. cit.*, p. 37.

31. See Schaeffer, *The God Who Is There*, *op. cit.*, pp. 141–43.

32. *Ibid.*, pp. 112–13.

33. Montgomery, *History and Christianity*, *op. cit.*, p. 101; cf. pp. 99, 107.

but this does not answer the question of how one might verify this faith even for oneself, let alone for others.

It is also true that the rational approach does not always lead to a valid faith. But it appears that it would be much better off in view of this question of verification than would a faith which does not (or cannot) utilize any rational method at all. Indeed, an intelligent investor does not often risk funds on an enterprise which gives no valid reasons to make such an investment seem worthwhile. Even hunches and premonitions are usually based on some sort of knowledge or reason, even if it is "secret information." In a similar way, faith should also be based upon a rational groundwork.

Apart from an objective faith which is based upon a logical examination of the facts, there is no way to ascertain if such beliefs are valid or not. No amount of wishful thinking can make the facts any more truthful. No matter how intense one's faith is, one cannot make this faith any more valid. Faith must therefore have an objective basis or else one would not be able to ascertain if it is simply spurious.

Pannenberg also believes that we must reject a subjective Christian faith which is based on one's personal experiences. He does so for at least two reasons. First, such private experiences cannot be obligatory for others because they lack factual, objective evidence and therefore are usually only capable, at the most, of convincing oneself.[34] Second, this subjectivism disregards the fact that the very center of Christianity is based on Divine initiative. Men everywhere are able to investigate the foundations of this religion in order to ascertain as closely as possible if events such as the resurrection have actually occurred. The opportunity to investigate the claims of Christianity is open to anyone who wants to

---

34. It might be objected that perhaps one does not care to make his faith obligatory for others, thus keeping it simply on the subjective level. But here we must remember, first, that Christianity claims to be a propagating faith interested in bringing others to accept this same grace of God that it has received. It therefore does not thrive on one's keeping faith to oneself. Second, we have reasoned here that Christianity is most properly based on one's exercising faith as a result of facts which are believed to be true and not upon irrational explanations or private experiences apart from these facts. Thus this aforementioned objection falls prey both to the idea that the Christian faith is to be propagated and to the conviction that faith is based upon objective facts as opposed to subjective feelings. For some of these ideas see Pannenberg's *Basic Questions in Theology, op. cit.*, vol. 2, especially pp. 53–54; cf. pp. 28, 30–32.

study them and is not relegated to the perusal of a select few.[35] Therefore, the Christian faith is most properly objective, open to a rational confrontation with the facts and not subjective or irrational.[36]

The same conclusion that was reached with regard to trying to substantiate Christianity by one's personal, subjective experience also applies to those who endeavor to point to the proclaimed message as the basis for the faith. This approach also fails in that the obvious question concerns whether there is a real reason to accept it or not. If the reason is unconvincing, it would seem that we would lack a sound basis for accepting it. Further, the message apart from any rational coercion cannot show why it should be accepted over another alternative, or even over a contrary view. In other words, the message is not self-authenticating but must also provide objective reasons to back up its claim to truth.[37]

By "objective reason" we are referring to the need for faith to investigate the historical (or other) evidence and make its decision upon which facts best fit the case. For Schaeffer, faith is based upon just such an examination of the events which Christianity claims have already occurred in history, such as the resurrection. One cannot be asked to exercise faith in the Christian message until the evidence has been investigated.[38] Montgomery agrees that faith begins in an investigation of the objective, historical events and rests in the probability of the findings.[39] But we must remember that faith is based on the events and not vice versa.[40] In other words, faith is not formulated apart from the facts, hoping that there is some evidence to support this venture. Rather, one believes because the facts appear reasonable. Pannenberg also stresses this last point, asserting that an individual does not bring an already existing faith to the events, but exercises this faith only after an open-minded look at the events.[41]

As for the question of importance, we found earlier that reason was temporally primary while faith was more important in a theological

---

35. Pannenberg, *Revelation as History, op. cit.*, pp. 135–39.

36. *Ibid.*, especially p. 138. See also *Basic Questions in Theology, op. cit.*, vol. 2, pp. 30, 53–54.

37. See Pannenberg's *Basic Questions in Theology, Ibid.*, vol. 2, pp. 33–34.

38. Schaeffer, *The God Who Is There, op. cit.*, p. 141; cf. p. 92.

39. Montgomery, *History and Christianity, op. cit.*, pp. 75–76, 79–80, 107–8.

40. *Ibid.*, p. 107.

41. Pannenberg, *Revelation as History, op. cit.*, p. 137.

context. We found this to be true for two main reasons. First, the whole of Christian teachings and belief cannot be explained completely in terms of reason. Second, when we speak in a theological context belief takes on a central importance, as it transcends reason. Faith must personally appropriate the facts, which involves ethical implications for one's life. This is chiefly because we are dealing with the existence and teaching of God (the Greek *theos*, root word of theology), a doctrine which cannot be dealt with adequately in the realm of reason alone. The importance of faith is primary here, as witnessed by centuries of Christian thought.

Does contemporary thought offer similar reasons for giving faith the place of primary importance while placing reason first temporally? We must answer here in the affirmative. It is especially noteworthy that the same scholars who we have been dealing with in our previous discussion, those who hold that reason and knowledge are the foundation for belief, also place faith in the place of prime importance in the end. Even the same two reasons used above (or very similar ones) are employed. First, Pannenberg notes that the doctrines of Christianity can never be explained completely in terms of reason. There will always be a remainder.[42] Second, Pannenberg further relates that no one can come to know God strictly by his own reason. A good example here is the Christian teachings concerning salvation. Even though reason provides the original basis, knowledge is still not capable of securing salvation because it depends finally upon the appropriation of faith and reliance in God and personal surrender to Him.[43] Thus faith is based upon rational probabilities, but the final expression of it transcends the rational.

Montgomery also comes to similar conclusions. Faith is based upon the probabilities which emerge from an investigation of the objective facts and the final step of salvation is an appropriation of this fact by means of faith. As such, faith and commitment to God through Jesus Christ is the final step of salvation, as it accomplishes something which reason could never do.[44]

---

42. Pannenberg, *Basic Questions in Theology, op. cit.*, vol. 2, p. 48.

43. *Ibid.*, p. 37 and *Revelation as History, op. cit.*, pp. 137–39.

44. Montgomery, *History and Christianity, op. cit.*, pp. 79–80, 107.

Wand adds an interesting point here. While faith is dependent upon reason and builds upon its more conclusive basis, faith is still more important in that it is more intimate and personal than knowledge. Thus it makes use of the framework of reason and then goes beyond the rational.[45]

It may become apparent at this point that reason and faith, when properly understood, actually compliment each other. Both have their own roles to play and each are very important.[46] These roles, as we have shown above, consist of faith operating on the basis of reason.[47] However, the two are not in competition with each other, but rather cooperate together. In this way they are found to be quite compatible.[48] The result is that head and heart should ideally work with, not against, each other.[49]

The conclusion which we have reached in this chapter is that faith can only be built upon reason, meaning that reason is temporally first in this process. This has been found to be the case both from an investigation of definitions and from a logical examination of the evidence. From the first study we found that we cannot even think in the way we are accustomed to, let alone exercise faith, apart from a rational process. For instance, real faith involves convictions and mental action. These can only be held by some variety of thinking and they also require reason, however naive. One can exercise valid faith, however, even if one is not able to personally investigate the facts, as mentioned above. From the latter study we have not only verified this, but we have concluded in addition that a subjective, irrational faith can provide no logical grounds as to why it should be accepted. If there is no rationale for this faith, there can be no objective criteria on which its claim to truth can be based. Therefore one cannot ascertain if the message based on such a faith should be accepted or not. Without any criteria or objective data on which to judge its contents, there is no logical way to distinguish one faith-message from a rival one. In fact, one is hard pressed for any evidence on which one's religious experience may be distinguished from any other human emotion, unless it is grounded in logical reason and investigation. Even an intense faith

---

45. Wand, *op. cit.*, p. 34.

46. *Ibid.*

47. Pannenberg, *Basic Questions in Theology, op. cit.*, vol. 2, pp. 36–37.

48. *Ibid.*, pp. 34–35, 47.

49. Brauch, *op. cit.*, p. 12.

apart from such an objective basis cannot make faith any more valid. Therefore, we hold that for faith to be intelligible it must be based on a rational knowledge.

We must be careful to point out once again that a rational approach to faith may not solve every last problem, but it does provide the best grounds on which to base faith, as shown above. Without this approach there would be no real way that one could verify these conclusions with any confidence. We thus encounter historical probabilities once again, as it appears that arguing from objective, historical data and logical evidence seems to provide the best way of arriving at the most probable results. So while the rational approach is not infallible, it does provide the best means of gaining a testable and verifiable foundation for faith. If we abandon the rational, we must also abandon our hopes of gaining such objective and verifiable results.[50]

An irrational or strictly subjective faith is not capable of providing such answers. It cannot verify itself or demonstrate its own validity. Neither can it answer the question of whether its grounds for faith are solid or not. Because of this lack of evidence it cannot show why it should be accepted over other possibilities. Such a faith cannot provide a logical reason as to why it should be accepted, since there are no testable grounds on which to base this claim. Neither can such belief make faith any more truthful. There is no logical reason to accept this faith.

Although reason is temporally first, faith was found to be the most important as an end result. This is because, first, all of Christian belief cannot be accounted for rationally. Second, in the context of theology, faith can do what reason cannot quite accomplish in dealing with the existence and teachings of God. Although based upon reason, faith transcends the rational in providing a means by which one can trust in the reasonable findings of one's aforementioned investigation, applying the results to one's life.

Lastly, we discussed the need to bring reason and faith together. We must present them henceforth as being entirely compatible and not in competition with each other, recognizing that each has a role to play.

---

50. Schaeffer, *The God Who Is There, op. cit.,* p. 113 and Pannenberg, *Basic Questions in Theology, op. cit.,* vol. 2, p. 28.

Reason forms the basis and is temporally first while faith is more essential and important.

In the historical and logical investigation which will now follow, we will endeavor to combine the essentials of our last three chapters. The scientific worldview can no longer be used to rule out the miraculous. Rather we must speak in terms of probabilities and investigate each miracle-claim. Here history also plays a part. Utilizing the concept of historical investigation outlined above, we will examine the possibilities of belief and nonbelief in the resurrection of Jesus. Again we must decide upon historical probability and accept as factual that explanation which best fits the facts. The philosophical discussion just concluded will also be utilized here. We must maintain throughout this relationship between reason and faith.[51]

It is advantageous to turn now to our historical and logical investigation of three key possibilities (and several related ones) concerning belief and nonbelief in the resurrection of Jesus. The findings in the fields of physics, history, and philosophy will be combined in an effort to ascertain which possibility best fits the facts.

---

51. Notice that in all three instances we have concluded that *probabilities* play a decisive part. *Science* has demonstrated the need to explain issues statistically, thus relying on probabilities. As we have shown above, *history* has also adopted this procedure as the best method of discerning facts about the past. Even in the *philosophical treatment* of reason and faith we spoke of the importance of faith making its decision on the probability of the rational investigation. Thus faith acts upon the most probable solution as well. We have here a striking confirmation of this belief.

PART 2

Possible Solutions to
the Question of the
Resurrection of Jesus

CHAPTER V

Possibility Number One:
That the Resurrection Did Not Occur

A. DAVID HUME: AN INTRODUCTION

The first possibility to be dealt with here is that the resurrection did not literally occur. We will begin by investigating the views of one very important scholar who held this opinion, turning later to several other related views.[1] The scholar we will use as a representative example is historian and philosopher David Hume (1711–1776).

This choice of Hume as the primary scholar to be dealt with here is one based on several closely related reasons. It is quite doubtful that an author could be chosen who has had more influence on this question of miracles. Hume's essay "Of Miracles" has been so influential that one can hardly even deal with this question at all without discussing his work.[2] The importance of this short writing has been reflected by its enormous affect upon contemporary theology and philosophy.[3] Even conservative theologian Wilbur M. Smith admits that this essay contains the strongest argument ever presented

---

1. In each of the three possible approaches to the resurrection which are covered in this work, we will likewise concentrate on one major scholar who we think is a representative example of that view. In the introductions to each chapter we will also outline the reasons for such choices. However, we will not be confined to just these three single opinions but in all three instances we will also entertain other similar views in the next chapter.

2. See, for example, McNaugher's treatment of miracles, which also deals with Hume's essay, *op. cit.*, pp. 91–118.

3. Montgomery, *The Suicide of Christian Theology, op. cit.*, p. 38.

against the belief in miracles.[4] Therefore Hume is an excellent example of
one who rejects belief in any miracle such as the resurrection. The popularity and high repute of his essay among other scholars who hold similar
views further reflects the trustworthiness of this choice.[5]

In order to more correctly understand Hume's contribution to the
question of miracles, it is important to look briefly at some of the intellectual trends of the time in which he lived. According to Heick, English
deism is a movement which may arbitrarily be said to have covered the
century and a half from Herbert of Cherbury in 1624 to Hume in 1776.
Deistic trends were intrinsically in agreement with similar proclivities in
French and German thought.[6]

During the seventeenth and eighteenth centuries in England we find
the popularity of various types of deism that sometimes allowed for varying amounts of Divine revelation. However, these brands of deism were
generally not of the variety which is often referred to today as "the clock-
maker's theory," whereby God was said to have made the world and later
abandoned it to its own existence without any guidance whatsoever. This
is a later definition of the word, formulated when it became necessary
to differentiate between atheism, theism and pantheism. In eighteenth-
century England, therefore, the word was not often used as a conscious
attempt to differentiate between deism and theism, as it is today. Rather,
the word was used to describe scholars who were opposed to atheism.[7]

In defending religion, the deists of this period depended upon reason
to justify faith. In fact, reason was usually perceived to be the most important part of one's belief. Traditional Christian dogmas were attacked as not
conforming to the application of this reason. Some of the emerging views
were quite radical for these times. For instance, the results included doubts
of traditional revelation and authority, and an opposition to Supernatural
miracles and wonders. There was a growing conviction that the search

---

4. Wilbur M. Smith, *The Supernaturalness of Christ* (Boston: W. A. Wilde, 1954), p. 142.

5. Later we will deal more fully with Hume's influence on theology, specifically viewing other
scholars who also reject all miraculous events and who believe that Hume's essay is the apex of
critical thought on this subject.

6. Heick, *op. cit.*, p. 52. Heick does note, however, that Hume differed from deism at several
points, such as the reliance upon reason and the desire to prove the existence of God. By turning
from such notions, Hume contributed to the demise of deism by taking this stance in favor of
empiricism (*Ibid.*, pp. 65–66).

7. *Ibid.*

for a natural religion was valid and that a "common ground" should be found among other religions, since all were believed to be ways to God.[8] Attempts at formulating such a natural approach to faith based upon the different religions were developed in works such as Herbert of Cherbury's "Common Notions Concerning Religion."[9]

One major development of a large portion of English deism was the emerging emphasis on empiricism, culminating in Hume. Experience was believed to be the criterion for obtaining knowledge. Even a very brief survey of some of these trends reveals this emphasis. An early empiricist, Francis Bacon, based his experiments and other observations upon the experience arrived at by the senses. This experience was gained by an application of the inductive method of ascertaining truth. Thomas Hobbes also sought to base all knowledge upon the criteria of sense experience. For John Locke, men acquire ideas by experience. In fact, even Divine revelation is perceived by reason and experience.[10]

Hume also followed the emphasis on experience. He believed that this experience was the foundation for all knowledge.[11] Although this method is not infallible, postulates were to be judged according to the probability of the experience. As we shall see below, this forms the center of his polemic against miracles.[12]

Hume's work is by no means limited to this field of philosophy. He is well known in this area, but in the middle of his scholarly career he turned away from such studies to other interests like history and ethics.[13] In fact, his best known work is very probably his multi-volumed masterpiece entitled *The History of England*.[14] It was poorly received by the public in

---

8. *Ibid.*, pp. 51–52; cf. also Vergilius Ferm's article "Deism," in Runes, *op. cit.*, p. 75.

9. This essay can be found in Owen C. Thomas, editor, *Attitudes Toward Other Religions* (New York: Harper & Row, 1969), pp. 32–48. Of course, not all scholars of this period held to all of these more radical beliefs. For instance, see John Locke's *The Reasonableness of Christianity*, edited by I. T. Ramsey (Stanford: Stanford University Press, 1958). Cf. here also Ferm, "Deism," in Runes, *Ibid.*

10. Heick, *op. cit.*, pp. 53–58, 65.

11. *Ibid.*, pp. 64–66.

12. See Hume's position in his work edited by Cohen, *op. cit.*, pp. 124–25.

13. Becker, *op. cit.*, pp. 38–39; cf. pp. 33–35.

14. David Hume, *The History of England*, 6 vols. (London: Gilbert and Revington, 1848).

the initial stages, but soon became a well-recognized and very popular work. It was considered a classic for many years.[15]

Earlier several reasons were observed for choosing David Hume as a representative example of one who holds that the resurrection, as a miracle, could not occur. Also just completed was a brief look at the background of the period in which he lived. It is desirable now to turn our attention to his extremely influential essay "Of Miracles."

B. DAVID HUME'S ARGUMENT
AND A CRITIQUE

In his essay "Of Miracles," David Hume argues from what he is convinced is mankind's experience against all real miraculous events. At the outset, miracles are defined as events which violate nature's laws. Hume postulates further that such events, if proven to have occurred, must be caused by some Supernatural power or other such agency.[16]

In order to determine if such events have actually happened, one must test the available data empirically. This consists of viewing the experiential evidence for the miracle-claim on the one hand and the experience of the reliability of the laws of nature on the other. Then one can ascertain which is more strongly attested. This test is therefore one based, once again, on the testimony of *experience*. The experience of miracles is pitted against the experience supporting the uniformity of nature. Here Hume concludes that it is more probable that the experience favoring the laws of nature is more reliable and the miracle is therefore rejected. Since each case of miracle comes against similar experiential data, these occurrences are rejected as a whole.[17] An important note here, however, is that Hume realized that his argument had not disproved the existence of God.[18]

---

15. E. W. F. Tomlin, *The Western Philosophers* (New York: Harper & Row, 1967), pp. 194–95.

16. Hume, "Of Miracles," in *Essential Works of David Hume, op. cit.*, p. 128. See the discussion of Hume's definition of miracle above. We will also return to this topic in the critique below. It is important to note here that this is not an obscure essay by Hume. This well known essay on miracles is Section X of his work *An Enquiry Concerning Human Understanding*. See *Ibid.*, pp. 123–42.

17. *Ibid.*, pp. 125–29. See Edwin A. Burtt, *Types of Religious Philosophy*, rev. ed. (New York: Harper & Row, 1939), pp. 212–16. Cf. Swinburne, *op. cit.*, pp. 13–14.

18. Burtt, *Ibid.*, p. 258.

Thus we perceive that for this scholar, the experience of miracles is to be rejected in favor of the experience of the laws of nature. In addition to the reasoning given above, Hume also makes use of four supportive points. First, there are no historical accounts of miracles which are attested by enough reputable men so as to make the event probable. Second, people are inclined to want to speak of extraordinary experiences, even to the point of fabricating the miraculous in order to spread religious truths. Third, miracles are cited as having occurred mainly in areas of ignorance or even barbarism. Fourth, the miraculous events in one religion destroy the probability that those of another faith are also true and vice versa. Therefore, accounts of such Supernatural events in different religions nullify each other. Thus, all are eliminated by the others.[19]

Now at the outset we must agree that this appears to be quite a reliable system in which to test relevant data. Hume seems to have found a valuable method and one can easily see how it has appealed to scholars. But in order to ascertain if these first impressions are correct ones, let us proceed to the text itself. It is the conviction of this writer that there are at least four major problems with Hume's approach to miracles—four chief criticisms which endanger the very heart of his polemic.

The first major criticism of Hume's essay is that he incorrectly defines both the essence of a miracle and the nature of the evidence for and against it. He states:

> A miracle is a violation of the laws of nature; and as a firm and unalterable experience has established these laws, the proof against a miracle, from the very nature of the fact, is as entire as any argument from experience can possibly be imagined.[20]

As in the actual definition of miracles stated by Hume above, we again observe that these events are perceived to contradict and violate nature's laws. They are said to do so because the *totality* of experience relates that these laws cannot be interfered with or broken. This experience is "firm and unalterable." Later Hume describes it as "uniform experience."[21]

---

19. Hume "Of Miracles," in *Essential Works of David Hume, op. cit.,* pp. 129–34; cf. Swinburne, *op. cit.,* pp. 15–18.

20. Hume, *Ibid.,* p. 128.

21. *Ibid.*

Immediately we can perceive a logical error in reasoning here. Hume fails to begin the investigation with an impartial look at the facts. Rather, his very definition rules miracles out because of an arbitrary and unproven assumption and it is therefore not a valid one. His definition is based upon the idea that the totality of experience rests against the miracle, when such is far from proven. There definitely are miracle-claims that are experientially based, but these are brushed aside by the assumed superiority of other varieties of experience. But Hume cannot know if the claims made by supernaturalists are able to invalidate the claims made against miracles apart from an investigation of the facts.

An example of this could readily be provided. Hume is definitely thinking at least somewhat in terms of the miracles of Jesus.[22] But rather than speaking specifically concerning the chief miracle-claim of the Christian faith, which is the resurrection of Jesus, he speaks only generally of the resurrection of any dead individual and then promptly informs his readers that such an occurrence has never happened when he has not presented any examination of the facts. He has no evidence that this has never occurred. He further concludes from this (without any new evidence) that in a similar way all experience opposes every miracle.[23] Therefore we have here a good example of circular reasoning. Dead men are assumed never to rise, and because all experience is arbitrarily perceived to stand against such an event, all experience also must oppose other miracles as well. The evidence for miracles is simply ruled out. But this can only logically be done *after* an investigation of the evidence. Thus Hume assumes that which he must demonstrate.

Oxford scholar C. S. Lewis also recognizes this weakness and develops it into a trenchant criticism of Hume's position. Lewis relates:

> Now of course we must agree with Hume that if there is absolutely "uniform experience" against miracles, if in other words they have never happened, why then they never have. Unfortunately we know the experience against them to be uniform only if we know that all reports of them are false. And we can know all the

---

22. *Ibid.*, p. 124.
23. *Ibid.*, p. 128.

reports to be false only if we know already that miracles have never occurred. In fact, we are arguing in a circle.[24]

Lewis has clearly perceived the problem here. Hume can only claim that all experience supports his view if he has first ascertained that all other experience is false. But since he has not investigated the other evidence, he can only state that it is false by assuming that miracles cannot occur. Thus he reasons circularly.

It goes without saying that one cannot disallow miracles simply by defining them so that they cannot happen. Circular definitions are clearly unsatisfactory.[25] But, as we have seen, Hume defines miracles to be impossible in light of the experience which testifies to the existence of laws in nature. This is done without any real investigation to determine if the experience on behalf of miracles can establish their validity. He must somehow know this latter experience to be false and he can only know that it is so by assuming that miracles cannot occur in the first place, as Lewis explains.

It may be that one agrees with Hume's conclusions that nature does rule out miracles. But the point here is that one cannot define this to be the case or arrange the "facts" in such an order that this assumption is supported. It is a matter of philosophical and historical debate.[26]

A further issue here is the place that should be given to experience for the laws of nature. We mentioned above in chapter two that we also agree with Hume in asserting that nature behaves by certain laws. We could not speak of miracles as being abnormalities apart from recognizing a normal pattern.[27] But Hume asserts that the existence of these laws is sufficient to disprove all experience of miracles.[28] At this point there are many scholars who would disagree.[29] Just because there are laws in nature does not mean that occasional abnormalities cannot occur. Such

---

24. Lewis, op. cit., p. 105.

25. W. Edgar Moore, Creative and Critical Thinking (Boston: Houghton Mifflin Company, 1967), p. 188 for instance.

26. Cf. Swinburne, op. cit., p. 15 and Ramm, op. cit., pp. 126–28.

27. See McNaugher, op. cit., p. 92.

28. Hume, "Of Miracles," in Essential Works of David Hume, op. cit., see pp. 127–29, 133, 139.

29. Cf. Lewis, op. cit., p. 60, McNaugher, op. cit., pp. 99–103 and Ramm, op. cit., p. 128, for instance.

laws regulate the inner workings of nature and describe what will happen
if the system is left to itself. But these laws do not dictate the possible results
of Supernatural interference from the outside. Now we have not as yet
established if such Supernatural influence is possible. But the point here
is that Hume is simply begging the question when he assumes that the
experience for the laws of nature is superior to experience (if established)
for the miraculous.[30] This is so in that the very experience which he dismisses as non-existent or as inferior, if established to be probable, would
overrule the supposedly stronger experience for the laws of nature. This
is because miracles involve the Supernatural intervention into nature, and
if such intervention was shown to be probable via a miracle, it would
show that the laws of nature *could* be temporarily suspended. Thus, valid
experience for a miracle would actually be superior to experience for the
laws of nature. Yet Hume fails to sufficiently investigate this experience
for the miraculous. Therefore Hume cannot use the laws of nature as an
absolute rule which cannot ever be broken.[31]

C. S. Lewis also accepts this last criticism of Hume as a valid one. He
points out:

> Probabilities of the kind that Hume is concerned with hold inside
> the framework of an assumed Uniformity of Nature. When the
> question of miracles is raised we are asking about the validity or
> perfection of the frame itself. No study of probabilities inside a
> given frame can ever tell us how probable it is that the frame itself
> can be violated.[32]

In other words, Lewis charges Hume with only answering questions which
fall into the framework of his assumed view of a completely uniform
nature, when in reality we should be asking whether the frame itself can
be violated. Thus Hume is concerned with things which might or might
not occur within a limited system when he should rather be concerned

---

30. Hume, "Of Miracles," in *Essential Works of David Hume, op. cit.*, see the obvious examples of
this attitude on pp. 127–128, 139.

31. See Lewis' essay "The Laws of Nature," contained in a collection of some of his other works
of this type entitled *God in the Dock*, edited by Walter Hooper (Grand Rapids: William B. Eerdman's
Publishing Company, 1973), pp. 76–79, especially p. 77.

32. Lewis, *Miracles, op. cit.*, p. 106.

with the system outside of this restricted area. Is it possible that this little system of nature, as trustworthy as it might be in and of itself, could be interrupted from the outside (as with a miracle)? Burtt levels a similar criticism at Hume.[33]

It is now easier to understand why experience in favor of miracles, if found to be probable, is so important here. If such was found to be the case, it would demonstrate that the laws of nature could be temporarily suspended, thus making the empirical claims in favor of the miracle dominant over the empirical claims for nature's laws. But by refusing to investigate such miracle-claims, Hume thereby rejects evidence that could easily disrupt his assumptions and show a miracle to be probable.

Therefore we see that Hume is guilty both of formulating a circular definition and of begging the question with regard to the importance of experience concerning the laws of nature. But these two errors are in turn used improperly as the heart of his polemic. Hume further states about miracles:

> There must, therefore, be a uniform experience against every miraculous event, otherwise the event would not merit that appellation. And as a uniform experience amounts to a proof, there is here a direct and full *proof*, from the nature of the fact, against the existence of any miracle.[34]

Here we see three more obvious errors of logic. First, Hume persists in formulating a circular definition of miracles, assuming that they cannot occur from the very outset. As we have said above, he can only know that there is uniform experience against all miracles if he has investigated all of the serious claims. Since he has not done so, he can only know that all experience opposes miracles by ruling that they cannot happen in the first place. This is clearly circular and has already been adequately shown to be an incorrect procedure. In addition, he still is working only within the framework of the laws of nature and thus does not take account of

---

33. See Burtt, *op. cit.*, p. 213, footnote 5 where it is also asserted that Hume fails to entertain this view which allows God to interfere with nature's pattern from outside the system.

34. Hume, "Of Miracles," in *Essential Works of David Hume, op. cit.*, p. 128. Italics are Hume's.

possible interferences from the outside. This, likewise, has been shown to be incorrect.

Second, we perceive an additional misuse of experience. Experience is now *uniformly* allied against all miraculous events. As we mentioned above, the reason all experience is assumed to agree with Hume's first prohibition against miracles is that these events have already been determined not to take place, by definition. Therefore, all *reliable* experience will indeed coincide with this since the opposite is defined as an impossibility. But it is clearly not possible to assume an important statement like this. It is not logically correct to argue circularly in order to answer supernaturalists who cite experience *for* miracles simply by defining all experience so that it opposes or even eliminates miracles. But this is exactly what Hume does, as experience is explicitly defined so that if it does not provide evidence against such events, then the said occurrence "would not merit that appellation."[35] This is a new prohibitive placed against miracles by experience. In other words, unless all experience stands against an event, it cannot be referred to as a miracle. In order for a miracle to be claimed as such, its existence must immediately be opposed by all experience. This is done without proof or investigation of the miracles. Is this a proper approach? Thus a second circular definition and subsequent begging of the question is introduced and the problem is further compounded. First, experience of nature, and second, the uniformity of experience are both placed against miracles in such a way (without any evidence) that these events are said to be impossible. The burden of the second (uniformity of experience) rests on the solidity of the first (experience of nature), whose solidity has all but been proven. The moment an event becomes designated as a miracle, it is snuffed out of existence arbitrarily.

Third, and in spite of all of this lack of proper evidence, Hume insists on stating that this constitutes a proof—"a direct and full *proof*" against any brand of miraculous event.[36] The argument thus moves from a first circular definition and begging of the question to a second of the same and on to the concluding "proof."

---

35. *Ibid.*
36. *Ibid.* The italics are Hume's.

But this "proof" turns out to be nothing more than an assumed conclusion. It is a good example of an *ipse dixit* or an unsupported assertion.[37] If one premise of a syllogism breaks down, the whole is invalidated.[38] One can demonstrate anything if definitions are allowed to be all-inclusive and contain the conclusion which is to be proven as a given. Therefore we perceive that Hume's "proof" fails. It indeed relies on the previously given definition of a miracle. It is a solid example of circular reasoning.[39]

It is easier now to see why many scholars have objected to various aspects of Hume's approach to miracles. He assumes here that which he wishes to prove, but which he has not investigated.[40] In spite of claiming to deal with the miracles of the Christian faith,[41] he refuses to deal with any specific New Testament miracles, but simply rules them out as being impossible.[42] In fact, one scholar notes that Hume felt so strongly about the impossibility of miracles which are part of the basis of faith for religious systems that claims to the contrary did not even have to be examined specifically.[43] This sounds like anything but an honest attempt to arrive at the proper facts concerning opinions which disagree with one's own! It is indeed an intellectually secure person who can know that these events can never occur without any investigation whatsoever. But judging from the work in question, this appears to be the attitude of this scholar.

Again, C. S. Lewis points to yet another example of circular reasoning in this essay on miracles. For Hume the two questions "Do miracles occur" and "Is the course of nature absolutely uniform?" are one and the same, simply asked differently. But "by sleight of hand" Hume answers "Yes" to the second question and then uses it for answering "No" to the first question. The real issue which he endeavors to answer is never really dealt with at all. We still do not know if nature's patterns can be interrupted or not and thus we do not really know if miracles occur. Therefore Hume

---

37. See McNaugher, *op. cit.*, p. 101 for a similar charge against Hume.

38. Moore, *op. cit.*, pp. 13–20.

39. Montgomery agrees that Hume's *a priori* and circular argument obligates no one to accept such a view of experience (*Suicide of Christian Theology, op. cit.*, p. 38).

40. Smith, *op. cit.*, p. 147; McNaugher, *op. cit.*, pp. 101–3.

41. Hume, "Of Miracles," in *Essential Works of David Hume, op. cit.*, p. 124.

42. Smith, *op. cit.*, p. 146.

43. Burtt, *op. cit.*, p. 215.

"gets the answer to one form of the question by assuming the answer to another form of the same question."[44] Again we find an example of circular reasoning.

We have found, first of all, that Hume commits a *series* of logical errors. In particular, these usually consist of arguing circularly (especially with regard to a definition of miracles) and by begging the question in using unproven and unsupported assumptions (especially in reference to the believed absolute authority of the laws of nature and the negligible value of any experience of miracles). These arguments alone are enough to invalidate Hume's entire thesis against miracles. We could also "prove" that miraculous events *do* occur by definition and by accepting all experience for miracles, while rejecting all experience for the laws of nature. Then we could conclude that all other experience must agree with this. To do so would of course prove nothing. But it could be made as logically valid as Hume's argument. However, there are yet three other points of attack that we must make with regard to Hume's work on miracles.

The second major criticism of Hume's essay concerns his use of the four supportive points which appear to expand his beliefs against miracles.[45] It is our contention that he then ignores a series of miracles which he even admits fulfills these four "conditions," leaving the way open to the possibility that other miracles also fulfill them. The case in question concerns a series of reputed miracles performed among the Jansenists in seventeenth-century France. Hume's own investigation of these occurrences proves very interesting indeed, in light of his four supportive points.

Pertaining to the first point, Hume admits that these miracles were "proved upon the spot, before judges of unquestioned integrity, attested by witnesses of credit and distinction" and lists several very reputable persons who were reported either to have witnessed them personally or who investigated the cases later. These include such persons as a well-known and respected lieutenant of police, a number of physicians, a duke,

---

44. Lewis, *Miracles, op. cit.*, p. 106.

45. Hume asserts that these four supportive points, which are summarized above, prove all miracles to be untrustworthy. We will briefly restate these four here. First, no historical accounts of miracles are attested by enough reputable witnesses. Second, people delight in telling miraculous stories, even lying in order to spread these teachings. Third, miracles are found mostly among people of backward nations. Fourthly, accounts of miracles in one religion nullify the accounts of those in other belief systems. See Hume's essay "Of Miracles," in *Essential Works of David Hume, op. cit.*, pp. 129–34.

a well-respected cardinal, 120 witnesses who were quite influential in Paris and even a list of several famous scholars (including Pascal and Racine).[46] Surely these can be counted as a satisfactory number of reputable witnesses.

As for the second point, Hume also admits that these reported miracles were investigated by the Jesuits and other groups who were enemies of these teachings. This group included the previously mentioned lieutenant of police, whose job it was to expose or suppress the reported miracles. His attempt was unsuccessful. The Molinist party also tried to discredit these occurrences and ended up attributing the miracles to the devil, thus admitting that they occurred. In another instance, the acting queen of France also wished to expose these miracles. She sent her personal physician to investigate them, only to have him return as a Jansenist convert. In fact, none of the antagonists who were sent to investigate this situation were apparently able to uncover any falsehoods at all.[47] We are not making any judgments as to what may or may not have happened here.[48] But it is plain to see that the many *enemies* of these reports were not lying to make the miracles appear plausible. Nor were they trying to delight in the spreading of these reports, for it was their own desire to expose these facts. Indeed, they had a private interest in disproving them. Even Hume admits to the fact that many of the witnesses were reliable.[49] Therefore we can assert that these witnesses have not upheld the second point.

Concerning the third supportive point, neither can we hold that these events occurred among ignorant and backward peoples. Not only did they occur in one of the more advanced countries of the world not long before Hume's own time, but Hume explicitly states that all of this happened "in a learned age." Once again he admits that the conditions stated in one of his points do not pertain to these miracles.[50]

---

46. Hume, "Of Miracles," in *Essential Works of David Hume, op. cit.*, pp. 135–37, especially footnote number two.

47. *Ibid.*

48. Our purpose here is by no means to determine if these Jansenist miracles actually occurred or not. Rather, we purpose to determine exactly what Hume's own reaction is when a miracle admittedly fulfills his four conditions. This we will perceive later.

49. Hume, "Of Miracles," in *Essential Works of David Hume, op. cit.*, pp. 135–37.

50. *Ibid.*, p. 136.

Hume's fourth supportive point also fails as an adequate explanation here. Even if the miracles purported to have occurred in some religions were able to cancel those in other faiths (which is a dubious assertion), the logical procedure would be first to investigate instances of these reports. If there were some instances which appear to be better documented than others, as in the case cited here, it would not be logical to abrogate these because of the existence of so-called lesser miracles which are also reported in other religions. It would be more reasonable to uphold the events which best fit the facts, as outlined above. Here it is curious to note that Hume adopts a similar procedure. He investigates what he feels are two such lesser miracles before discussing the Jansenist reports. The first two are clearly found to be falsehoods.[51] Later he recognizes that the Jansenist reports fit the facts better. But he apparently does not endeavor to rule out the latter accounts by using the former two, and logically so.[52]

Hume's fourth point would only be plausible if one assumed that all accounts of miracles were true, thereby causing some to believe that there was a possible conflict of ideologies. But since all are clearly not factual, we are left most logically with the need to investigate each case on its own merits. Thus we cannot rule out an event which is well-attested simply because other accounts of miracles also exist, for we cannot know but that the latter ones are the falsehoods and the former one factual. This can only be determined by an investigation of the miracle-claims. Therefore the last point is also found not to be applicable here as a critique of these miracles.

For these reasons we can perceive that Hume's four supportive points do not succeed as a valid critique of the miracles in the case of the Jansenist reports. Nor have they disproved the testimonies. In other words, these four prerequisites for miracles have all been fulfilled. In fact, Hume seems willing to admit his assertion. The following statement could be construed as his acknowledgment that the first three in particular meet the requirements. Speaking of the Jansenist claims he states:

---

51. *Ibid.*, pp. 134–35.

52. *Ibid.*, p. 137. However, Hume seems to believe that just because the fourth point does not hold in this instance because of the superior testimony of the authorities involved (*Ibid.*), it still may apply in other instances (*Ibid.*, pp. 137–38).

But what is more extraordinary; many of the miracles were immediately proved upon the spot, before judges of unquestioned integrity, attested by witnesses of credit and distinction, in a learned
age, and on the most eminent theatre that is now in the world.[53]

Here Hume informs us that there were reputable witnesses of these occurrences (point one), men of sufficient integrity and unquestioned character
so as to militate against the charges both of lying (or forgery) and of the
unscrupulous spreading of tales in order to tickle the ears of men (point
two). In addition, these reports were proclaimed to have happened in an
intellectual age in one of the most advanced countries of the world (point
three). We have already shown above that the fourth point also cannot
be used here because we cannot rule out a well-attested event *a priori*
simply because of the testimony of other similar events which often do
not fit any of the facts at all. We can only judge on the evidence at hand.
Neither does Hume specifically assert that the fourth point applies here.

We have now established that Hume felt that the Jansenist miracles
were well-attested cases. The human testimony in favor of these occurrences is impressive, especially in view of the fact that it concerns claims
of Supernatural events.[54] Therefore it would be very valuable to see how
Hume responded to the question of whether these were valid claims to
the miraculous or not. To this suggestion Hume responded concerning
these events:

Where shall we find such a number of circumstances, agreeing to
the corroboration of one fact? And what have we to oppose such
a cloud of witnesses, but the absolute impossibility or miraculous
nature of the events, which they relate? And this surely, in the
eyes of all reasonable people, will alone be regarded as a sufficient
refutation.[55]

It appears that Hume's dismissal of the miraculous is here a very arbitrary one. Even when all of the information adds up in support of a fact,

---

53. Hume, *Ibid.*, pp. 135–36.

54. We must state here once again that we are not ourselves concerned as to whether these
Jansenist claims are valid or not.

55. Hume, "Of Miracles," in *Essential Works of David Hume, op. cit.*, p. 137.

it cannot be maintained to be true if it is Supernatural in origin. Even if it is one of the most corroborated facts in terms of human testimony and experience, Hume says we must reject it simply because miracles are impossible. A more blatant case of circular reasoning may be difficult to produce. When evidence is found for a miracle, it is held not to apply simply because such events do not occur when this may be the very evidence capable of demonstrating that they *do* occur. One would just naturally assume that Hume was really interested in exploring the possibility of miracles in an essay of this scope. Rather, we find that his belief is that miracles do not occur and that no examination of experience for them can establish that they even probably do.[56] Thus we hold that Hume first assumes that miracles could never occur and then disregards the evidence on behalf of them.[57]

Even if one could show that Hume did have an adequate reason to distrust these reported Jansenist miracles, the former charge that he arbitrarily dismisses possible evidence in favor of miracles for faulty reasons can still be maintained for two reasons. First, he makes a similar statement earlier in the essay which is not related to the Jansenist issue. After his circular definition of miracles which is dealt with above, he remarks that

> no testimony is sufficient to establish a miracle, unless the testimony be of such a kind, that its falsehood would be more miraculous, than the facts, which it endeavors to establish ... always reject the greater miracle.[58]

Again we perceive that Hume is convinced that no amount of testimony can establish a miracle. Even when his criteria (the presence of sufficient

---

56. *Ibid.*, p. 139 for instance.

57. Philosopher Swinburne arrives at similar conclusions about this exact passage in Hume's work. He also realizes that Hume dismisses the Jansenist miracles not because the evidence is not adequate, but because such evidence is seen to be irrelevant (*op. cit.*, p. 16). We might wonder just how Hume is able to disregard such an admittedly adequate amount of experience for these events when such examination and research is the foundation of history. The acceptance of past events as having actually occurred is based upon the existence of an adequate amount of historical evidence. But even though Hume realizes that such has been produced he still rejects the miracle, as Swinburne also notes. Such a double standard of rejecting miracles when they are evidenced by the same (or an even greater) amount of experience which is viewed as being adequate in other instances of establishing historical fact certainly seems unscholarly. It is such circular reasoning that invalidates his argument.

58. Hume, "Of Miracles," in *Essential Works of David Hume, op. cit.*, pp. 128–29.

experience of the event) has been satisfied he holds that miracles are impossible. Therefore, as explained in the first major objection to Hume's essay given above, Hume is also guilty of employing unsupported assumptions. Miracles are rejected just because they are Supernatural even when they are found to have adequate experience supporting their reality.

Second, even if Hume continued to rely on other conclusions (such as the miracles in other religions) to oppose the miraculous in the instance of the Jansenist reports, he disregards the fact that the available evidence might be sufficient to establish this experience as miraculous even if no other miracles had ever occurred. In other words, the evidence that is dismissed might be enough to demonstrate the reality of these events as the supreme example of the Supernatural whether other such claims were valid or not. If an event has occurred it is made no less realistic because there are other claims to similar occurrences in existence.

Therefore we find that this second major criticism of Hume's essay is also valid. His four supportive points are highly objectionable in the first place, mainly because a large portion of our currently accepted history would be subject to much doubt if these were viewed as the norm by which facts are to be judged as being correct. For instance, how much of our accepted world history is made up of events which were not attested by a goodly number of unquestionably intelligent and educated men who in themselves are sufficient to guard against *all kinds* of error and delusion? One might indeed question large amounts of history because of a lack of conformity to this rule. Or how much of our history is prejudiced by the fact that the person reporting stood to gain much by the acceptance of these events, such as Julius Caesar's reports of his victories over the barbarians? And surely many other events took place among ignorant or backward nations? Since Hume includes the Greek and Roman civilizations as falling into this category (because miracles were reported by them),[59] are we to doubt the history of these entire periods, to say nothing of ancient Babylon, for instance? One begins to note the many problems involved in such an application of these four criteria to history. Yet this history is accepted as being quite reputable and trustworthy. As Richard Whately once so aptly noted, the same method which Hume employed to

---

59. *Ibid.*, pp. 132, 134.

dismiss the miracles from the life of Jesus would also remove the unique
elements from the life of Napoleon. Such reconstructing of history is correctly seen as being self-condemning and very problematical.[60]

But as we have also found, Hume fails to do justice to miraculous
events even when they have attained a high level of credibility because
of the weight of the experiential testimony in their favor. Such evidence
would most likely be sufficient to corroborate other historical events.
Therefore it appears that we would be impelled to grant probability to
certain miracles if they best account for the available evidence. And if
Hume errs in his evaluation in cases such as the above, it is also reasonable
to hold that other well-documented miracles can be held to be probable
events if they are found to be the best explanations for what occurred.[61]

The third major criticism of Hume's essay revolves around the fact
that this entire work depends upon an assumed uniformity in nature.
Hume rejects miracles because of man's experience of this uniformity.
But in order to do this one must hold to the validity of cause and effect
by assuming that the course of nature will continue (and that it always
has continued) exactly as it is now perceived. However, the fact is that
we know only a small part of nature and cannot be sure that what we do
know will continue to be the same in the future (or that it has continued
this way throughout the past).

What makes this argument all the more persuasive is that Hume himself recognized the fact that we cannot accept cause and effect as being
valid.[62] This is especially evident in his little work *An Abstract of a Treatise
of Human Nature*,[63] where Hume explains why we cannot reasonably

60. Montgomery, *The Suicide of Christian Theology, op. cit.*, 43–44, footnote 13.

61. If such miracles can be shown to exist, of course. We are still not making any judgment about the facticity of the Jansenist miracles, or saying that they are probable. This is because we have relied on Hume's presentation of the evidence and therefore have not investigated the evidence for ourselves. As mentioned above, the main object here was to perceive how Hume viewed occurrences which *he thought* were well-documented. This was accomplished here.

62. For Hume's rejection of cause and effect, see, for instance, his work entitled *A Treatise of Human Nature*, edited by L. A. Selby-Bigge (Oxford: The Clarendon Press, 1964), Book I, Part III, Section II, pp. 73–78, especially p. 76. Cf. also Heick, *op. cit.*, p. 65.

63. David Hume, *An Abstract of A Treatise of Human Nature* (Cambridge: The University Press, 1938). For a perceptive discussion concerning the author of this work, see the Introduction by J. M. Keynes and P. Spaffa, pp. v–xxxi; cf. Bronowski and Mazlish, *op. cit.*, p. 474, footnote number three.

accept this notion. It is customary to expect an effect to follow a cause, but there are no reasonable or logical grounds for it.[64]

Since cause and effect are no longer held to be valid,[65] there is really no logical reason for believing that the uniformity of the laws of nature can rule out the miraculous. Neither can we assert that the state of nature has ruled out miracles in the past, because the uniformity needed for such an assertion also cannot be demonstrated. In other words, Hume's contention that the experience of mankind does not know of any valid cases of miracles because of the uniformity of nature is not only invalid, but it contradicts his own statements to the contrary.

This is actually a very powerful argument against Hume's entire essay, which relies on man's supposed experience of the uniformity of the laws of nature.[66] This experience, based upon the reliableness of nature's laws, is the very center of his polemic against miracles, as shown above.[67] It is so central that it is held that no miracle could have occurred, simply because of this uniformity. Hume holds that even if one could find a probability or proof for a miracle, it would then run up against the "proof" of this uniform conception of nature, meaning that it could never occur anyway.[68]

But now we find that this method can no longer be used as a basis for this rejection of miracles. There is not only a lack of proof that nature must act in this way, but we have even found that we cannot speak of this type of causality in nature because it is no longer a valid concept (see especially chapter 2 above). This means that the entire basis of Hume's system as it now stands must be abandoned. If such a probability for a miracle were found to exist, as postulated above, there is therefore no "proof" from nature left to oppose it. This would also apply to instances of miracle-claims in past history, if they were shown to be probable, because these new concepts of nature would have applied then as well. Once again we perceive that miracles cannot be opposed by a uniform, causal view of nature. Hume's objection to miracles is therefore quite defective.

---

64. Hume, Ibid., especially p. 16. Cf. Bronowski and Mazlish, Ibid., pp. 474–75.

65. Cf. Bronowski and Mazlish, Ibid. See chapter 2 above.

66. Hume, "Of Miracles," in Essential Works of David Hume, op. cit., p. 128.

67. Ibid.

68. Ibid., p. 139.

C. S. Lewis agrees in this critique of Hume. He states in a similar vein of thought:

> The whole idea of Probability (as Hume understands it) depends on the principle of the Uniformity of Nature. … We observe many regularities in Nature. But of course all the observations that men have made or will make while the race lasts cover only a minute fraction of the events that actually go on. Our observations would therefore be of no use unless we felt sure that Nature when we are not watching her behaves in the same way as when we are: in other words, unless we believed in the Uniformity of Nature. Experience therefore cannot prove uniformity, because uniformity has to be assumed before experience proves anything. … The odd thing is that no man knew this better than Hume. His *Essay on Miracles* is quite inconsistent with the more radical, and honorable, skepticism of his main work.[69]

Here Lewis also recognizes that Hume's entire argument depends on the uniformity of nature. But there is no way we can know, much less prove, this belief. We observe nature by our senses and incorporate it into our experience. But all of the experience of mankind is but a small part of the whole. To say that nature acts completely uniformly with *no* interruptions (as Hume asserts) would be to know all of nature. This is once again circular reasoning because, as Lewis points out, one must assume uniformity in all of nature in order to say that we experience the same when we do not know the whole of it. We must simply believe it is the same. In other words, one must already have assumed that nature is completely uniform and acting in a causal way when the evidence indicates otherwise. Lewis also notes that Hume accepted similar arguments against the causality of nature in his other works.

Our two former conclusions must therefore stand in light of this knowledge. First, Hume's basis for rejecting miracles is not valid. One cannot reject a miraculous event if it best fits the evidence simply because of an assumed uniformity in nature, especially when such uniformity has been shown not to exist. Cause and effect would have to be in operation

---

69. Lewis, *Miracles*, op. cit., pp. 105–6. Italics are Lewis'.

before Hume's arguments could even begin to be asserted. But even Hume himself rejects this view of nature. Thus nothing is left but to abandon the very basis of his reasoning. Second, this means that the question now concerns which facts best fit the evidence, turning us once again to an investigation of these facts. If a miracle in past history is found to offer the best explanation of the evidence, it can no longer be opposed because of the belief that these things simply do not happen or because nature opposes such an event.

Our fourth major criticism of Hume's essay arises from the second and third criticisms. A positive aspect of Hume's philosophy is that he relies heavily upon probabilities, which has been shown above to be the conviction of modern thought. In addition, Hume rejected many of the then-popular theories concerning cause and effect and the accompanying implications based upon a closed universe. In an age when it was popular to accept a mechanistic view of the universe, Hume insisted that it remain open.[70] In this sense, at least, his thoughts may be viewed as a forerunner of some of the modern theories which also postulate an open universe.

However, a problem arises when we try to reconcile Hume's belief in an open universe with his previous rejection of miracles. Rather than allowing the evidence to speak for itself (since evidence for miracles cannot be ruled out *a priori* or by an improper view of nature), as might be expected when one holds the above positions with regard to nature, Hume transgresses his own position to rule out miracles. He does not allow the miraculous even when the evidence is sufficient to point to a probability (criticism two) and then he dismisses the miraculous as a whole by accepting a view of nature which he himself has already dismissed (criticism three).

Therefore a fourth major criticism is arrived at here. While he accepts quite a modern view of the universe in many senses, he becomes a pre-modern in his treatment of miracles. In other words, he is not self-consistent in his philosophy. His treatment of miracles shows signs of a pre-modern critical consciousness, for he proposes to accept an open

---

70. Hume's rejection of cause and effect has been noted above. For his emphasis on probability, see, for instance, his work *Essays, Literary, Moral and Political* (London: Ward, Lock and Bowden, Limited, n.d.), pp. 341–43 and also the essay "Of Miracles" in *Essential Works of David Hume, op. cit.*, pp. 125–29.

universe but rejects miracles because of a closed view of nature,[71] and he proposes to base his work on probabilities but arbitrarily rules out a probable miracle. Thus he is internally inconsistent and reverts to this pre-modern consciousness.

We therefore hold that all four of these major criticisms of Hume are valid. He is first guilty of committing a series of logical blunders. He argues circularly[72] several times, usually with regard to his definition of miracles and often begs the question by using unsupported assumptions, such as the negligible value of any experience of miracles. He also fails here in refusing to investigate any of these events when this very investigation could reveal a valid miracle. Second, Hume fails to accept miraculous events even when they are found to be well-attested by human experience. He still rejects them for arbitrary reasons even after he admits the high credibility of this attestation. Third, Hume rejects miracles because of a view of nature that not only was false, but that he even rejected himself. Yet the belief in this uniformity of nature is the center of his polemic against miracles. Therefore the very apex of his polemic against miracles must be rejected. Fourth, while Hume is modern in many of his conceptions of nature (opting for the use of probabilities and rejecting cause and effect and the subsequent uniform view of nature), he reverts to a pre-modern stage in his attempt to prove that no actual miracles have ever occurred. In arguing against miracles he gives little weight to miraculous probabilities and employs an incorrect view of nature which he even rejected. Thus he is both pre-modern and inconsistent here.

It is obvious that these criticisms invalidate Hume's treatment of miracles. These errors and improper conclusions in Hume's work were not as readily detected in the eighteenth century because the Enlightenment intellect continued to prevail in scholarly circles. As will become even more apparent in chapter 6, the desire was usually to reject miracles in

---

71. Montgomery also feels that Hume's argument against miracles is based on a closed view of the universe. See Montgomery's *Suicide of Christian Theology, op. cit.*, pp. 262–63, 351, note 15. Once again, we also believe that there are laws in nature, as pointed out above. To speak of miracles as out of the ordinary there must be an ordinary course of nature. The question is not if these laws exist, but if they can be temporarily suspended.

72. Even William Hordern, a scholar sympathetic to certain trends in contemporary, critical theology, states that Hume argues circularly in this essay. See his work *A Layman's Guide to Protestant Theology* (New York: The Macmillan Company, 1956), p. 37.

the first place and Hume's essay provided the needed authority for such a venture.

It thus goes without saying that Hume's polemic against miracles, while appearing to be a strong argument at the outset, fails when closely investigated. This system cannot therefore be used at all to invalidate or rule out miracle-claims. A more proper approach may have been to define miracles without any inherent statement as to the possibility of their occurring. Then it would have been possible to investigate the available experience in order to determine the extent of its agreement. We are thus confronted once again with the need to investigate the evidence to better ascertain what has occurred. Such a historical investigation of the documents making such miracle-claims is therefore needed, as concluded in chapter 4 above. In the specific case of the resurrection of Jesus, empirical claims have been made which report experiential evidence for the appearances of the risen Lord. These are the accounts which must be examined in order to ascertain if this event is the best explanation for the facts.

CHAPTER VI

Possibility Number One:
Other Similar Views

I t is hard to estimate exactly the influence that Hume's essay "Of Miracles" has had upon the intellectual world since its appearance in 1748. However, we may most assuredly determine that its affect upon theology has been extremely great. Many scholars have viewed it as the determining argument against the existence of any miraculous event. This is true both of the older nineteenth-century liberal theologians and of the more contemporary twentieth-century theologians. Some refer directly to Hume as the source for this rejection of miracles while others make anonymous references to their dismissal of the miraculous as being due to the belief that our experience of nature completely opposes any such violation of its laws. It is important to look briefly at both this direct and indirect evidence for Hume's influence.

We are informed by John Hermann Randall, Jr. that since the appearance of Hume's essay, religious liberals have rejected any belief in miracles. Nineteenth-century liberalism[1] as a whole became convinced by this work that there could be no interference with nature from any miraculous events.[2]

---

1. Briefly, we will refer to religious liberalism in this work as the predominant trend of theological thought in the nineteenth century (cf. Daniel Fuller, *op. cit.*, chapter 3). More specifically we might date this movement's prominence from the publishing of Schleiermacher's work *On Religion: Speeches to Its Cultured Despisers* in 1799 to Karl Barth's *The Epistle to the Romans*, which appeared in 1918. Cf. here this work by Schleiermacher, translated by John Oman (New York: Harper & Brothers, 1958). See the Introduction by Rudolf Otto, especially pp. ix, xii. Cf. also Burtt, *op. cit.*, p. 284 and William Hordern, *Introduction*, vol. 1 of *New Directions in Theology Today*, edited by William Hordern, 7 vols. (Philadelphia: The Westminster Press, 1966), p. 15.

2. John Herman Randall, Jr., *The Making of the Modern Mind*, rev. ed. (Boston: Houghton Mifflin Company, 1940), pp. 553–54. Concerning Randall's statement that liberalism rejected miracles because

Montgomery agrees with this assertion that nineteenth-century liberal theology followed Hume's rejection of miracles.[3]

An excellent example of this rejection is seen in the works of German theologian David Strauss, one of the most vigorous critics of the New Testament who ever lived. In his two-volumed work *A New Life of Jesus* (first translated into English in 1865, shortly after the German edition), Strauss specifically asserted that Hume's essay was so conclusive in disproving miracles that the question had now been settled.[4] Miracles simply could not be allowed to contradict nature.[5]

Strauss' stance on this question, one which follows Hume's critique, is a typical one taken by nineteenth-century liberalism. Friedrich Schleiermacher was also of the opinion that a real miracle would involve the suspension of the laws of nature. Such miracles occur most often where there is little knowledge of these laws. We should abandon such miracles as being superfluous, for they are not able to bring us closer to a recognition of Christ. Besides, science and religion agree here that there are no absolute instances of such an event. A more perfect view of God, one requiring man's absolute dependence, needs no such miracles to support its cause.[6] For this reason, Schleiermacher preferred to see all events as being miraculous, including the most common and natural ones. In fact, events such as those which were supposed to have broken the laws of nature by Supernatural intervention are really not miracles at all.[7]

Other instances such as these are common in liberal theology. Bruno Baur followed Strauss in strongly insisting that we can admit of no events which deny the laws of nature. Rather, nature's laws are upheld by religion and not insulted by occurrences such as miracles.[8] Ernst Renan postulated

---

of the influence of Hume's essay, it appears that Randall is also speaking of liberalism as a predominately nineteenth-century movement (*Ibid.*).

3. Montgomery, *The Suicide of Christian Theology, op. cit.*, pp. 27–28.

4. David Friedrich Strauss, *A New Life of Jesus*, 2nd ed., 2 vols. (London: Williams and Norgate, 1879), vol. 1, p. 199.

5. *Ibid.*, pp. 199–201.

6. Friedrich Schleiermacher, *The Christian Faith*, edited by H. R. Mackintosh and J. S. Stewart, 2 vols. (New York: Harper & Row, 1963), vol. 1, pp. 71, 178–84; vol. 2, pp. 448–49.

7. Schleiermacher, *On Religion: Speeches to Its Cultured Despisers, op. cit.*, pp. 88–89, 113–14, explanation number 16.

8. Albert Schweitzer, *The Quest of the Historical Jesus*, translated from the 1906 German edition, *op. cit.*, p. 154.

that Jesus was not aware that there were any laws in nature at all. Because of this lack of knowledge about the lawful pattern of nature, Jesus believed that miracles were very common occurrences and nothing about which one should be surprised.[9] Adolf Harnack also held that ancient peoples had no concept of the strictures of the laws of nature. But today we realize that no events can occur which interrupt nature. As a result, miracles do not happen and we cannot believe in the accounts of them.[10]

This rejection of the miraculous, revealing a dependence upon Hume's thesis, is not relegated only to nineteenth-century theology, however.[11] As shown above, contemporary twentieth-century critical theology has pursued a similar pattern of thought. It usually espouses either the belief that miracles cannot (and should not) be validated, or, often relying directly on Hume's arguments, that all miracles should simply be dismissed as impossible.[12]

For instance, Paul Tillich holds that miracles cannot interfere with the laws of nature. Any theology attempting to make them do such is distorting the Biblical view of God.[13] Bultmann believes that our modern conception of nature has rendered miracles impossible. The natural laws are such that they make the world a reality that is closed to the miraculous. We are thus too advanced to believe in the New Testament accounts of such Supernatural workings.[14] John A. T. Robinson likewise believes that miracles such as Jesus' incarnation can only be described as myths because in our scientific age we realize that natural processes cannot be interrupted by Supernatural intervention. The entire New Testament cosmology must be ruled out for these reasons.[15] We have briefly explored some

---

9. Ernst Renan, *Life of Jesus*, vol. 1 of *The History of the Origins of Christianity* (London: Mathieson and Company, n.d.), pp. 147–55, especially p. 148.

10. Adolf Harnack, *What is Christianity?*, translated by Thomas Bailey Saunders, 3rd ed. (London: Williams and Norgate, 1912), pp. 25–31.

11. Randall asserts that from Hume's time until today few learned men have questioned his conclusions against miracles (*op. cit.*, p.293).

12. Montgomery, *The Suicide of Christian Theology*, *op. cit.*, pp. 37–38; cf. p. 28.

13. Paul Tillich, *Systematic Theology*, 3 vols. (Chicago: The University of Chicago Press, 1971), vol. 1, pp. 115–17. Cf. Alexander J. McKelway, *The Systematic Theology of Paul Tillich* (New York: Dell Publishing Company, 1964), pp. 81–83.

14. Bultmann, "New Testament and Mythology," in *Kerygma and Myth*, *op. cit.*, pp. 4–5.

15. John A. T. Robinson, *Honest to God* (Philadelphia: The Westminster Press, 1963), pp. 11–18, 64–68.

major theories proposed by those who follow Hume in arguing against the occurrence of all miraculous events. Many scholars utilized these and similar views which opposed all miracles in deducing from them specific hypotheses against the belief in a literal resurrection of Jesus.

To be sure, the milieu of the eighteenth century, in which Hume formulated his anti-miraculous argument, was different from the milieu of the nineteenth and twentieth centuries, in which these religious liberals applied Hume's views. In the nineteenth century there were the philosophical systems of Immanuel Kant, stressing morality, and Friedrich Hegel, who emphasized a theology of reason and development.[16] In the latter half of the nineteenth and on into the twentieth centuries, Darwinism extended its influence. Historical events such as the French Revolution and the two World Wars also added to this climate of change. The secularity of the twentieth century affected still more worldviews. In spite of these differences, however, on the question of miracles these liberal theologians ever since the eighteenth century continued to follow Hume, believing that such events were impossible.

A. HEINRICH PAULUS

Very possibly the most noteworthy scholar who endeavored to apply Immanuel Kant's thought to New Testament studies was Heinrich Paulus.[17] This German theologian also rejected miracles for reasons which were quite similar to those listed above. The Biblical witnesses are believed to have had a deficient knowledge of the laws of nature, especially in not knowing of nature's secondary causes. Therefore they wrongly believed that Supernatural events actually occurred. However, when we discover the true workings of nature, we are said to find that the events which were once considered to be miraculous can no longer be considered as such. This is because these occurrences are found to proceed according to natural law. Thus Paulus proceeded to employ naturalistic explanations for the New Testament accounts of miracles.[18]

---

16. Heick, *op. cit.*, pp. 92–102, 119–27; especially p. 92.

17. Daniel Fuller, *op. cit.*, p. 38; cf. Schweitzer, *op. cit.*, pp. 51, 53.

18. Schweitzer, *Ibid.*, pp. 49, 51–53.

The resurrection of Jesus was also given such a natural explanation. For Paulus, Christ did not die on the cross. He was taken down before death overcame him and later resuscitated gradually in the grave. The spear wound in the side had not immediately killed him, but had merely served as a blood-letting device and encouraged his recovery. Later an earthquake was additionally helpful in rolling away the very large stone from the front of the grave, thus enabling Jesus' escape. He obtained the apparel of a gardener and then proceeded to arrange for a meeting with his disciples. After several visits with them, he realized that he was dying. He then held one last meeting on the Mount of Olives. As he moved away from them, he was obscured from their sight by a cloud and was not seen by them again. Jesus died, but in a place unknown to the twelve, who referred to this event as an "ascension."[19]

According to this conjecture, usually referred to as the "swoon theory" of the resurrection, Paulus plainly conceived of this event as one operating by natural processes. There was no Supernatural intervention involved. Thus Jesus was not believed to have risen from the dead.

The swoon theory did not originate with Paulus, but was quite popular with several other scholars throughout the first half of the nineteenth century. It was an especially common interpretation of the resurrection found in the so-called fictitious accounts of the life of Jesus which appeared during this same period of time.[20] These works were imaginative portrayals of the life of Jesus, often very similar to novels. The use of fiction was quite apparent, as the author weaved various plots and counterplots into an attempt to portray Jesus' life in a certain light. The nonhistorical ingenuity of the writer was usually quite noticeable. As a result, these works were seen as having little credibility or esteem.[21] Paulus' work differed in that it was not one of the above imaginative lives. His work was both more logical and more respectable than the fictitious lives and thus he was a more reputable exponent of this theory.[22]

---

19. Ibid., pp. 53–55.

20. For some of those who held this view, see Ibid., pp. 46–47, 64, 161–66; cf. pp. 43, 60.

21. Ibid., p. 38.

22. Cf. Ibid., pp. 48–50.

Strangely enough, various liberal theologians were some of the most ardent critics of the swoon theory. By far the most famous critique was given by David Strauss himself. He pointed out that in order for this theory to be true, Jesus would have come forth from the grave half dead, one who was quite visibly ill and weak, badly in need of medical help and care, later even succumbing to death because of these wounds. But Strauss persuasively argues that it would be impossible for such an individual to have convinced the disciples that he was the Conqueror of death, the Victor over the grave, or the Prince of life. If Jesus did not die on the cross, he could only have convinced his followers that he was someone to be pitied and cared for by them. They would have immediately perceived the facts as they were in reality. At any rate, Jesus' condition could not have changed the disciples' sorrow into happiness. Nor would it have convinced them to worship Jesus as the Messiah.[23] Strauss' criticism is a very pointed and accurate one. As we noted above, Paulus did indeed conceive of Jesus as a victim of blood-letting, one whose appearance was changed due to tremendous suffering and who still felt weak and sickly, finally dying of the wounds.[24] And this is just how a survivor of a crucifixion would appear. But could such a limping, bleeding, stoop-shouldered individual convince even his loved ones that he had conquered death forever? The answer is obviously a negative one.

Most theologians have therefore agreed that Strauss' critique has settled the issue for good.[25] Indeed, Schweitzer even judged that Strauss' reasoning was the absolute death stroke to the swoon theory.[26] Renan was also careful to point out the assurance we have of Jesus' death on the cross.[27]

The New Testament records claim that Jesus was *nailed* to the cross (Luke 24:39–40; John 20:25–27). If this could be shown to be valid, Strauss' view would be strengthened all the more.[28] And we do find, in

---

23. Strauss, *op. cit.*, vol. 1, p. 412.

24. Schweitzer, *op. cit.*, p. 54.

25. Cf., for instance, McNaugher, *op. cit.*, p. 148; Smith, *op. cit.*, p. 208; Miller, *op. cit.*, pp. 37–38.

26. Schweitzer, *op. cit.*, p. 56.

27. Renan, *op. cit.*, pp. 244–45.

28. Anyone who has had the misfortune of even stepping on a nail knows the discomfort and pain so caused, including the forced limp! This writer has done so several times. Once only a small nail was enough to incapacitate him for three days, making it impossible to recover completely until the fourth and fifth day. Imagine the results of crucifixion with a spike bearing one's weight for several

fact, that Strauss' critique has received striking archaeological confirmation in recent years. Paul Maier reports the following:

> In the summer of 1968, archaeologist V. Tzaferis excavated some stone ossuaries in East Jerusalem dating from the first century A.D. These were chests in which bones of the dead were reburied after the flesh had decomposed following original burial in a cave. One of the ossuaries, inscribed with the name Yohanan Ben Ha'galgol, contained the bones of a man who had obviously been crucified, the first such victim ever discovered. A large, rusty iron spike, seven inches long, had been driven through both heel bones after first penetrating an acacia wood wedge or plaque that held the ankles firmly to the cross. The nail must have encountered a knot on being driven into the cross, for the point of the spike had been bent directly backward. Slivers still clinging to it show that the cross was made of olive wood. ... In addition to the iron spike, evidence of crucifixion included a deep scratch on the right radius bone, showing that a nail had penetrated between the two bones of his lower forearm just above the wrist, which abraded them as the victim writhed in agony. ... Yohanan, at any rate, had his lower arms pierced with nails.[29]

This is indeed important evidence bearing on this question. Maier further corroborates this evidence with three photographs which plainly show the affected bones of this victim. One displays a hind view of the heel bones as they were found, pierced by a large iron spike. The end of the spike is curved upward. A second photograph reveals the portion of the right arm where the radius bone was scared by another nail. The third photograph displays a side view of the left heel bone after the spike

---

hours! We could not avoid Strauss' illustration of the condition in which a wounded crucifixion victim would emerge from the grave. Considering the feet *only* (even if we were to momentarily disregard the other wounds), it would not be possible to walk so soon afterward. Detection of such a wounded victim would indeed be both inescapable and inevitable. He would not pass for someone who was resurrected, at any rate.

29. This portion is quoted from Maier's *The First Easter, op. cit.*, pp. 78, 80. Page 79 contains three photographs of the above-mentioned crucified victim's bones, which were affected by the piercing of the nails.

had been removed, clearly showing the very large hole thus created by the wound.[30]

Strauss' critique of the swoon theory therefore appears to be even stronger. There is no reason to doubt the New Testament accounts of the nail wounds inflicted upon Jesus, especially in light of this archaeological evidence.

It is possible to adduce other considerations against the swoon theory as well. For instance, secondly, there is strong evidence to demonstrate that Jesus was dead prior to the burial. We are told in John 19:31–35 that the legs of the other two crucified men were broken in order to hasten their deaths.[31] But since Jesus was found to be already dead, his legs were not broken. Rather, a Roman soldier pierced his chest with a spear in order to make sure that he was not simply feigning it. This portion has both long and often been recognized as a proof that Jesus was dead by many scholars of differing theological positions. The general tendency by those who prefer this approach is to perceive this spear wound and the subsequent appearance of blood and water as signifying one of two medical explanations. It is thought either that the spear punctured the heart via the pericardium (a thin sac surrounding the heart, which contains a watery liquid) or that the heart had ruptured (in which case the pericardium would be filled with blood and fluid). In either case the presence of both blood and water is medically explained and Jesus would have been dead.[32] The question here concerns whether this account in John is a reliable testimony as to crucifixion procedure.

Again we find some corroboration of these facts in the archaeological evidence already supplied by Maier. The bones of the crucified victim bring evidence to bear that this account of the spear wound and breaking of the legs is also based on historical information (as claimed in John 19:35). Maier relates that:

---

30. *Ibid.*, p. 79.

31. For the most likely reasoning behind the breaking of these men's legs in order to speed up their deaths, see Jim Bishop's analysis in *The Day Christ Died* (New York: Harper & Row, 1965), cf. p. 280 with pp. 289–90.

32. For a few of those who hold one of these views, see Renan, *op. cit.*, p. 244–45; McNaugher, *op. cit.*, p. 148; Miller, *op. cit.*, pp. 38–39; Charles C. Anderson, *op. cit.*, p. 168; Maier, *op. cit.*, p. 112.

Even the detail of the two criminals having their legs broken at the close of Good Friday to induce death—the *crurifragrium* has an exact parallel here: Yohanan's right tibia and the left tibia and fibula were all broken in their lowest third segment at the same level, indicating a common crushing blow, probably from a mallet or sledge.[33]

Now it is true that this evidence does not mention a spear wound. But once the custom of breaking the legs of the criminals has been established, it is a short step to this next point. After all, the object of each was to insure the victim's death. If one was found to be already dead, the logical thing to do would be to make sure. The spear, being a natural part of the Roman military repertoire, would be the most likely weapon. And where could one more likely kill a person with a spear than by piercing his heart? The Romans were responsible for making sure that the victim was dead, as he had been sentenced by a Roman official, and they were very efficient in such tasks.[34]

In addition, since at least this first portion of this gospel statement has been verified, there is no sufficient reason to assert that the interrelated item of the spear wound was not also historical. The two belong together, because if Jesus had not been pierced, he would most likely have had his ankles smashed as well. Both meant that he died. The best conclusion is that both are fact.

A third great difficulty for this theory is that Jesus would have to have been an impostor of one sort or another. He would have been guilty of proclaiming his resurrection when such would clearly not have been the case. He, of all people, would certainly know the facts.[35] To honestly ignore them would be to make himself worse than an imposter, as it would then most likely entail some sort of mental insanity. Yet, the world almost unanimously views Jesus at least as a great moral teacher, in all probability incapable of such a grand example of deceiving others. Whatever else might be postulated, he cannot be found to be such an impostor.

---

33. Meier, The First Easter, *op. cit.*, p. 80. Italics are Meier's.

34. For this last point, see Charles C. Anderson, *op. cit.*, p. 168.

35. Cf. Miller, *op. cit.*, p. 38.

Thus the swoon theory fails as an adequate explanation of the facts. Other points could also be made against it.[36] But suffice it to say that there is very little doubt among scholars today that Jesus was actually dead.[37] First, as pointed out by Strauss, he could not have convinced his disciples that he had conquered death and was victor over the grave in his physical condition. They would have known immediately that he needed medical help, not that he was immortal. Second, the facts point strongly to his actual physical death on the cross, which occurred no later than the time of the spear wound (and actually before this time). Third, Jesus was certainly not an impostor of this sort.

It is therefore no wonder that the swoon theory appeared short-lived in its popularity. By 1908 Scottish theologian James Orr could remark that no one held this view any longer.[38] Similarly, today this view is also rejected as being outdated and insufficient to account for the facts at hand.[39] Frank Morison could even assert that the swoon theory is today best regarded as a theological curiosity of the past.[40]

B. DAVID STRAUSS

As noted above, Strauss was one of nineteenth-century liberalism's most ardent New Testament critics. His *Life of Jesus* appeared in 1835 and occasioned a great theological furor. One result of this work was the immediate signaling of a raging battle concerning the nature of myth in the

---

36. What of Jesus' embalmed body? Could he move the stone in front of the tomb? How and where did he actually die? Questions such as these are most difficult for this theory. Cf. Charles C. Anderson, *op. cit.*, p. 168.

37. McNaugher, *op. cit.*, p. 149.

38. James Orr, *The Resurrection of Jesus* (Grand Rapids: Zondervan, 1908 edition reprinted in 1965), p. 92.

39. Karl Barth, *The Doctrine of Reconciliation*, vol. 4, part 1 of *Church Dogmatics*, edited by G. W. Bromiley and T. F. Torrance, 13 vols. (Edinburgh: T. & T. Clark, 1961), pp. 340–41.

40. Frank Morison, *Who Moved the Stone?* (London: Faber and Faber Limited, 1962), p. 96. It is true that this theory reappears from time to time, almost always establishing many of the older presuppositions and often, once again, in the form of a novel. One such modern attempt is Hugh Schonfield's *The Passover Plot* (New York: Bantam Books, 1967). That such attempts to revive this theory are generally met with scholarly disdain (see, for instance, Montgomery, *The Suicide of Christian Theology, op. cit.*, p. 39 and especially note number 44 on p. 46 and J. N. D. Anderson, *op. cit.*, pp. 63–65; cf. pp. 93–94) is easily conceivable since this theory still has to adequately answer the objections raised here and other similar problems.

New Testament accounts.[41] A second result was Strauss' dismissal from his teaching post at Tübingen because of the radical nature of his work. Large amounts of criticism directed toward his theories were to follow, as much printed material opposed his efforts. One book even humorously demythologized David Strauss himself![42]

One element of the New Testament which was clearly rejected by Strauss was the accounts of miracles. Ever since David Hume's essay on miracles, these occurrences could no longer be thought to be possible. Miracles cannot break the laws of nature. Explanations other than the Biblical ones must be found.[43]

Concerning the resurrection of Jesus, Strauss is most explicit. Jesus was definitely dead and thus the swoon theory is inapplicable here.[44] Rather, Strauss preferred and popularized the subjective vision theory of the resurrection. According to this view Mary Magdalene was probably the first to perceive psychological visions of the risen Christ. Next the apostles also had subjective visions convincing them that Jesus was indeed alive.[45]

However, Strauss explains, the disciples were not in the proper frame of mind to be open to visions immediately after the death of Jesus or for even days afterward. They were too despondent to have any hope at all so soon. Therefore both a change of locality is needed (away from Jerusalem) and a period of "recovery" before the visions could begin. Strauss thus transfers the disciples' first apparitions to Galilee in the north. The time which passed before the first "appearance" is also expanded to a much longer period than is stated in the New Testament narratives.[46]

The result was internal visions which occurred because of the presence of fervent imagination and much excitement.[47] Because of this deception on the part of the disciples when they mistook their subjective experiences

41. Schweitzer, *op. cit.*, pp. 71–72, 96–120. Cf. Charles C. Anderson, *Critical Quests of Jesus* (Grand Rapids: William B. Eerdman's Publishing Company, 1969), p. 18.

42. Schweitzer, *Ibid.*, pp. 70–72, 96–97, 111.

43. Strauss, *op. cit.*, vol. 1, pp. 199–201; vol. 2, pp. 149–280. Cf. Schweitzer, *Ibid.*, pp. 82–83.

44. Strauss, *Ibid.*, vol. 1, pp. 408–12.

45. *Ibid.*, vol. 1, pp. 427–29; cf. also Strauss' work *The Old Faith and the New, op. cit.*, vol. 1, pp. 81–82.

46. Strauss, *The New Life of Jesus, Ibid.*, vol. 1, pp. 430–37 and *The Old Faith and the New, Ibid.*

47. Strauss, *The New Life of Jesus, Ibid.*, vol. 1, p. 440.

for objective reality, Strauss asserts that the resurrection itself has there-fore become a worldwide illusion.[48]

This theory which Strauss developed gained popularity in the nine-teenth century. Scholars such as Renan and Ghillany, among others, pre-ferred it as the most probable explanation for the appearances of Jesus.[49] Its popularity has diminished in the twentieth century.[50]

However, several of the nineteenth-century liberals opposed this view as well. Schleiermacher asserted that any version of the vision theory was entirely unacceptable because its suppositions do not fit the facts.[51] Another rejection of this theory was given by Paulus, whose own views we have discussed above. He likewise felt that visions were not possible in view of the available facts, for there was sufficient evidence to prove that Jesus was actually alive and present with the apostles.[52] Therefore he preferred the swoon theory. This rejection of visions by Paulus is a very interesting one, because we have already pointed out that Strauss had likewise ruled out Paulus' theory. Thus we see that each attempted to negate the theory of the other.

---

48. Strauss, *The Old Faith and the New, op. cit.*, vol. 1, p. 83.

49. Renan, *op. cit.*, pp. 249, 309–10; Schweitzer, *op. cit.*, pp.170, 187. Renan's work has already been cited above. Ghillany, writing an imaginative life of Jesus under the pseudonym of Richard von der Alm, also preferred this view. Other liberals accepted this theory as well.

50. Comparatively few scholars hold the vision theory today. More common are views which are based upon some personal experience of the disciples which convinced them that Jesus was somehow still alive. The exact details vary from one view to the next. Charles Anderson (*The Historical Jesus: The Continuing Quest, op. cit.*, pp. 169–71) and Paul Maier (*First Easter, op. cit.*, p. 107) rightly include such views in the same category with the vision theory because, even though hallucinations are rejected here, a subjective experience of one sort or another is generally perceived to be based upon some form of pre-existent faith on the part of the disciples. Thus it is still a case of these believers becoming convinced of the resurrection because of their own projected faith issuing forth into a belief in objective reality. Probably the best-known theory of this type is Paul Tillich's "restitution theory." For Tillich, the resurrection is not to be conceived of in terms of the reappearance of either a person or a spirit. In fact it is not any type of literal appearance of any kind. Rather, the disciples experienced the spiritual presence of Jesus. Like Strauss, Tillich feels that it was actually an ecstatic experience which convinced them that Jesus was the New Being. It is possible for believers today to have this same experience (Tillich, *op. cit.*, vol. 2, pp. 156–58. For a similar interpretation of Tillich's view, see McKelway, *op. cit.*, pp. 170–71, 181–82). Theories such as Tillich's will also be included in this treatment of visions (as Charles Anderson and Paul Maier also do). Most of the problems involved in postulating a pre-existent faith and in the subsequent application of subjective criteria to objective conviction also apply here and render such an experience quite impossible, as will be shown below.

51. Schleiermacher, *The Christian Faith, op. cit.*, vol. 2, p. 420.

52. Schweitzer, *op. cit.*, pp. 54–55.

The most noteworthy nineteenth-century criticism of Strauss' vision theory came from another liberal theologian, Theodor Keim. Schweitzer notes that Keim's study of Jesus' life, which was published in three volumes from 1867–1872, was the most important critical work on this subject that had appeared in many years.[53] In it he presented a substantial critique of all hypotheses which made subjective visions and inner experiences the basis for the disciples' belief in objective, outward appearances of Jesus.

Keim rejected the vision theory for several key reasons. First, the over-abundance of self-generated emotion and excitement which Strauss felt had to be present[54] to produce these visions is not found in the early church. Other inward experiences and visions found in the early texts are likewise not characterized by this extreme excitement. Second, visions in the New Testament are numerous. But these are never confused with the resurrection appearances, so as to admit the difference between them. Third, the appearances of Jesus are characterized by calmness and reticence. Those involved are usually reserved and not at first ready to accept Jesus with joy and exuberance. Fourth, religious visions tend to multiply and grow more numerous. But the appearances of Jesus come to a sudden cessation. For these and similar reasons, this theory is rejected as not adequately explaining how the appearances of Jesus could possibly have been subjective visions.[55] Some of Keim's points are well-taken and are

---

53. *Ibid.*, pp. 193, 211.

54. See, for instance, Strauss' *The New Life of Jesus, op. cit.*, vol. 1, p. 440.

55. W. J. Sparrow-Simpson, *The Resurrection and the Christian Faith* (Grand Rapids: Zondervan, 1911 edition reprinted in 1965), pp. 113–115. The theory popularized by Keim is commonly referred to as the "telegram theory." According to this hypothesis, Jesus rose spiritually from the dead (not bodily) and returned to God. Afterward he communicated the knowledge of his spiritual existence to the apostles by means of "telegrams" or messages from heaven. The appearances of Jesus recorded in the New Testament were therefore not subjective visions or hallucinations but objective impressions sent by both Jesus and God. Keim admits that this communication to the disciples of the truth that Jesus had risen required Divine intervention (*Ibid.*, pp. 117, 119; McNaugher, *op. cit.*, pp. 155–56). But such a theory falls prey to at least four major criticisms. First, is this view any less a miracle than the view recorded in the New Testament? The miraculous is admittedly involved here as well and we still have the teaching that Jesus *actually* rose and is alive (although in spiritual form). Second, would God and the risen Jesus send messages and reveal appearances which would deceive the disciples into thinking that Jesus was physically there with them? Such deception has moral (or amoral!) implications and fails to explain why Jesus did not actually appear instead of sending the impression that he had actually done so. Third, these impressions would not be objective enough to make them think that Jesus had actually risen bodily. Fourth, it fails to explain the empty tomb. (For these and similar criticisms, see Tillich, *op. cit.*, vol. 2, p. 156; McNaugher, *Ibid.*; Lewis, *Miracles, op. cit.*, pp. 152–53; Smith, *op. cit.*, pp. 219–20; Tenney, *op. cit.*, pp. 189–92.)

still employed today as negative evidence that opposes this theory, as we will perceive presently. At any rate, many scholars believe that Keim dealt the death-blow to Strauss' theory of visions, just as Strauss had earlier done the same to Paulus' hypothesis.[56]

Today there are at least four major reasons why the subjective vision theory is rejected. First, the apostles were not in the proper frame of mind to presuppose visions. There is a needed psychological precondition for such hallucinations, this being the *expectation* of the event in question and a strong *belief* that it will happen. Otherwise there would be no impetus for the mind to produce such subjective projections.[57] But the disciples were not in such a state of mind. They were very despondent and did not have such faith and expectation that Jesus would rise. Pannenberg expresses this point as follows:

> To maintain, first, that the appearances were produced by the enthusiastically excited imagination of the disciples does not hold, at least for the first and most fundamental appearances. The Easter appearances are not to be explained from the Easter faith of the disciples; rather, conversely, the Easter faith of the disciples is to be explained from the appearances. All the attempted constructions as to how the faith of the disciples could have survived the crisis of Jesus' death remain problematic precisely in psychological terms, even when one takes into account the firm expectation of the imminent end of the world with which Jesus presumably died and in which his disciples lived. It cannot be disputed that, in spite of all this, Jesus' death exposed the faith of the disciples to the most severe stress. One could hardly expect the production of confirmatory experiences from the faith of the disciples that stood under such a burden. Certainly such psychological considerations by themselves are as little suited to support any conclusions as to support the criticism of the New Testament traditions.[58]

56. Sparrow-Simpson, *Ibid.*, pp. 113–15; Orr, *op. cit.*, p. 219; McNaugher, *Ibid.*, p. 155.

57. McNaugher, *Ibid.*, p. 152. See especially George E. Ladd, *I Believe in the Resurrection of Jesus* (Grand Rapids: William B. Eerdman's Publishing Company, 1975), p. 138.

58. Wolfhart Pannenberg, *Jesus—God and Man*, translated by Lewis L. Wilkins and Duane A. Priebe (Philadelphia: The Westminster Press, 1968), p. 96.

As Pannenberg clearly states here, it is psychologically problematical to endeavor to explain how the disciples' faith could have withstood the stress placed upon it by the death of Jesus. We could not expect the collectively forlorn faith of these men to respond positively by producing visions which, by their nature, require enthusiasm, excitement, and especially belief. Therefore we find that the *appearances* of Jesus gave rise to the post-Easter faith and were not produced by an already-existing faith.[59]

This position is well-attested by various others as well. Eminent Scripture scholar Raymond E. Brown notes that most theologians also agree that faith in the resurrection of Jesus arose because of the appearances rather than the appearances being caused by a pre-existing faith.[60] An examination of the facts will show that this is the case, thus making visions an impossibility.

The disciples were simply too despondent to have produced such hallucinations, especially in so short of a time. Even Marxsen realizes that the disciples' faith was a result of external experiences and not inward impulses, thus making the vision theory untenable.[61] William Barclay agrees that the disciples could not contemplate themselves into a situation where visions would be possible so soon. Therefore this theory itself is perceived to be unreasonable.[62] Ramsey likewise asserts that any theory which proclaims that the resurrection appearances arose because of a prior belief of the disciples, as this theory does, can be dismissed because of the problems involved.[63]

It is not overly difficult to comprehend this criticism raised against Strauss' subjective vision theory. The disciples had expected Jesus to redeem Israel and bring in the heavenly Kingdom of God (see Luke 24:21). They had followed him for a few years, expecting this result. But now his death was unexpected and caused much despondency. Such a reaction is a natural psychological response when so much was at stake and believed

59. *Ibid.*

60. Raymond E. Brown, *The Virginal Conception and Bodily Resurrection of Jesus* (New York: Paulist Press, 1973), p. 84.

61. Marxsen, *op. cit.*, p. 116.

62. William Barclay, *The Mind of Jesus* (New York: Harper & Row, 1961), pp. 304–5.

63. Ramsey, *op. cit.*, p. 41.

to be dependent upon Jesus' remaining alive. Their long-awaited hopes and dreams were dashed to pieces. To expect an ecstatic, enthusiastic faith-affirmation capable of producing inward visions from these men is therefore not very possible.

An interesting concession here was made by Strauss, who also realized that, as the facts stand, visions would not have occurred. The disciples could not have escaped such despondency in such a short period of time. Thus, unless one rearranged the available data, the theory would fall.[64]

Therefore we find that the disciples were too despondent to have been subject to such excited visions entailing a believing frame of mind. As Marxsen concludes, we must reject the vision theory because it does not agree with the textual facts.[65] McNaugher reminds us that such hallucinations have psychological rules and these had not been fulfilled.[66]

In addition, we find that the disciples did not expect Jesus to rise from the dead.[67] Ramsey notes that they were not able to anticipate this event at all because of their aforementioned doubt and bewilderment.[68]

In fact, the disciples did not believe immediately even *after* the appearances, but doubted the evidence.[69] Orr believes that this doubt on the part of the disciples is the most historical portion of the resurrection records.[70] Reginald Fuller finds this doubt to be a part of the earliest tradition and a very natural inclination for these early witnesses.[71] Both Marxsen[72] and Ramsey[73] note the effect of this doubt on the disciples. It is important to realize here that if the vision theory were true, such persistent doubt could not exist, because the supposed presence of the pre-existent faith

---

64. Strauss, *The New Life of Jesus, op. cit.*, vol. 1, pp. 430–31. Cf. also Sparrow-Simpson, *op. cit.*, pp. 111–12.

65. Marxsen, *op. cit.*, p. 116.

66. McNaugher, *op. cit.*, p. 152.

67. The narratives sufficiently establish this point. See Luke 24:12, 21; John 20:9, 19; cf. the Markan appendix, 16:10. Cf. also Brown, *op. cit.*, p. 106, footnote 176.

68. Ramsey, *op. cit.*, p. 41.

69. The witness to this is even greater than that of the previous point. See Matthew 28:17; Luke 24:11, 22–24, 27; John 20:25; 21:4; Cf. the Markan appendix, Mark 16:11, 13, 14. Cf. also Brown, *op. cit.*, p. 106, footnote 176.

70. Orr, *op. cit.*, p. 225.

71. Reginald Fuller, *op. cit.*, pp. 81–82; cf. pp. 100–101.

72. Marxsen, *op. cit.*, p. 67.

73. Ramsey, *op. cit.*, p. 41.

would mean that the appearances would have already been regarded as genuine. In other words, if the disciples' faith in a risen Jesus had produced visions, this same faith would automatically accept the resulting visions as true. But we find that such was not the case. The doubt was both genuine and persistent.

Thus we see that, first, the disciples were not in the proper frame of mind for visions to occur. They were too despondent to have had hallucinations in so short a time.[74] In addition, they did not expect Jesus to rise and did not readily believe the appearances even after they occurred.

The second main reason that the vision theory is rejected is because of the problems involved concerning the number of people who claimed to have seen Jesus after his death and the different places and times in which these appearances were believed to have taken place. It is true that visions can be experienced by more than one person at a time.[75] But we have been speaking of a theory which proposes subjective hallucinations—visions with no real objective stimulus. Therefore if one of the disciples (or others who claimed to have experienced the resurrection appearances) actually did hallucinate, it would not by any means be automatic that others would also experience the same vision. Rather, each would also have to go through the process of developing a prior faith and of being psychologically ready for such an experience. This is because hallucinations are essentially private events and are experienced by more than one person only when these above conditions are present for *each* individual.[76] But, as Pannenberg notes, the narratives record several different appearances which occur under many different circumstances and

---

74. Even Gordon Kaufman, one of the comparatively few scholars who still hold the vision theory today, realizes that a prior belief must exist before visions can be produced. However, he fails to show what positive factors there were that would be sufficient to give rise to this optimistic faith, a faith which would absolutely have to be present *before* the events themselves. This is quite damaging to his viewpoint, especially in view of the fact that he admits that the disciples were quite disillusioned at Jesus' death and were therefore subject to despair. He realizes that their hope had disappeared. But we may wonder what spontaneous factors caused such a reversal of thought and made the disciples believe that Jesus was alive *before* they received any confirmation of the fact. See these admissions in Kaufman's *Systematic Theology: A Historicist Perspective* (New York: Charles Scribner's Sons, 1968), especially pp. 415, 422.

75. *Ibid.*, p. 421; footnote 20; Orr, *op. cit.*, p. 219.

76. Edwin G. Boring, Herbert S. Langfield and Harry P. Weld, editors, *Foundations of Psychology* (New York: John Wiley and Sons, 1956), p. 216; Yamauchi, *op. cit.*, March 15, 1974, p. 6; McNaugher, *op. cit.*, p. 153; Smith, *op. cit.*, p. 217.

times and even include different participants. This invalidates this theory which relies upon a mental reaction which spread from one individual to the next. The various conditions simply do not support such a view.[77]

The above objections are persuasive especially when one remembers that in order for this theory to be valid, each individual would have to have responded to personal stimuli at each of these various times and places. The different personalities involved would mean that many would not be in the proper state of mind, especially when all the records indicate that exactly the *opposite* reaction prevailed, as shown above.

Surely some of the participants would not have experienced these appearances at all if they were due to visions, for they would not all be in the correct state of mind. But such was not the case. Even New Testament *critics* are agreed that all the disciples genuinely believed that Jesus had appeared to them after his death. In other words, whatever may have been the cause of the appearances, the disciples *believed* that Jesus had been raised from the dead.[78] In fact, Johannes Weiss pointed out that the early proclamation of the resurrection would not have been possible at all had the disciples experienced even the simplest doubt in an objective resurrection.[79] This undoubting belief would hardly be the consequence if we were to rely on visions to such large numbers of people as are recorded in the narratives. As mentioned above, all would not be prepared for such visions.

An instance where this would be true occurs in the oldest resurrection narrative. Here Paul relates that on one occasion Jesus appeared to over 500 people at once (1 Cor 15:6). That Paul cites this as a proof of Jesus' resurrection is evident from his further explanation that most of these 500 witnesses were still alive at the time of his writing (and thus available to testify of the reality of this event).[80] As Brown asserts, it is hardly possible to imagine a synchronized but personal experience which

---

77. Pannenberg, *Jesus—God and Man, op. cit.*, pp. 96–97.

78. Bultmann, "New Testament and Mythology," in *Kerygma and Myth, op. cit.*, p. 42. See Orr, *op. cit.*, p. 115, with regards to this admission by critic Kirsopp Lake.

79. Johannes Weiss, *Earliest Christianity: A History of the Period A.D. 30–150*, edited by Frederick C. Grant, 2 vols. (Magnolia: Peter Smith, Publishers, 1959), vol. 1, p. 28.

80. Bultmann, *Kerygma and Myth, op. cit.*, p. 39; cf. Reginald Fuller, *op. cit.*, p. 29. See also Archibald T. Robertson, *Word Pictures in the New Testament*, 6 vols. (Nashville: Broadman Press, 1931), vol. 4, p. 188.

would convince each that Jesus had objectively risen.[81] A collective hallucination in which all saw visions would be to ignore the above-mentioned evidence to the contrary.

Another instance where the vision theory appears especially improbable is Luke's recording of the walk to Emmaus (Luke 24:13–33). This narrative, complete with proper names (such as Cleopas, Emmaus, and Jerusalem), convinced Martin Dibelius that the pure form of the event had been preserved at this point.[82] This incident has received much respect from critics who have rejected other aspects of the resurrection accounts.[83] Here we find that the shifting scenes, continual conversation, and the time element involved all militate strongly against the reality of visions.[84] Paul's list of appearances in 1 Corinthians 15:1–8 is also problematical for this viewpoint as well.[85]

It would be advantageous here to recall two of Keim's criticisms made last century which were discussed above. First, the New Testament writers distinguish between the resurrection appearances of Jesus and visions which occur at later times (such as 2 Cor 12:2–4; Acts 7:55–56; 18:9; 23:11; 27:23).[86] This would not be the case if the resurrection appearances were of the same variety as the later visions, as all would be viewed as being of the same type. This is an acute point because it demonstrates that the resurrection experiences were regarded as being unique and were therefore not of a subjective visional character.[87] Second, if these appearances of the risen Jesus had not been perceived to be unique, then one would not expect them to have ceased so suddenly. Rather, they would tend to have been related to the later visions. That they did stop indicates that the early church did not want them to be confused with spiritual visions.[88]

Therefore we perceive once again the second chief criticism of the vision theory. Many factors have contributed to this probability that the

---

81. Brown, *op. cit.*, p. 91.

82. See Ramsey, *op. cit.*, pp. 61–62.

83. Orr, *op. cit.*, p. 176. Cf. Reginald Fuller, *op. cit.*, p. 107.

84. This conclusion was verified for the writer by a discussion with a psychology professor on Dec. 18, 1969, who spoke of the various impossibilities of relying on visions in this instance.

85. Pannenberg, *Jesus—God and Man, op. cit.*, p. 97.

86. Sparrow-Simpson, *op. cit.*, p. 114.

87. See Reginald Fuller, *op. cit.*, pp. 32, 170.

88. Sparrow-Simpson, *op. cit.*, p. 114.

number of visions, the number of people who saw them, and the way in which these occurred simply do not correspond to the required data for the disciples to have experienced such manifestations.

The third major criticism of this theory is that real subjective hallucinations are comparatively rare, as proper causes are usually lacking. They are, by definition, experiences in which something is perceived to be present, but for which there is *no* objective reality. Thus they differ from illusions, where a reality is mistakenly identified.[89] Thus it can be ascertained that such occurrences are generally rare. The perception of something that not only is not present but for which there is *no* objective reality at all therefore requires an explanation. Usually such hallucinations are caused by mental illness of some kind, drugs, or extreme methods of bodily deprivation.[90] To suppose that all of the witnesses of the resurrection appearances were in such a state of mind thus becomes nonfactual. We can now better understand how an extreme pre-conditioned hope and expectation must exist, combined with other factors. Such conditions as the above clearly did not exist in order for all of the disciples to imagine something that was only "thin air."[91] Therefore Pannenberg rightly concludes that to describe the resurrection appearances as hallucinations or subjective visions is completely unsatisfactory.[92]

The fourth major reason why the vision theory is rejected today (and the last which we will deal with specifically) is that cautions were actually taken in order to demonstrate that the appearances were not hallucinations. We have already mentioned the theme of doubt in the gospels and the consequential conviction of contemporary scholars that the disciples were convinced that Jesus was actually alive only *after* the appearances and not before.[93] We have likewise spoken of the conviction of the New

---

89. See, for instance, William James, *The Principles of Psychology*, 2 vols. (Dover Publications, 1950), vol. 2, pp. 114–15. Cf. also Yamauchi, *op. cit.*, March 15, 1974, p. 6 and Pannenberg, *Jesus—God and Man, op. cit.*, p. 95.

90. Yamauchi, *Ibid.*; Pannenberg, *Ibid.*, pp. 94–95, footnote number 93.

91. Kaufman admits that the objection that the vision theory is too subjective to account for such objective appearances of Jesus is a strong one. He also notes that his work had thus far (*op. cit.*, pp. 426–27) not sufficiently handled this problem.

92. Pannenberg, *Ibid.*, pp. 95–97.

93. Marxsen, *op. cit.*, p. 67; Reginald Fuller, *op. cit.*, pp. 81–82; cf. pp. 100–101; Brown, *op. cit.*, pp. 84, 106, footnote 176.

Testament authors that the appearances of the risen Jesus were different from later visions. Reginald Fuller especially notes here that Paul did not confuse these appearances with the *subjective* visions which were experienced later.[94]

In addition, we find that other steps were also taken to disprove visions as the origin of the appearances. We find these safeguards in *both* the earlier and the later narratives which deal with this subject. The emphasis in Matthew, Luke-Acts, and John on Jesus' resurrected body being both spiritual and material is well-known.[95] We find an emphasis on being able to see and handle the body of Jesus. In Luke especially it is related that it occurred to the disciples that they were seeing just such a spiritual hallucination—a bodiless apparition.[96] Although these gospels were written later than Paul's description of the resurrection appearances, it is recognized by many scholars that the description of Jesus' body in the gospels may have been derived, at least in part, from the same source as Paul's conception of a spiritual body. In other words, it is often recognized that both Paul and the gospels speak of a resurrected body composed of both spiritual and material qualities (with varying emphases) and that these concepts were in turn based on the reports of the original eyewitnesses.[97]

What is often not realized is that Paul's list of appearances in 1 Corinthians 15:1–8 also contains a polemic against theories such as that of subjective visions. As Brown properly notes, Paul's reference to 500 people having seen Jesus at one time means that Paul conceived of the appearances as being other than purely internal experiences. Thus hallucinations were not possible in view of his testimony.[98] This is especially

---

94. Reginald Fuller, *Ibid.*, pp. 32, 170. Cf. Marxsen, *Ibid.*, pp. 100–102.

95. See, for example, Orr, *op. cit.*, p. 197. See also Reginald Fuller, *Ibid.*, pp. 71–154.

96. Luke 24:36–43 relates this scene. The disciples though that they were viewing a bodiless apparition or spirit (Greek *pneuma*; cf. Matt 14:26, 27). Jesus had to convince them otherwise by presenting his body for observation. We are told that they only believed that they were not seeing "ghosts" when it was thus proven to them. See Robertson, *op. cit.*, vol. 2, p. 296. Other verses where it is either stated or implied that Jesus' body was handled include Matthew 28:9; John 20:17, 26–28; cf. Acts 1:3.

97. Cf. Robert M. Grant, *Miracle and Natural Law* (Amsterdam: North-Holland Publishing Company, 1952), pp. 229–30; Brown, *op. cit.*, pp. 85–89; Charles Anderson, *op. cit.*, pp. 161, 163–66; Smith, *op. cit.*, pp. 194–95. Concerning Paul's list being based upon eyewitness testimony, see Brown, *Ibid.*, p. 92 and Reginald Fuller, *op. cit.*, pp. 28–29.

98. Brown, *Ibid.*, p. 91; Ladd, *op. cit.*, p. 138; cf. p. 105.

true when we remember that Paul adds that most of these witnesses were still alive and thus could be questioned. Therefore, this testimony in 1 Corinthians 15:6 is regarded by Paul himself as proof against subjective visions.[99]

Thus we see that there were precautions taken in both Paul's account and in the gospels to guard against the view that the appearances were due to subjective visions and therefore not genuine. This motif is more developed in the gospels, where we are told that Jesus' body was touched on various occasions, demonstrating its reality.[100] But we have seen how Paul also includes a proof against such a theory as well.[101] That this is the case in the New Testament is only natural when we consider man's psychological impulse to investigate both strange occurrences and the testimony of others who claim to have experienced such.[102]

Therefore we perceive that the vision theory cannot account for the resurrection appearances of Jesus. Several major points militate against such a view. The disciples were not in the correct psychological frame of mind. There is also a problem concerning the number who claimed to have seen Jesus and the time and place factors involved. In addition, real hallucinations and visions are rare and do not fit the facts. Lastly, the early sources explain that various cautions were taken to prove that visions were not applicable in these instances. Many minor points could also be mentioned against this theory.[103] Most of these objections can also be applied to theories relying upon other subjective experiences of the apostles as well.[104]

---

99. Cf. Bultmann, "New Testament and Mythology," in *Kerygma and Myth, op. cit.,* p. 39 and Reginald Fuller, *op. cit.,* p. 29.

100. This is also reported by Ignatius in section three of his *Epistle to the Smyrneans.* See J. B. Lightfoot, editor and translator, *The Apostolic Fathers* (Grand Rapids: Baker Book House, 1971), p. 83; cf. p. 85.

101. See Sparrow-Simpson, *op. cit.,* p. 110.

102. Orr, *op. cit.,* p. 180.

103. For instance, if the vision theory were true, the empty tomb would be left unexplained. And what happened to Jesus' body? In addition, this writer has compiled a list of 34 total reasons why this theory is inadequate.

104. Theories like those of Tillich (*op. cit.,* vol. 2, pp. 156–58) and Van Buren (*op. cit.,* pp. 132–33) which rely on some unexplained subjective experience of the disciples face practically all of the same difficulties. For instance, the disciples' despondency and doubt must still be changed to faith *before* the experience itself in order for these to occur in the first place, which encounters the difficulties raised above. There is likewise the same problem of how many would have been convinced in this manner,

We thus conclude that the visional theory simply does not fit the narratives. For hallucinations to have occurred, all of the facts must be changed around. There are psychological laws which these hallucinations must abide by, and these were not present.[105] No matter how inviting a theory may appear, if it fails to account for the evidence, it must be rejected.[106]

Today the vision theory is held by comparatively few scholars. Brown notes that this nineteenth-century view is not even respectable any longer.[107] Based upon the fear and dejection of the disciples, Bornkamm asserts that we cannot resort to any explanation which depends upon the inner, subjective experience of these men.[108] McLeman agrees that the nineteenth-century vision theorists such as Strauss and Renan presented views which were quite extravagant in their claims.[109] Even Schonfield rejects this theory as not fitting the evidence. Whatever theory may be proposed, it cannot validly be this one.[110]

C. OTTO PFLEIDERER

In the last portion of the nineteenth century a movement appeared from within the ranks of Protestant liberalism. It became designated as the History of Religions school of thought. It opposed several of liberalism's suppositions, such as trying to find a "Jesus of history." In fact, it was believed that very little historical information could be gathered about

---

as well as with the various time and place factors. Even more acute is the disciples' mistaking such subjective experiences for objective ones and how they became convinced that Jesus had *literally* risen from the dead. The disciples knew the difference between the resurrection appearances and later experiences, as explained above. We also find psychological causes lacking here. What would give rise to such experiences? As with visions, there is also the objection that cautions were deliberately taken in the narratives to prove that the experiences were objective and not subjective. These are a few of the key objections to these subjective theories. As we have observed, they are practically the same as those listed above. See McKelway (*op. cit.*, pp. 170–71, 181–83), Charles Anderson (*op. cit.*, pp. 169–73) and Maier (*The First Easter, op. cit.*, pp. 112–13) for similar criticisms and other objections to this theory.

105. Orr, *op. cit.*, pp. 27, 222.

106. Brown, *op. cit.*, p. 75, footnote number 127.

107. Raymond E. Brown, "The Resurrection and Biblical Criticism," *Commonweal* (November 24, 1967): 233, 235.

108. Bornkamm, *op. cit.*, pp. 184–85.

109. McLeman, *op. cit.*, pp. 212–13.

110. Schonfield, *op. cit.*, p. 152.

the life of Jesus.[111] This was mainly due to the legendary growth which was said to have built up around the life of Christ. These legends were believed to have accumulated in stages until the embellished material became quite detailed.[112]

The History of Religions school sought to study Christianity in terms of the other religions. The Christian faith came to be seen as being syncretistic and therefore it was not unique in the sense that it did borrow from the other faiths. It was now postulated by these scholars that Christianity borrowed quite freely from Judaism and from other systems of belief such as the Babylonian, Egyptian, and Persian religions.[113] It was postulated that Christianity was especially influenced by the Old Testament and by the teachings of these other faiths. Myths were believed to be extremely prevalent at this time and were perceived to be spreading from one region and religion to another. Each then accepted ideas from the other that were advantageous to its own purposes. As a result, these scholars constantly compared almost every individual category of the Christian faith to similar ideas which were a part of other religions.[114]

One scholar who had many beliefs in common with this emerging school of thought was German theologian Otto Pfleiderer. For instance, he also postulated that there were many affinities between Christianity and other ancient religions. The influence from Judaism was also noteworthy. Myths were said to be present in all of these faiths and there were similarities, especially in the transmission of events requiring Supernatural intervention. Especially noticeable is Pfleiderer's tendency to compare different aspects of the Christian faith with similar ideas and occurrences in these other religions. Parallels are found, for instance, in Jesus' relationship to Satan, in the miracles of Jesus, and in the accounts of the resurrection.[115]

Pfleiderer also believed that very little could be known about the beginnings of the Christian faith. He likewise based this conclusion upon

---

111. Charles C. Anderson, *Critical Quests of Jesus* (Grand Rapids: William B. Eerdman's Publishing Company, 1969), pp. 55–57.

112. McNaugher, *op. cit.*, p. 157.

113. Anderson, *Critical Quests of Jesus, op. cit.*, pp. 55–56; Orr, *op. cit.*, p. 235.

114. Anderson, *Ibid.*, p. 56; Orr, *Ibid.*, p. 238; McNaugher, *op. cit.*, p. 157.

115. Cf. for instance, Pfleiderer's work *The Early Christian Conception of Christ* (London: Williams and Norgate, 1905), see pp. 63–83 for his account of some of the similarities between Jesus' miracles and those found in other ancient religions.

the thesis that legends grew profusely around the life of Jesus in the early church. It is now too difficult to know for sure which reported events actually occurred and which did not.[116]

The History of Religions school rejected any belief in the resurrection of Jesus. Rather, they popularized the view that the narratives of this occurrence were later additions to the gospel, ones which grew mainly from the influence of stories of other such events found in other religions. At any rate, the resurrection was considered to be a legend which was added to the story of Jesus' life.[117]

Pfleiderer follows this pattern and also views the resurrection of Jesus as myth that did not occur literally. But he does so for two main reasons. First, the resurrection is believed to be legend added to the story of Jesus' life by his earliest followers. It was not a real occurrence at all, for Jesus never actually rose from the dead. Rather, the narratives were added by the disciples, who were convinced that Jesus must be alive. The legends continued to grow until they were detailed accounts of a victory over death. In addition, stories of resurrected gods in other religions served as a basis for the rise of the Christian legends about Jesus. These more ancient myths provided the impetus for the formulation of the New Testament accounts of Jesus rising from the dead.[118]

Second, Pfleiderer believes that this theory based upon the formation of legends must also be supplemented by the subjective vision theory of the resurrection.[119] Visions apparently account for the *source* of the conviction that Jesus was alive, while the subsequent legends explain the present form of the narratives.[120] We have already dismissed the vision theory above, and we will turn presently to the possibility that the

116. Otto Pfleiderer, *Primitive Christianity*, translated by W. Montgomery, 4 vols. (Clifton: Reference Book Publishers, 1965), see vol. 1, pp. 1, 5, 23–25 for instance.

117. Orr, *op. cit.*, pp. 235–61; McNaugher, *op. cit.*, p. 157.

118. Pfleiderer, *Primitive Christianity*, *op. cit.*, vol. 1, pp. 5–6, 24–25; vol. 2, pp. 186, 371–72; vol. 4, p. 76. See also *The Early Christian Conception of Christ*, *op. cit.*, pp. 84–133.

119. Friedrich Ghillany was another nineteenth-century scholar who likewise combined visions with legends which were influenced by myths from other ancient religions (Schweitzer, *op. cit.*, pp. 167, 170).

120. Pfleiderer, *The Early Christian Conception of Christ*, *op. cit.*, p. 157–58; *Primitive Christianity*, *op. cit.*, vol. 1, pp. 10–14; vol. 2, pp. 115–16, 125.

narratives are due to legends. We will henceforth refer to this hypothesis as the mythical or legendary theory of the resurrection.

Even in the twentieth century the mythical or legendary theory of the resurrection can be found.[121] Probably the best-known theologian today who advocates a somewhat related form of this theory is Rudolf Bultmann.[122] He freely recognizes his indebtedness to the History of Religions school of thought, especially in his understanding of the meaning of myth. For Bultmann, New Testament mythology is made up of elements quite similar to concepts found in both Jewish apocalypticism and the redemption myths of gnosticism.[123] All have several features in common. As a result, we find that many of the gospel miracles, for instance, are close to those in the Hellenistic narratives. Bultmann draws parallels between some of these gospel miracles and those of other ancient peoples in a way much reminiscent of Pfleiderer's attempt spoken of above.[124]

Also similar to Pfleiderer is Bultmann's twofold treatment of the resurrection. First, there is a stress on the presence of legendary material in the New Testament accounts. For instance, this event is viewed as being a myth constructed by imagination and legend.[125] But, second, while in his discussion of the resurrection Bultmann laid much more emphasis on the part played by this legendary growth, it is noteworthy that he also felt that the vision theory was also a very possible explanation, at least in part.[126] While the narratives of Jesus' rising from the dead do have significance when we view them as being pointers to the uniqueness of Jesus'

---

121. For instance, Hooke favors the partial use of this view. See his work used above (op. cit., pp. 173–79).

122. Bultmann does not actually offer much rationalization for the resurrection. Neither does he appear very interested in developing theories as to why it did not occur. Therefore it is hard to label him at this point. However, he does believe that this occurrence is a myth, in some ways similar to other ancient myths, as will be perceived below. Because his treatment is nevertheless quite similar in several ways to these we have been discussing, we will include him here. The critique of this theory also applies to his views about this event.

123. Bultmann, "New Testament and Mythology," in Kerygma and Myth, op. cit., p. 10, footnote number two, and pp. 15–16.

124. Bultmann, "The Study of the Synoptic Gospel," in Form Criticism, op. cit., pp. 36–39.

125. See, for instance, Ibid., pp. 66, 72.

126. Bultmann, "New Testament and Mythology," in Kerygma and Myth, op. cit., p. 42.

death, the resurrection is nonetheless a myth devoid of historical reality and thus not an actual historical event.[127]

For Bultmann, the New Testament church combined and mingled Greek and Jewish (Old Testament) mythology.[128] It is no surprise, therefore, that this scholar postulated that the resurrection also had similarities to beliefs in other religions and systems of thought. The affect of such beliefs upon this Christian doctrine of a risen Jesus might partially be realized, for instance, in Paul's speaking of the resurrection in gnostic terms.[129] The gnostic influence on such narratives is also found in other portions of the New Testament.[130] Bultmann holds that Jewish sources also influenced the faith that the early church had in Jesus' resurrection. Old Testament verses were reinterpreted as predictions of this event. In fact, one of the early proofs of this occurrence was what the Christians felt was just such Jewish Scriptural support.[131] We therefore find that certain aspects of the New Testament's teaching about the resurrection were influenced by other ancient faith systems. As a result of these and other legendary features involved in the Christian faith, little can actually be known about the historical Jesus with any degree of certainty.[132]

Earlier we saw how nineteenth-century liberal theology as a whole followed Hume in its rejection of miracles.[133] We should also note that Pfleiderer was no exception here. He likewise accepted the view that science had discovered the laws of nature which were so regular that they could not be violated.[134] Even in the twentieth century this view was accepted by Bultmann (as shown above), who rejected the miraculous

---

127. Ibid., pp. 34, 38, 42.

128. Ibid., pp. 15–16; see also Bultmann's History and Eschatology (New York: Harper & Row, 1962), p. 7.

129. Bultmann, "New Testament and Mythology," in Kerygma and Myth, Ibid., p. 40 and Theology of the New Testament, op. cit., vol. 1, p. 345; vol. 2, p. 153.

130. Cf. the references in footnote 129 with History and Eschatology, op. cit., pp. 54–55.

131. Bultmann, Theology of the New Testament, op. cit., vol. 1, pp. 31, 82.

132. Bultmann, "The Study of the Synoptic Gospels," in Form Criticism, op. cit., pp. 60–61.

133. Randall, op. cit., pp. 553–54; cf. p. 293.

134. Otto Pfleiderer, Philosophy and Development of Religion, 2 vols. (Edinburgh: William Blackwood and Sons, 1894), vol. 1, pp. 5–6.

both because it was perceived to contradict the laws of nature and because we live in too modern of an age to accept such occurrences as fact.[135]

It is apparent that there are several similarities between Bultmann and Pfleiderer on the concept of mythology, especially with regard to the treatment of the resurrection. Therefore Bultmann's position will also be included in the discussion and critique in this section.

We will turn now to an examination of what we will term the legendary or mythical theory of the resurrection of Jesus.[136] Ancient mythology relates various tales concerning "vegetation gods." In their earlier forms these stories, in other words, celebrated the yearly death of vegetation during the fall season and the birth of the vegetation in the spring season. These myths originally dealt only with an expression of man's observances of this yearly cycle of vegetation. Later they were transformed into narratives expressing religious beliefs about the gods.[137]

Various versions of such myths circulated around the ancient world. The details vary from culture to culture, but they do appear to have the most prominent features more-or-less in common, as they revolve mainly around the death of a vegetation god. The god is in love with a goddess but becomes separated from his lover, often by death. She usually mourns for him and sometimes receives him back into the land of the living.[138] The Sumerian form of this myth concerns the god Dumuzi and the goddess Inanna.[139] The Babylonian version is about Tammuz and Ishtar.[140] The Egyptian rendering speaks of Osiris and Isis.[141] Other cultures depict their gods and goddesses directly patterned upon these major versions. For instance, Phoenician mythology presents Adonis and Astarte and Phrygian mythology concerns Attis and Cybele, both of which are the

---

135. Bultmann, "New Testament and Mythology," in *Kerygma and Myth, op. cit.*, pp. 4–5.

136. We note here once again that since the vision theory has been perceived above to be an inadequate explanation to account for the resurrection, we will not reopen the subject here even though both Pfleiderer and Bultmann seem to also prefer this theory *along with* the mythical or legendary theory.

137. Pfleiderer, *Early Christian Conception of Christ, op. cit.*, pp. 91–93.

138. Cf. Orr, *op. cit.*, p. 237.

139. Hooke, *op. cit.*, pp. 20–23.

140. *Ibid.*, pp. 39–41.

141. *Ibid.*, pp. 67–70.

equivalent of the Babylonian Tammuz and Istar.[142] The Greek equivalent
to the Egyptian god Osiris is Dionysus.[143]

It is generally asserted by those who hold the legend theory that these
myths concerning the vegetation gods not only permeated Christian circles, but that they formed the basis for the Christian belief in the resurrection of Jesus. The foundation thus laid by the influence of these ancient
myths then is believed to have provided the framework for later legendary
accumulations, which continued to grow.[144]

There are at least four major reasons (and several addition minor
ones) as to why the legend theory of the resurrection attracts the attention of comparatively few scholars today. First, there is ample proof from
contemporary theological studies that Jesus' resurrection lies at the very
roots of New Testament belief. In other words, it is not simply a flatter-
ing tale added to the origins of Christianity years after the death of Jesus.

It is agreed by all that Paul's account of the resurrection in 1 Corinthians
15:3–8 is the earliest witness to this occurrence. It is also almost entirely
unanimous that Paul is not passing on material which he has formulated
himself, but rather is citing a much earlier tradition.[145] In other words, the
earliest account of the resurrection appearances was formulated before
Paul actually wrote this book and thus it is earlier than the composition
of the book in which it appears.[146]

The key question is how near this ancient formulation of these appearances is to the actual events. Pannenberg believes that the creed is *quite
close* to the original appearances of Jesus.[147] Most others agree with him for
several reasons. First, Paul's words "I delivered" and "I received" are technical jargon referring to the Jewish custom of the transmission of ancient

---

142. Pfleiderer, *Early Christian Conception of Christ*, op. cit., pp. 94–95; Orr, op. cit., p. 237;
Yamauchi, op. cit., March 15, 1974, p. 4.

143. Pfleiderer, *Ibid.*, p. 97.

144. Orr, op. cit., p. 235 and Pfleiderer, *Primitive Christianity*, vol. 1, pp. 5, 23–25 for instance.

145. Reginald Fuller, op. cit., p. 10; Marxsen, op. cit., p. 80. Even Bultmann recognizes this
(*Theology of the New Testament*, op. cit., vol. 1, p. 45).

146. See, for example, Marxsen, *Ibid.*, pp. 52, 80; cf. p. 86; Brown *The Virginal Conception and
Bodily Resurrection of Jesus*, op. cit., p. 81; Reginald Fuller, *Ibid.*, pp. 10–14, 28.

147. Pannenberg, *Jesus—God and Man*, op. cit., p. 90.

data.[148] Second, there are words in this portion which are non-Pauline, pointing to an earlier formulation by others.[149] Third, at least Jeremias believes that the origin of these words is Aramaic and not Greek, thus dating back to the earliest sources.[150]

For these and other similar reasons, it is the belief of most theologians today that this formulation reported by Paul is about as close to the original appearances as is possible for such a formalized creed. This is because a little time would be required for this process of formalization into a list of appearances. We do not know if Paul preserved the list exactly in its original form or if he added to it or modified it, but the core material concerning the appearances of Jesus dates to just a short time after Jesus' death.[151]

In all likelihood, Paul received this information about Jesus' resurrection from Peter and James when he visited Jerusalem after his conversion (Gal 1:18–19).[152] This is especially likely when we remember that there are single appearances of Jesus to both Peter and James in this early traditional formulation (1 Cor 15:5, 7). Therefore, Reginald Fuller states that the very *latest* that this list could have been formulated would be five years after the original appearances, or about 35 AD when Paul made this visit to Jerusalem.[153] Pannenberg dates this visit and the subsequent receiving of this information as occurring six to eight years after these events.[154] But Fuller rightly notes that this is the *latest* that the tradition could have been formulated (so that Paul could have received it at that time). It very well could have crystallized much earlier.

Therefore, we find that the disciples taught the resurrection of Jesus from the very beginning. There was no period of inactivity when this was

---

148. Brown, *The Virginal Conception and Bodily Resurrection of Jesus*, op. cit., p. 81; Reginald Fuller, op. cit., p. 10; Pannenberg, *Jesus—God and Man*, op. cit., p. 90; Ladd, op. cit., pp. 104–5.

149. Reginald Fuller, *Ibid.* Fuller lists some of these phrases which are foreign to Paul's speech patterns in footnote number 1, chapter 2, p. 199.

150. For an evaluation of this conclusion see Brown, *The Virginal Conception and Bodily Resurrection of Jesus*, p. 81, footnote number 140 and Reginald Fuller, *Ibid.*, pp. 10–11.

151. Reginald Fuller, op. cit., p. 10; Ladd, op. cit., p. 105.

152. *Ibid.*, pp. 14, 28; Brown, *The Virginal Conception and Bodily Resurrection of Jesus*, op. cit., p. 92; Pannenberg, *Jesus—God and Man*, op. cit., p. 90; Ladd, op. cit., p. 105.

153. Reginald Fuller, op. cit., pp. 48–49, 70.

154. Pannenberg, *Jesus—God and Man*, op. cit., p. 90.

not their central theme for preaching.[155] The early formulation cited by Paul demonstrates that the proclamation of the resurrection rests upon the testimony of the original eyewitnesses and not upon a legendary process. Therefore this carefully worded tradition in 1 Corinthians 15:3–8 reveals explicitly that the appearances of Christ were experienced by groups of early Christians and *not invented* as a part of later legendary development. This early date caused Pannenberg to conclude that

> under such circumstances it is an idle venture to make parallels in the history of religions responsible for the *emergence* of the primitive Christian message about Jesus' resurrection.[156]

Thus we see, first of all, that myths in ancient religions in all probability cannot be made to account for the rise of the belief in Jesus' resurrection from the dead because the New Testament accounts are simply too close to the events themselves to be legends, as we have seen here.[157]

The second reason that the legend or myth theory is rejected is in some ways similar to the first. In addition to the very early date given to the earliest tradition which reports the appearances of the resurrected Jesus, we are also informed that we have the testimony of *eyewitnesses* to this fact. Above we discussed the probability that two of the original persons to whom Jesus appeared, Peter and James, were the ones who had passed this information to Paul. But there is additional New Testament evidence that must now be discussed which demonstrates that the original eyewitnesses agreed with Paul in teaching that Jesus both rose from the dead and that he appeared to them. To show that such eyewitnesses also believed and taught that this event occurred after Jesus' death and that they witnessed the appearances would of course be an extremely strong point against the legend theory. We will deal more with this below, showing why this point is so acute.

In 1 Corinthians 15 we have not only the earliest testimony concerning Jesus' resurrection appearances to the apostles and to others (vv. 1–8), but we also have Paul's statement that these same apostles also

---

155. Reginald Fuller, *op. cit.*, p. 48; Morison, *op. cit.*, p. 107.

156. Pannenberg, *Jesus—God and Man, op. cit.*, p. 91. Italics are Pannenberg's.

157. Orr, *op. cit.*, p. 246.

preached these same facts. Paul thereby asserts that the message which he was preaching about the resurrection appearances was the same as that to which the other apostles were also testifying (1 Cor 15:11).[158] Later he mentions three times that these original eyewitnesses to the appearances were also preaching of their experiences with the risen Jesus (1 Cor 15:14, 15). Even the critics admit that Paul is here witnessing to the content of the early disciples' message—that *both* Paul and these other *eyewitnesses* were proclaiming a risen Lord who had appeared to them.[159] In other words, those who had seen the risen Lord were now relating this to others. And they did so immediately after the events occurred. Paul additionally explains that the 500 who had also beheld an appearance of the Lord, while they perhaps were not themselves actively preaching about their experience, were still available for questioning, as most of them were still living (1 Cor 15:6). Therefore we see that a number of eyewitnesses were either preaching or available for questioning concerning their experiencing of various appearances of the risen Jesus. This testimony did not take place only years later, but immediately after the original manifestations.

We also receive confirmation of Paul's testimony in the gospels and the book of Acts. Although some critical scholars do not believe that any eyewitnesses were the authors of any of the four gospels, most believe that at the very least some can be traced to eyewitness testimony. Therefore we can at least say that, in all probability, Mark received much material from the apostle Peter, Matthew from the apostle Matthew, Luke-Acts from various eyewitnesses (Luke 1:1–4) and John from the apostle John.[160]

---

158. J. N. D. Anderson, *op. cit.*, pp. 90–91.

159. Reginald Fuller, *op. cit.*, pp. 29–50; Marxsen, *op. cit.*, p. 81.

160. It is not within the scope of this paper to thoroughly examine the question of the authorship of the four gospels. But suffice it to say that most critical scholars recognize at least some eyewitness testimony behind these four books. Matthew is often taken to be the author of the Q document and thus is an eyewitness testimony for one of the major sources of the first gospel. The author of the second gospel is usually asserted to be John Mark, who is believed to have recorded the testimony of Peter, another eyewitness and apostle. Most scholars believe that Luke is the author of the third gospel and the book of Acts, with many recognizing that Luke claims to have collected his information from eyewitnesses (Luke 1:1–4). Part of the reason for the new resurgence of interest in the authority of the fourth gospel is that it is often recognized that this book is very close to the eyewitness testimony of the apostle John. For these and similar conclusions, see Archibald M. Hunter, *Introducing the New Testament*, 2nd ed. (Philadelphia: The Westminster Press, 1957), pp. 41–43, 49–50, 55–56, 61–63; Ladd, *op. cit.*, pp. 74–78; Robert M. Grant, *An Historical Introduction to the New Testament* (London:

These, then, also point to eyewitness testimony concerning the resurrection appearances of Jesus.

The importance of eyewitness testimony such as this is hard to overestimate. We have seen how virtually all agree that the earliest church, including those who were the original observers, proclaimed Jesus' resurrection from the dead.[161] That these first witnesses did not simply fraudulently invent the narratives, fully believing that Jesus was still dead, is evident and admitted by all. Men do not risk their lives and even die[162] for what they know to be only a fabricated falsehood. Also, as J. N. D. Anderson points out, the quality of the ethical teaching of the early disciples and the fact that none ever recanted under the threat of losing their lives further repudiates any theory based upon such fraud. In addition, the psychological transformation of the disciples is left unaccounted for if they invented the stories.[163] Thus they actually *believed* that Jesus had risen from the dead.[164]

But under these conditions the legend theory is impossible. This is obvious not only because those who witnessed the appearances proclaimed the exact opposite. Of course, proclaiming something does not necessarily make it true. But since we have ruled out any chances of a

---

Collins, 1963), pp. 119, 127–29, 134–35, 160; George A. Buttrick, editor, *The Interpreter's Bible*, 12 vols. (New York and Nashville: Abingdon-Cokesbury Press, 1951–1956) vol. 7, p. 242 and vol. 8, pp. 9–10, 440–41; Raymond E. Brown, *New Testament Essays* (Milwaukee: The Bruce Publishing Company, 1965), pp. 129–31; William Hamilton, *The Modern Reader's Guide to John* (New York: Association Press, 1959), pp. 13–15; Daniel Fuller, *op. cit.*, pp. 188–94.

161. See Fuller, *Ibid.*, p. 48.

162. For the traditions concerning the martyr's deaths suffered by all of the twelve apostles (except John) and other early prominent Christians like Mark and Luke, see Marie Gentert King, editor, *Foxe's Book of Martyrs* (Westwood: Fleming H. Revell Company, 1968), pp. 11–13 for instance. Cf. also the witness of Eusebius' *Ecclesiastical History*, translated by Christian Frederick Cruse (Grand Rapids: Baker Book House, 1969), pp. 58, 75–80.

163. J. N. D. Anderson, *op. cit.*, p. 90.

164. Even Bultmann admits this, as we saw above ("New Testament and Mythology," in *Kerygma and Myth*, *op. cit.*, p. 42). There is a difference between saying that the resurrection was a legend or myth and that it was fraud. The former, which is the theory we are discussing here, advocates that the disciples and other early Christians formulated the stories because they really believed Jesus was alive (such as the view of Pfleiderer and Bultmann). The second theory advocates that the disciples simply invented the story in spite of believing that Jesus was dead. Some still hold the former theory (legends or myths). But it is obvious why the latter (fraud) is rejected. The psychological improbabilities of someone dying only for a known fraud, as well as the other reasons against this theory as listed above, therefore make it impossible.

fabricated story or lie on the part of the disciples,[165] there has to be a reason *why* these men would come to believe that Jesus had risen from the dead. The other leading theories (the swoon and the vision theories) have also failed as adequate solutions, as shown above. Therefore these cannot be used as the impetus for this faith. So the legend theory also fails because *some event* had to have happened at the very beginning to convict the disciples that a resurrection had actually occurred. There could have been no gradual build-up of legends because these events were reported from the very first to be true. Neither do other naturalistic theories help to explain this conviction and unquestioning belief on the part of the earliest witnesses.

To proclaim that other ancient myths are the basis for these appearances merely begs the question. To proclaim that Jesus rose because ancient mythology relates such a scheme for the so-called "vegetation gods" does not solve the problem of the origin of faith which convinced the disciples that this event had actually occurred. It also fails to account for the need of the disciples to fabricate appearances of the risen Jesus as narrated in the early formulations. They would obviously know that Jesus had not risen unless they were otherwise deceived (as by a swoon, or by visions). But the conditions for such deception are obviously lacking and this therefore renders such suppositions useless. We are thus caught in a hopeless bind.

The third major criticism of the legend or myth theory (as well as the fourth) even challenges the supposition that any parallels at all can be drawn between the New Testament proclamation of Jesus' resurrection and the resurrection claimed for the vegetation gods of other ancient religions. The main difference between Christianity and the myths of the vegetation gods centers in the fact that Jesus was a historical person, but these gods and heroes were not.[166] The person of Jesus is histori-

---

165. This theory, usually referred to as the "fraud theory," is not held today among theologians to the knowledge of this writer. This is because of the reasons given above. This also includes theories of the disciples stealing the dead body of Christ, for this would once again involve their lying about the appearances when they would have known that Jesus was not alive. Men do not die for a known lie. For these and the other objections already given, this expansion of the fraud theory is also unanimously rejected.

166. This point is admitted by both Pfleiderer (*The Early Christian Conception of Christ, op. cit.,* pp. 157–58) and by Bultmann ("New Testament and Mythology," in *Kerygma and Myth, op. cit.,* p. 34).

cally accessible, whereas those of the mythical characters such as Dumuzi, Tammuz, Osiris, and the others live only in the tales spread about them. For instance, many claimed to have seen the resurrected Jesus, but not so with these mythical figures.[167]

Therefore we perceive that there are no historical grounds upon which we can compare the two types of resurrection stories. Neither are there any historical grounds upon which to compare even the lives of Jesus and of these other gods and heroes. Here we find no close connections.[168] In fact, in none of these mythical characters do we find belief in a *historical* resurrection from the dead as is presented in the New Testament concerning Jesus. This is an important point because it means that, far from having so many resurrection tales after which the disciples could have "patterned" Jesus' resurrection as some of these theorists would have us believe, there were no previous stories of a historical person among these vegetation gods being raised. Jesus' story is therefore unique.

The fourth major criticism against the legend or myth theory is that there is considerable doubt about just how much the teaching of resurrection is found in this ancient mythology at all. Therefore the question yet remains as to the extent that the New Testament was influenced by the resurrection myths of other religions. For instance, Orr feels that these ancient myths are too vague and fluctuating to determine the amount of their influence. Their lack of historical reality adds to this confusion.[169]

In addition, the assumed diffusion of ideas of the resurrection of gods into Judaism and Christianity has anything but been proven. Even the critic Kirsopp Lake believed that the difficulty with the legend theory was in ascertaining how much was based upon real fact and how much was due to overzealous guessing.[170] Pannenberg agrees that this diffusion has not been proven. In first-century Palestine there are almost no traces whatsoever of any influence from these ancient cults of resurrected gods.[171]

It was this last point that once baffled Oxford scholar C. S. Lewis when he was an atheist. After coming to accept the dependence of the

---

167. Orr, *op. cit.*, p. 236; Pfleiderer, *Ibid.*, p. 102.

168. Orr, *op. cit.*, p. 246; McNaugher, *op. cit.*, p. 157.

169. Orr, *Ibid.*, p. 236.

170. *Ibid.*, p. 247, footnote number one.

171. Pannenberg, *Jesus—God and Man*, *op. cit.*, p. 91.

New Testament upon ancient mythology, he was nonplussed by the so few times that any reference was made to any death and rebirth patterns similar to those in ancient mythologies. He also found that such elements were essentially absent from Jesus' teachings as well, which was hard to comprehend if the aforementioned influence was so great.[172]

Orr also believes that the legend theory is too arbitrary, as well. It desires to choose points of similarity while disregarding differences. He feels that it is not hard to use the imagination in order to find isolated areas of agreement.[173] Pfleiderer agrees that the mistake is often made where points of difference are neglected in order to bring about a connection between the facts which are more similar.[174] An example here is appropriate. Pfleiderer himself seems to lay a certain emphasis on the myths which present the resurrection of a god on the third day.[175] But he fails to stress as much the celebration of Adonis' acclaimed resurrection on the first day after the period of mourning[176] or Attis' acclaimed resurrection on the fourth day.[177]

But even after all of these doubts, the key matter concerns the problem of the extent to which a resurrection from the dead is really found in any of these myths. For instance, the key manuscripts in the Sumerian Dumuzi-Inanna myth break off before the ending and therefore contain no account of a resurrection at all. In fact, a recent discovery of one fragment reveals that Inanna allows Dumuzi to be taken to the underworld rather than rescuing him from this realm of the dead.[178] In the Babylonian myth of Tammuz-Ishtar there is also no specific mention of a resurrection. Rather, Tammuz is only inferentially (not explicitly) thought to have been raised,[179] and some even question this.[180] In addition, it has been shown that there is no sign of any resurrection in the early accounts of

---

172. Lewis, *Miracles, op. cit.*, pp. 117–18, 120.

173. Orr, *op. cit.*, pp. 249–50.

174. Pfleiderer, *The Early Christian Conception of Christ, op. cit.*, pp. 153–54, 159.

175. *Ibid.*, pp. 153–55; cf. p. 103.

176. *Ibid.*, p. 94.

177. *Ibid.*, p. 103; cf. p. 155; Orr, *op. cit.*, p. 252.

178. Hooke, *op. cit.*, pp. 21–22; Yamauchi, *op. cit.*, March 15, 1974, p. 4.

179. Hooke, *Ibid.*, p. 40; Pfleiderer, *The Early Christian Conception of Christ, op. cit.*, p. 99.

180. Yamauchi, *op. cit.*, March 15, 1974, p. 4: Orr, *op. cit.*, p. 250

Adonis. The texts which refer to such an event date from no earlier than the second century AD and thus *after* the time of Christ's resurrection.[181] Likewise, the god Attis is not presented as being resurrected until after the middle of the second century AD.[182] One early critic who preferred the legend or myth theory, P. Jensen, cited the Gilgamesh myths as providing a background for Jesus' resurrection, when these myths say nothing at all about such an occurrence.[183]

For these reasons, it is doubted just how much the idea of resurrection can be found in such ancient religion. The references that we do find are fewer than expected, somewhat ambiguous, and not enough to account for the prominence that this belief supposedly reached.[184] Therefore Yamauchi asserts that the only god for which we have both clear and early evidence (before Christ's life) of a resurrection is the Egyptian Osiris. However, this god provides no inspiration for the Christian concept of resurrection, especially since Osiris is always pictured as a mummy. He did not stay on earth after his return to life, but rather descended to rule the underworld. This is a far cry from Jesus' appearances to his followers in this world. We must look elsewhere to find any inspiration for the narratives of Jesus' resurrection as depicted in the New Testament.[185]

Therefore we perceive that there is actually much less of a basis for the ancient belief in the resurrection of gods than was originally thought. A few questionable references to such occurrences do not provide the needed proof. There is especially little basis for the theory that these beliefs in other cultures were just "floating around" and that they are the foundation and background for the Christian teachings.[186]

Thus we see here a converging negative result when the legendary or mythical theory of Jesus' resurrection is examined. First, the earliest narratives concerning this occurrence are too close to the events themselves

181. Yamauchi, *Ibid.*, p. 5. See also J. N. D. Anderson, *Christianity and Comparative Religion* (Downers Grove: InterVarsity Press, 1974), p. 39.

182. Yamauchi, *Ibid.*; Anderson, *Ibid.*, p. 38.

183. Orr, *op. cit.*, pp. 242–43, 251.

184. See, for instance, *Ibid.*, p. 257

185. Yamauchi, *op. cit.*, March 15, 1974, p. 5. Cf. Hooke, *op. cit.*, p. 68.

186. Orr, *op. cit.*, pp. 247, 256–57. Cf. also Pannenberg, *Jesus—God and Man, op. cit.*, p. 91. For some of the general *disbelief* in the Judaeo-Christian concept of resurrection, note the Hebrew and Greek responses to the idea in Mark 12:18; Acts 17:31–32; 26:8.

to allow any time for legends to have formed at all. This is especially true of Paul's list of appearances in 1 Corinthians 15:3–8. There was no gradual build-up of legends here. Second, the direct and indirect testimony from eyewitnesses is a very strong objection to this view. That these witnesses were not lying is agreed by all, for men do not suffer tremendous discomfort and even death for what is known to be a lie. It is also agreed by all that they at least actually *believed* that they had really *seen* something. Therefore it is impossible to assume that they reported a legend or ancient myth as having actually occurred, for they would both know that they were lying when they narrated literal appearances of Jesus and they could not have actually believed that they had really seen him. Some *event* had to have occurred which convinced them that Jesus was risen, otherwise there would have been the need to invent the narratives. This is why this theory is usually coupled with another. A legend does not provide such realistic impetus. But the other key theories (swoon and visionary) were also found to be inadequate.

Third, there are some primary differences between the nonhistorical resurrection of vegetation gods and the resurrection of a historical person. The parallels between the two types of beliefs have very little in common. Fourth, a comparison of the New Testament narratives with the stories of these vegetation gods reveals further that the supposedly similar characteristics are usually missing. In addition, there is real doubt as to the presence of real resurrection stories in ancient mythology and the extent to which they appear. There is certainly no actual basis to believe that these myths were simply "floating around" in Jesus' time. For these and other reasons, this theory must be rejected as being inadequate to explain Jesus' resurrection.[187] As Orr asserts, it simply lacks any historical foundation and relies too much on highly questionable comparisons. We cannot dismiss facts just by pointing to artificial mythical origins.[188]

Bultmann's modification of this theory also fails for similar reasons. First, his reliance on gnostic influences upon the resurrection of Jesus

---

187. Other reasons could also be given against the legendary or mythical theory. For instance, we are left without any adequate explanation for the beginnings of the church or for the belief in the empty tomb if this theory were correct. This writer has formulated a list of 33 total reasons (revolving around points such as these enumerated in the four major criticisms above) for rejecting this theory.

188. Orr, *op. cit.*, pp. 245–46, 253.

must be rejected for almost the same reasons as those raised above for rejecting the influences from other ancient mythologies. The comparisons are not as close as might be expected with regards to the resurrection and these myths surely could not have given rise to the belief in this event, as already explained. Bultmann must have realized this himself, however, because he does not try to make gnostic sources account for the basic foundation of the New Testament resurrection narratives. Rather, we have noted above that he utilizes these myths to explain *periphery portions* of the resurrection such as Jesus' exaltation over all cosmic powers. This does not explain the core proclamation of a risen Jesus at all and thus cannot be the basis of these claims in the earliest church.

Second, Bultmann's scientific worldview is outdated. We can no longer rule out miracles a priori because of *a belief* in a mechanistic, closed universe that rejects the miraculous from the outset (as pointed out in chapter 3 above). Yet, this is what Bultmann does, as we have already seen.[189] Physicist Werner Schaaffs[190] and philosopher Gordon Clark[191] both agree in this criticism. Miracles cannot be excluded in this way because of the modern scientific world in which we live today. Such an approach is not valid.

Third, theologian John Macquarrie also criticizes Bultmann for his arbitrary dismissal of the resurrection without any investigation whatsoever[192] due to his lack of studying the historical evidence. As with Hume, just such an investigation may have revealed the resurrection to be a probable event. Macquarrie also notes the defective scientific view involved.[193]

These second and third criticisms are very substantial ones indeed. They are some of the strongest arguments against Bultmann, who is seen as using an outdated and ineffective view of science, as well as neglecting

---

189. Bultmann, "New Testament and Mythology," in *Kerygma and Myth, op. cit.*, pp. 4–5 for instance.

190. Schaaffs often directs his attack specifically at Bultmann for using an outdated scientific worldview, a criticism which nullifies Bultmann's rejection of the miraculous. It is not possible to handle miracles in such a way, as if they were strictly impossible from the start. See Schaaffs, *op. cit.*, pp. 13, 15, 24–25, 31, 60, 64.

191. Clark also realizes that Bultmann's defective scientific understanding cannot be used to rule out miracles today. See Clark, "Bultmann's Three-Storied Universe," in Gaebelein, *op. cit.*, pp. 218–19.

192. Bultmann, "New Testament and Mythology," in *Kerygma and Myth, op. cit.*, p. 38 for example.

193. Macquarrie, *op. cit.*, pp. 185–86.

any historical investigation at all. The resurrection of Jesus can no longer be rejected for these reasons. In order to ascertain if this event has actually occurred, it must be investigated. It cannot be ruled out *a priori* as done by Bultmann.

In addition, Bultmann's view still falls prey especially to the first and second major criticisms listed above. The earliest narratives are too close to the events to refer to them simply as myths. Also, the eyewitness testimony rules out this theory. As mentioned above, to refer to the resurrection as a myth does not explain why the original disciples came to relate their experiences with the risen Jesus. Even Bultmann admits that they really *believed* that Jesus rose from the dead.[194] But something had to cause this belief. Myths in other religions or the development of later legends cannot account for the *beginning* of this belief because this is no basis from which to project the *original* resurrection appearances, which would otherwise be pure lies. The disciples would not have actually *believed* that *they* had seen Jesus, no matter how prominent other such stories may have been (and we have seen that they were not that common). They could not therefore have believed that Jesus had *actually* appeared to them *personally* unless they had been otherwise deceived. This is probably why Bultmann suggests visions as the answer.[195] But, as we have seen, this and other such theories of deception are also quite inadequate. But legends or myths are especially inept at providing the needed impetus. Therefore Bultmann also fails in his attempt to explain away the literal resurrection of Jesus.

As pointed out by Brown, this legend or myth theory is rejected by most theologians today.[196] Bornkamm points out that there is a decisive lack of common ground between this theory and the New Testament narratives.[197] Pannenberg likewise asserts that such legends cannot account for Jesus' resurrection.[198]

---

194. Bultmann, "New Testament and Mythology," in *Kerygma and Myth, op. cit.,* p. 42.

195. *Ibid.*

196. Brown, "The Resurrection and Biblical Criticism," *op. cit.,* p. 233.

197. Bornkamm, *op. cit.,* p. 185.

198. Pannenberg, *Jesus—God, and Man, op. cit.,* pp. 90–91.

CHAPTER VII

Possibility Number Two:
That the Resurrection Did Occur, but
That It Cannot Be Demonstrated

A. SØREN KIERKEGAARD: AN INTRODUCTION

The second major possibility to be dealt with is that the resurrection of Jesus did occur, but that this occurrence cannot be demonstrated. We will first examine the views of a very significant scholar who held this opinion. This theologian and philosopher, Søren Kierkegaard (1813–1855), is probably the best-known representative of this viewpoint.

Although Kierkegaard was not the first scholar to formulate a hypothesis such as this, he popularized this view in a way which has influenced twentieth-century theology immensely. He has been chosen here as the primary representative of this view because of the affect which his work has exerted on many contemporary theologians. This influence is especially apparent, for instance, in this scholar's treatment of miracles. Beginning with Karl Barth's *Epistle to the Romans* in 1918,[1] various theological schools of thought have followed Kierkegaard in postulating that the miraculous cannot be demonstrated to have occurred in any way. This is especially

---

1. For the relation between Barth and the nineteenth-century liberal theology which his thought was to replace, see the brief summation in chapter 6, footnote number 1. Barth's neo-orthodox theology as a whole was indebted to Kierkegaard for much of its framework and foundation, and for many of its key facets. See, for instance, Bernard Ramm, *A Handbook of Contemporary Theology* (Grand Rapids: William B. Eerdman's Publishing Company, 1966), pp. 89–92.

true of the resurrection. The occurrence of this event is often affirmed in various ways, with the understanding that there is no way that it can be verified or proven.[2] In fact, it is probable that even most of the theologians since Barth who *reject* any belief in a real resurrection of Jesus still manifest the influence of Kierkegaard in their belief that this event was not meant to be proven anyway. Such miracles are simply not open to objective verification.[3] We will deal with the reasoning behind such assertions below.

It is mainly for these reasons that Kierkegaard has been chosen here as the representative of this viewpoint. This Danish scholar has exercised much influence on twentieth-century theology. His view of miracles was especially influential. As will be shown in the next chapter, a very large portion of contemporary theology has followed Kierkegaard in holding that miracles cannot be demonstrated, whether these occurrences are accepted as really happening or not. He is thus an excellent example of one who believes that miracles such as the resurrection did occur but that any attempts at demonstrating their validity are fruitless and misleading.

Before we proceed to an examination of Kierkegaard's views concerning miracles, it will be advantageous to look briefly at some of the intellectual background for his polemic. Perhaps more than with most other well-known thinkers, much of this scholar's thought is derived from personal experiences, such as his observation of the conditions in his native land of Denmark.

Kierkegaard experienced a difficult boyhood. Apparently because of family problems and also because of a physical deformity (his back was crooked and he limped), he endured acute periods of melancholy which seemed to be continually present in his life.[4] By his own admission he suffered greatly from this daily depression, which was complicated by the conviction that he had been singled out in order to suffer for others.

---

2. See Daniel Fuller, *op. cit.*, pp. 80–84; cf. Ramm, *Ibid.*, pp. 74–76, 79–80, 89–92. In the next chapter we will discuss some of these theologians who were influenced by Kierkegaard in their acceptance of the resurrection with the stipulation that it cannot be demonstrated.

3. See, for example, Rudolf Bultmann, *Jesus Christ and Mythology* (New York: Charles Scribner's Sons, 1958), pp. 61–62, 71–72, 80, 84.

4. Martin J. Heinecken, "Søren Kierkegaard," in *A Handbook of Christian Theologians*, edited by Martin C. Marty and Dean G. Peerman (Cleveland: The World Publishing Company, 1965), pp. 125–26.

These emotions caused him a great amount of consternation and kept him from the real joy in life which might otherwise have been attainable.[5]

It was at least partially due to this intense melancholy and conviction that he must suffer for others that Kierkegaard encountered two other experiences which had a tremendous effect upon his life. First, he felt obliged to break off his engagement to his lover, Regina Olson. Although both loved each other very much, Kierkegaard felt that somehow the break was God's guidance and will for his life. But because he still loved her, he struggled much with his feelings. His writings reveal this battle which he waged with himself. His action seemed to be attributable to the melancholy from which he still suffered. But nonetheless, this broken engagement led to an immense amount on writing on his part. His time was now spent in publishing his views on various subjects, especially theology and philosophy. His rate of production over the coming years has rarely been equaled, especially in the diversity of the subjects which were covered.[6]

Second, Kierkegaard attacked a weekly news sheet named the *Corsair*. This publication openly denounced many public figures, embarrassing them in the process. Kierkegaard had hoped to expose this literary tirade with the help of other prominent men of Copenhagen who also disliked the methods of this paper. But he received no help and thus suffered all of the brunt of the return attack upon himself. And the *Corsair* was quite vicious in its presentations of this Danish thinker, deriding him because of his physical deformity. For instance, it made light of the unequal length of his two legs. This procedure continued in the paper for approximately one year and soon he was looked upon with much derision by the public. But Kierkegaard accepted this treatment as part of the suffering which was ordained for him. It caused him to become even more withdrawn from society and resolved to continue the work he had begun.[7]

One conviction that Kierkegaard continued to act upon was his polemic against the presence of Hegelian-influenced theology in Denmark.

---

5. Søren Kierkegaard, *The Point of View for My Work as an Author*, edited by Benjamin Nelson, translated by Walter Lowrie (New York: Harper & Row, 1962) pp. 76–80. Cf. also Heinecken, *Ibid.*, p. 125.

6. Kierkegaard, *Ibid.*, see Appendix A, written by the translator, pp. 162–63; Heinecken, *Ibid.*, pp. 126–27.

7. Kierkegaard, *Ibid.*, see Appendix B, written by the translator, pp. 163–65; cf. Kierkegaard's own assessment, pp. 94–95. Cf. also Heinecken, *Ibid.*, p. 128.

The Hegelian version of Christianity encouraged people to reason clearly, as if this was all there was involved in becoming a Christian. The popular belief in Denmark was that being a good Danish citizen and being a Christian were almost synonymous.[8] Kierkegaard attacked these presuppositions, pointing out that Christianity is much more than a life of easy living. Rather, it is a total transformation of the individual, based upon the personal recognition of one's being a sinner. It involves a commitment to God through faith in the death of Christ to pay for one's sins. The result is the imitation of Christ.[9] In fact, the chief theme of all of his writings was to speak to those living in "Christendom" to inform them about how they could become true New Testament Christians.[10]

This brief background will make the proceeding presentation of Kierkegaard's arguments more comprehensible. After endeavoring to understand the reasoning behind his treatment of miracles, a critique of these views will then be presented in order to ascertain their ability to support Kierkegaard's arguments. It should be mentioned before passing, however, that the two main texts which will be used here are Kierkegaard's *Concluding Unscientific Postscript*[11] and his *Philosophical Fragments*.[12] This is for a few very important reasons. The Danish scholar himself relates to us that the former volume is both the turning point of his work as an author and the transition between his aesthetic works and his religious ones.[13] In addition, quite a large portion of this work concerns one of the main topics which is to be discussed here and other related thoughts.[14] On the other hand, the primary problem treated by the latter work

---

8. Kierkegaard's polemic against the "Christianity" of his day is especially strong in his work *Attack Upon "Christendom,"* translated by Walter Lowrie (Princeton: Princeton University Press, 1972). For his evaluation of Danish Christianity such as spoken of here, compare pp. 132–33, 139, 145, 149, 164–65 for instance, or see the essay "What Christ's Judgment is About Official Christianity," *Ibid.*, pp. 117–24. For a brief discussion of Kierkegaard's attack against the influence of Hegelianism upon Danish Christianity as mentioned above, see also Heinecken, *Ibid.*, pp. 127–28, 134–35.

9. For Kierkegaard's own evaluation of what a real Christian is, including these points just mentioned, see *Ibid.*, pp. 23, 149, 210, 213, 221, 268, 280, 287, 290 for example. Heinecken agrees with this summary, *Ibid.*, pp. 131, 134.

10. Heinecken, *Ibid.*, p. 127.

11. This work is translated by David Swenson (Princeton: Princeton University Press, 1974).

12. This work is also translated by David Swenson (Princeton: Princeton University Press, 1974).

13. Kierkegaard, *The Point of View for My Work as an Author, op. cit.*, pp. 13–14, 53, 97.

14. Kierkegaard, *Concluding Unscientific Postscript, op. cit.*, pp. 86–97, 115–343 for example.

concerns whether or not the Christian faith can be based on historical events[15] and this is the key question to be dealt with in this chapter. After thus perceiving these introductory facts, it is now possible to proceed to our presentation of Kierkegaard's views.

B. SØREN KIERKEGAARD'S
ARGUMENT AND A CRITIQUE

As a theologian and philosopher, Kierkegaard's writings were not overly popular beyond Scandinavia and Germany until the twentieth century.[16] As pointed out above, he often reacted against both the "official Christianity" of his day, which was very defective in terms of the New Testament definition, and against the philosophy of Hegelianism.[17] Both trends were leading people away from real Christianity. It was at least partially as a result of his bold stand taken against these ideas that he was not very popular in his own time. However, his works were revived in this century by both secular and religious existentialism, including such scholars as Karl Barth, Martin Heidegger, and Jean-Paul Sartre.[18] Today one cannot even deal adequately with existentialism without noting the influence of Kierkegaard and the impetus which he gave to the beginnings of this philosophy.[19]

Kierkegaard formulated and defended the well-known philosophical statement that "Truth is subjectivity."[20] Therefore, while several forms of philosophy teach that the way to knowledge is to seek objective truth in one form or another, this is viewed as being impossible. We can only

---

15. *Ibid.*, p. 323. For instance, see *Philosophical Fragments, op. cit.,* pp. 93–110. For the importance of these two texts as the writings of Kierkegaard which most influenced contemporary theology and philosophy, see Heinecken's "Søren Kierkegaard," in Marty and Peerman, *op. cit.,* pp. 131–32.

16. Runes, *op. cit.,* p. 160.

17. In addition to the references listed above, see James Collins, "Faith and Reflection in Kierkegaard," in *A Kierkegaard Critique,* edited by Howard A. Johnson and Niels Thulstrup (Chicago: Henry Regnery Company, 1962), pp. 141–42, 147–48. Cf. Lev Shestov, *Athens and Jerusalem,* translated by Bernard Martin (No city: Ohio university Press, 1966), p. 242.

18. Daniel Fuller, *op. cit.,* pp. 80–81, 84; Heinecken, "Søren Kierkegaard," in Marty and Peerman, *op. cit.,* pp. 127, 142. Cf. Runes, *op. cit.,* p. 124.

19. See, for example, Wesley Barnes, *The Philsophy and Literature of Existentialism, op. cit.,* pp. 48, 56–57, 100–102; Ramm, *A Handbook of Contemporary Theology, op. cit.,* pp. 46–47.

20. Kierkegaard, *Concluding Unscientific Postscript, op. cit.,* title of part 2, chapter 2, p. 169.

achieve the truth by subjectivity. In fact, all eternal truth and values are based upon this subjectivity.[21]

Do objective approaches have any validity at all? For Kierkegaard, objective reflection can yield objective truth, such as mathematics and history. In other words, objective facts can be true, especially in an objective sense as with the above disciplines.[22] We might phrase it this way: a rational, objective approach to reality can yield *true* facts, but it cannot lead to eternal *truth*, which is a different concept.

An example which is introduced here by this Danish thinker will serve to illustrate this point. A patient from an insane asylum succeeded in escaping from the institution. He knew that he would have to express himself sanely when he arrived in a nearby city, lest someone perceive the truth of the matter and send him back. As he walked along he picked up a ball and put it into the pocket of his coat. This continually bounced against his body with every step that he took. Inspired by this, the patient began repeating to himself each time it happened, "Bang, the earth is round." When he reached the city he attempted to convince one of his friends that he was sane by speaking objectively. So he again repeated, "Bang, the earth is round." But, alas, instead of being able to convince the doctor that he was sane, he only impressed upon him that he was still sick and in need of medical assistance.[23]

The point that Kierkegaard thus expresses is the questionableness of objective truths. The statement which the patient from the asylum made was true, even objectively true (the earth *is* round). But it was of little consequence. Therefore we are to see that, while such objective statements can indeed be true, they do not lead us to eternal truth. In this respect they fail, because "Truth is subjectivity."

For Kierkegaard, this subjective factor finds its culmination in the idea termed "passion." The highest of the passions of human subjectivity is faith.[24] This concept is a central one in the thought of this scholar. It opposed that portion of Western philosophy which reached its apex in

---

21. *Ibid.*, p. 173.
22. *Ibid.*, pp. 173–74.
23. *Ibid.*, p. 174.
24. *Ibid.*, pp. 118, 177–78.

Hegel, a tradition which stressed the importance of reason as the basis for knowledge.[25]

This understanding of faith (as the highest of the passions) as the basis of knowledge is an important factor when we are speaking of Kierkegaard's approach to God. Since subjectivity is the way to truth and faith is the highest expression of subjectivity, it follows that we can only come to know the truth about God by this subjective, inward faith. It is an inner process, a faith-experience, by which we come to know about Him.[26]

Since God can only be known by subjectivity such as is expressed in faith, it is therefore plain that we cannot gain such knowledge by any forms of objectivity, such as by reason. In fact, when we try to approach God by reason we find that He is inaccessible. It is plainly impossible to discover truth about God objectively.[27]

The same is true of the Christian faith as a whole, because Christianity also opposes all objectivity. Kierkegaard even goes as far as to say that objective Christianity is paganistic.[28]

The culmination of these thoughts is in Kierkegaard's convictions that since God is a Subject, He can therefore only be known subjectively. Thus we cannot attempt any proofs for His existence, nor can we conjure up any arguments concerning God by the use of reason. It is little wonder that Kierkegaard does not try to demonstrate His existence.[29]

This brings us to the crux of this presentation. It has been shown that Kierkegaard rejected verification and proof for the existence of God and for the Christian faith as a whole. Such an objective approach is clearly improper. Christian truth is achieved by subjectivity.

For these same reasons, Kierkegaard also rejected any attempts to base the truth of the Christian faith on historical knowledge.[30] In this he followed his predecessor, Gotthold E. Lessing (1729–1781), who postulated

---

25. *Ibid.*, p. 176 and Ramm, *A Handbook of Contemporary Theology, op. cit.*, p. 97.

26. Kierkegaard, *Ibid.*, pp. 117–16, 178–79.

27. *Ibid.*, p. 178 and Kierkegaard's *Philosophical Fragments, op. cit.*, pp. 55–57.

28. Kierkegaard, *Concluding Unscientific Postscript, Ibid.*, pp. 42, 116.

29. *Ibid.*, p. 178 and Kierkegaard's *Philosophical Fragments, op. cit.*, pp. 49, 55; cf. Robert L. Perkins, *Søren Kierkegaard* (Richmond: John Knox Press, 1969), p. 17.

30. Kierkegaard, *Concluding Unscientific Postscript, Ibid.*, pp. 86–97. See also James Brown, *Kierkegaard, Heidegger, Buber and Barth* (New York: Collier Books, 1967), pp. 57–60.

that "accidental truths of history can never become the proof of necessary truths of reason."[31] By this Lessing explains his conviction and belief that one cannot support Christian doctrines by referring to historical events such as the resurrection. In other words, while Lessing asserts that he has no historical grounds on which to deny the resurrection of Jesus, this is no reason to believe other doctrines of the Christian faith as a result. One may, indeed, affirm the other doctrinal beliefs of Christianity (as Lessing claims that he does), but this must be on another basis other than that of the historicity of certain events. To argue from such events would be to reason from accidental historical facts to the necessary truths of one's faith, and this is not allowable.[32]

Lessing adds that this division between historical facts and religious faith "is the ugly, broad ditch which I cannot get across, however often and however earnestly I have tried to make the leap."[33] Thus we perceive that the gap between these two categories is what comprises the barrier over which Lessing cannot find a way. There is no means he can discover which will allow one to proceed from an argument in the first category to a belief in the second category.

It is doubtful, however, if Lessing actually believed in a historical resurrection like he appears to affirm (as noted above). For instance, when writing in another essay about eighteenth-century rationalist Hermann Reimarus' rejection of the resurrection, he admits that even if the objections which were raised were valid ones, Christianity would still exist because the acceptance of Christian doctrines depends upon faith and not upon historical events.[34] Even Kierkegaard realized that Lessing's affirmations about events such as the resurrection were actually only concessions made by him to highlight the point he was making.[35]

In addition, Lessing relates that historical truths cannot be proven anyway. Thus, even if it is held that events have occurred, it cannot be *proven* that they did. In a similar way, just because the resurrection is

---

31. Gotthold E. Lessing, *Lessing's Theological Writings*, edited by Henry Chadwick (London: A. and C. Black, 1956), p. 53.

32. *Ibid.*, pp. 53–55.

33. *Ibid.*, p. 55.

34. *Ibid.*, this essay about Reimarus appears on pp. 9–29. Cf. Daniel Fuller, *op. cit.*, p. 32.

35. Kierkegaard, *Concluding Unscientific Postscript*, *op. cit.*, p. 88. Cf. Fuller, *Ibid.*, pp. 34–35.

believed to have actually occurred, it cannot be *proven* to have been historical, but only accepted by *faith*.[36] We can therefore better perceive how Lessing could seemingly accept an event even when it could not be demonstrated to have happened and when it could not be the basis for other beliefs.

Lessing's formulation, whereby history is divorced from faith, has exercised much influence since his time. For example, Immanuel Kant borrowed from him in making a similar distinction between the truths of God and historical fact. Separating these two categories is "a mighty chasm, the overleaping of which ... leads at once to anthropomorphism."[37] Thus we find once again that religious truths of faith cannot be supported by history. And, as with Lessing, neither can events of history such as the resurrection be proven. In fact, this event cannot be demonstrated to have occurred literally because as such it is an offense to reason.[38]

Kierkegaard also followed Lessing in this belief that occurrences in history could not support religious truths of faith. Kierkegaard expressly states that "there can in all eternity be no direct transition from the historical to the eternal."[39] This is the case both for the eyewitnesses to the facts and for those who are removed by generations. Whether the believer was a contemporary of Jesus or not, he is not able to base faith on reason or history.[40]

This stance by Kierkegaard is actually the key to this discussion. Since truth is subjective, then objective approaches such as the historicity of certain events cannot lead one to a decisive faith or to eternal happiness.[41] To be sure, this scholar believes that Jesus was a historical person in that he entered the time sequence of this world as a man. It was also in history

36. Lessing, *op. cit.*, p. 53; cf. p. 54. See Fuller, *Ibid.*, p. 34.

37. Immanuel Kant, *Religion Within the Limits of Reason Alone*, translated by Theodore M. Greene and Hoyt H. Hudson (New York: Harper & Row, 1960), pp. 58–59, note. Cf. Fuller, *Ibid.*, p. 37.

38. Kant, *Ibid.*, p. 119, note. Cf. Fuller, *Ibid.*, pp. 37–38.

39. Kierkegaard, *Concluding Unscientific Postscript*, *op. cit.*, p. 89; cf. p. 47.

40. See *Ibid.*, pp. 38, 89, 190 and Kierkegaard's *Philosophical Fragments*, *op. cit.*, pp. 108–9 for instance. See footnote number 46 below.

41. Kierkegaard, *Concluding Unscientific Postscript*, *Ibid.*, p. 33, 42, 45. On Kierkegaard's belief that history is an objective approach, compare *Ibid.*, p. 173 for instance, in addition to the discussion above.

that Jesus lived, died, and rose again.[42] But even though these events actually occurred, they comprise the supreme paradox of the Christian faith because the doctrine of the incarnation is seemingly inexplicable and difficult to grasp logically. Such events are contradictory because they assert that God has become man, contrary to all reason. Even though this incarnation really did take place in history, one cannot historically (or otherwise) demonstrate such events in Jesus' life like the resurrection because it is impossible to demonstrate a contradiction (even one that really occurred). Historical proofs cannot make such events any less of a contradiction or paradox.[43]

Therefore, Kierkegaard postulated that these events cannot be the basis of faith, as mentioned above. But, in addition, they are to be believed even though it is not possible to demonstrate that they have occurred. Thus it is not only impossible to base one's faith on objective, historical events (since faith is subjectivity), but it is also impossible to prove these events. The various facets of Jesus' incarnation are an enigma to history and the objective discipline of history is too suspect and inexact to yield such proof.[44] For this reason, Kierkegaard discouraged arguing and debating about the truths of faith.[45]

The direct result of this emphasis upon theology is the very important concept termed the "leap." Kierkegaard, inspired here by Lessing, makes much use of this idea.[46] For Kierkegaard, God cannot be determined to exist by "proofs," as mentioned earlier. Neither can His existence be demonstrated by pointing to events in history such as the incarnation, as

---

42. *Ibid.*, pp. 188, 194. See also Heinecken, "Søren Kierkegaard," in Marty and Peerman, *op. cit.*, p. 131; cf. p. 138 and Brown, *op. cit.*, p. 59.

43. Kierkegaard, *Ibid.*, pp. 189–90; cf. p. 30. Cf. Ramm, *A Handbook of Contemporary Theology, op. cit.*, pp. 7, 94–95.

44. Kierkegaard, *Ibid.*, pp. 42–43 and Kierkegaard's *Philosophical Fragments, op. cit.*, p. 108. Cf. Brown, *op. cit.*, p. 59.

45. Kierkegaard, *Concluding Unscientific Postscript, Ibid.*, pp. 46–47.

46. See Brown, *op. cit.*, pp. 57–59; Perkins, *op. cit.*, p. 17; Ramm, *A Handbook of Contemporary Theology, op. cit.*, p. 79 and Schaeffer, *The God Who Is There, op. cit.*, p. 21. Kierkegaard does not accept this idea *exactly* as it appears in Lessing, however. For Lessing the leap is made by persons who are removed from the historical events by time (perhaps by hundreds of years), but who still wish to exercise faith. The leap from history to faith would not be needed if we had all been contemporaries of the event in question. But for Kierkegaard, the lean from historical events in the life of Jesus to faith in these events must be made by all believers because there is no benefit in being a contemporary (see Kierkegaard, *Ibid.*, p. 89; cf. Brown, *Ibid.*, pp. 58–59).

we have just seen. As long as we hold to such objective methods of verification, we will never understand God's existence. It is only when we let
go of such proofs and accept God by faith that we will realize that God
does indeed exist.[47] This act of abandoning all of our proofs and all of
our attempts to reach God by reason, however brief a moment it may be,
is termed a "leap."[48] This leap takes place when we let go of all of these
objective attempts to prove God by our reason and accept Him by faith.

So it is very clear that, for Kierkegaard, the resurrection of Jesus provides no basis for faith. Although this event is believed to be true, it cannot
be demonstrated to be such. It must simply be accepted by faith apart from
any historical logic. Once again we are required to reject this proof and
perceive God without such a crutch. Thus, we are to take the leap to God's
existence by faith, without any reliance upon historical fact. Lessing's
ditch is bridged by faith, as one leaps from the facts of Jesus' life to faith
in him apart from any verification.

So far, Kierkegaard's position concerning subjectivity has been investigated. To repeat briefly, this concept is viewed as being the proper way
to finding the truth. A very clear statement to this effect is "Subjectivity
is truth, subjectivity is reality."[49] This inward quality of transformation
reaches its apex in passion. In fact, passion itself is strictly a subjective
factor which cannot be objective at all.[50]

This obviously leaves very little room for objectivity. Indeed,
Christianity is opposed to all that is objective. If we rely on an objective
faith we are said to be reverting to paganism.[51] There is actually even a limit
placed on reason, dictating its boundaries. This is because Kierkegaard
believes that reason can only advance to a certain point, beyond which it
is not operative. For instance, it cannot prove God. But even when reason
is taken to its limit in relation to God, He is still no closer than before.[52]

We should also mention the *personal* quality of this faith. One believes
in God even though this exercise of faith is not based upon any logical or

47. Kierkegaard, *Philosophical Fragments*, op. cit., p. 53.

48. *Ibid.*

49. Kierkegaard, *Concluding Unscientific Postscript*, op. cit., p. 306.

50. *Ibid.*, pp. 51, 117, 177.

51. *Ibid.*, pp. 42, 116.

52. Kierkegaard, *Philosophical Fragments*, op. cit., pp. 53, 55, 57.

other objective grounds. Neither does this faith attempt to prove its own validity. Rather, the decision to act in faith involves the leap and one's subsequent embracing of subjective inwardness, which ultimately leads to a nonrational passion.[53]

It now remains for us to attempt to ascertain the accuracy of these views. We concluded above (in chapter 4) that in theological investigations, reason is temporally first while faith is more important, especially as an end result. But here we have seen that Kierkegaard gives no essential place to reason at all, while beginning and ending the theological process with faith. This leads to three major criticisms of Kierkegaard's approach, all of which are directed at the very heart of his polemic. One criticism concerns his exclusive use of faith and the other two revolve around his resultant denial of any essential place being given to objective, reasonable approaches to Christianity.

The first major criticism concerns this scholar's internal consistency, as it questions the very point of whether Kierkegaard was successful in his own attempt to leave the objective approach to Christianity out of his view of faith.[54] It was concluded earlier (in chapter 4) that reason, by definition,[55] was the grounds for all convictions and decisions. Any defense of a belief is also reason. Even the ability to think coherently is reason. This definition clearly shows, in full opposition to Kierkegaard's teaching, that rational thought (as opposed to subjective thought) is the very basis of our knowledge. In other words, Kierkegaard himself could not even provide such a polemic in defense of faith without relying on reason. This is because reason must be the basis of his conviction that faith is primary. Reason must likewise have compelled his decision to act through such a faith-commitment.

---

53. *Ibid.*, pp. 53–55 and Kierkegaard's *Concluding Unscientific Postscript, op. cit.*, pp. 118, 209 for instance.

54. To be sure, Kierkegaard did not assert that there were no objective truths. He did allow for such. However, objective approaches simply cannot lead to eternal truth and neither can the objective be the basis for faith. See Heinecken's "Søren Kierkegaard," in Marty and Peerman, *op. cit.*, pp. 139–41.

55. We also found scholarly support of this definition as well, so as not to attempt to settle such philosophical issues simply by referring to definitions.

Kierkegaard even makes use of logic and reason in his polemic in favor of the way of faith,[56] even though such an objective process also finds its basis in the rational. Thus there could not even be a defense of the primacy of faith apart from some sort of rational process. Even though Kierkegaard does see some value in the objective, as noted above, he does not believe that it occupies a place of importance in reaching God. Neither does he accept reason as being temporally primary. The objection here is not that he gives no place at all to the objective, but that he does not realize that he is making use of such reasonable approaches in his own approach to God. Therefore, even in his system, reason must be temporally first in order for Kierkegaard to assert the importance of faith.

This can be demonstrated more clearly when we remember how Kierkegaard postulated that truth is found in subjectivity and that objectivity was not the way to God. He could assert this, for instance, either by reasonable persuasion and rational argument or by intuitive conviction and knowledge. But now it is plain to see that reason, and not passion, is the origin of each. All processes of reasonable persuasion and rational argument obviously involve reason. But we have also seen that even the basis of such intuitive conviction or knowledge is reason. Should he try to demonstrate that this is not the case, this persuasion also becomes rational. One cannot show how subjectivity is central without utilizing reason.

Indeed, it would even be impossible for Kierkegaard to think in the sense that he was accustomed to at all, except by reason. He would be required to think through his position apart from the formulating of any convictions, without the formulating of any conclusions or without making any decisions in order to theorize apart from a rational process. It is therefore obvious that Kierkegaard did begin the process with reason, as he was not able to simply start with faith.

It is therefore somewhat ironic that the very element which Kierkegaard sought to separate from faith (namely, objectivity) was the basis upon which faith was built. His very arguments against this conclusion proved reason to be an essential element, since the very polemic was rational. Thus, however subjective or irrational the entire system may be, this

---

56. For Kierkegaard's use of logic and reason in his polemic, see Heinecken's "Søren Kierkegaard," in Marty and Peerman, *op. cit.*, p. 132; cf. pp. 127–28.

subjectivity has been formulated upon a rational process, albeit a disguised one. Otherwise such a theoretical construction would not have been possible.

It is because of these factors that subjectivity, passion, and faith cannot be held to be temporally first. This position belongs to reason, even though faith is more important, especially in the end.

The second major criticism of Kierkegaard's system is that he does away with all logical grounds which might support his thesis. Even though it has been shown that Kierkegaard himself relies on an objective foundation in spite of his protests to the contrary, he still insists that there be no objective verification of faith. It is, of course, this scholar's express intention to do away with these grounds, but in so doing there is no objective criteria on which his claims may be based. In other words, Kierkegaard is in error by first denying a place to any objective basis for faith even when he unknowingly utilizes such a reasonable basis himself (criticism number one above). But second, he continues to insist that faith cannot be verified at all. Therefore, even though it is his intention not to base faith on any objective foundation, it is because of this that one cannot ascertain if the subsequent message should be accepted or not. Since such faith is a personal, subjective experience, there is no reason someone else should likewise be compelled to accept it.

Or further, how would it be possible for one to know whether the Christian faith was the right religion? One could likewise urge faith in another system of belief. If no reasonable persuasion exists, how could Kierkegaard differentiate and choose between these options?

As stated earlier, since this faith which Kierkegaard proposes is so subjective, it is even hard to differentiate between it and human emotions such as elation, love, or even heartburn. In other words, Kierkegaard's subjectiveness is not capable of answering these questions and those raised above because it cannot demonstrate its own validity or tell if its own foundations are solid. In the end there is no real way to ascertain if such a faith has been exercised in the proper way.

Even if Kierkegaard prefers a subjective faith, this does not answer the question of how he might be sure that this faith is valid even for himself, let alone for others. Just because this scholar is not interested in any objective demonstration of the Christian faith, it is nevertheless very important to be able to know if the faith-commitment which he is expounding is valid or not. After all, faith is not simply a cerebral exercise devoid of consequences if it just happened to be false. Much is at risk for those who place high value (indeed, eternal value) in their faith if it is found to be illegitimate.

Kierkegaard speaks much of eternal truth, but it is hard to distinguish between real beliefs and false ones if there is no factual criteria. It is therefore essential to know if his system is probable. It becomes more obvious here that an objective, logical faith would thus be in a much better position to ascertain its trustworthiness than an irrational, subjective one.

For these reasons, for faith to be intelligible it must have some sort of objective groundwork. If the objective is rejected, as Kierkegaard does, then we must also abandon all hope of arriving at testable data about our beliefs. It is true that Kierkegaard was opposed to all such testing and demonstration, but without some criteria such as this, it would be almost impossible to know if such a faith was spurious or not. Therefore we see that Kierkegaard's system of positing a faith which culminates in passion and inwardness is simply too subjective. There must be some reasonable basis upon which to build this faith.

There is also the problem that Kierkegaard claims that his method of faith is the only way that a Christian can find eternal happiness. But we submit that to abandon a rational basis for faith and to disregard intellectual demonstration can lead to eternal happiness only if one simply *ignores* any faith-related questions that might arise, such as these which have been raised here. One would have to wear earmuffs and blinders of irrationality in order to forsake all needs and desires to rationalize just so that one might achieve a temporary and fleeting "eternal happiness" which lasts only until the next doubt arises. And the questions raised here would still remain unanswered—one would never know if one's faith-commitment was valid or even if it was warranted in the first place.

These first two criticisms alone are enough to provide an adequate critique of Kierkegaard's view of the Christian faith. But it is now possible to apply these two to his system with regards to his rejection of proofs and historical demonstrations as the basis of his way to God.

The third major criticism of Kierkegaard is that his rejection of any objective approach to the Christian faith, including historical verification, is no longer warranted in view of the preceding two criticisms. It has been shown that reason must remain temporally primary. Subjective factors such as faith and passion are unquestionably important, but these are to be based on reason. There must also be some objective grounds for faith. There are some definite implications in these conclusions.

It was stated earlier that the resurrection of Jesus was held by Kierkegaard as not being a valid basis upon which to rest the theological truths of faith. The reason for this was that the subjective was thought to be the true basis for belief. Such objective events were believed to be of a different category and are thus rejected.[57]

But all of these convictions must change when it is held (1) that reason is temporally first and (2) that faith should be objectively verified, both of which were concluded above. For instance, since reason is held to be temporally primary (criticism number one here and chapter 4 above), one can no longer hold that the subjective stands alone and apart from this objective basis and neither can one negate the effectiveness of objective historical events as a result. In other words, with the former basis for religious truths dissolved (namely, subjective faith), the former reason for rejecting historical events must also disappear. This is because it can no longer be maintained that historical verification is opposed to an exclusively subjective faith, because it has been found that this faith is already based on an objective element, namely reason. And since this is the case, it must be realized that this reason can be historical reason, logic, or another means of reasonable verification. At any rate, one could not be opposed to such reasonable historical demonstrations when the objective element of reason is already inherent in the concept of faith, thereby requiring some such objective approach. In fact, the way is opened for faith to be verified by any reasonable approach (or even several at once).

It was also postulated above that faith must have some objective criteria on which to base its claims so that it can be verified (criticism number two here and chapter 4 above). The use of historical research provides an excellent means by which such verification can be effected. Therefore, we perceive once again that Kierkegaard's thesis of subjectivity cannot

---

57. Kierkegaard, *Concluding Unscientific Postscript, op. cit.*, p. 89. See also Brown, *op. cit.*, pp. 38–39 and Daniel Fuller, *op. cit.*, pp. 34–35.

stand. When this scholar's emphasis on the exclusiveness of subjectivity fails, so does his polemic against such proofs as are shown to be probable. It has been shown that faith must be confirmed as being the proper approach to God. Thus we can no longer rule out the confirmation which is provided by verification, such as that from past events which are found to be probable. Such objective demonstration is in fact demanded by the very nature of the two conclusions which we have reached here, as faith must be shown to be valid.

For these reasons, an exact inverse of Kierkegaard's relationships has therefore occurred. Whereas it was formerly not possible to accept historical events as pointing to eternal truths (according to this scholar), we now understand that this is no longer true. Historical verification (and other such objective demonstrations) now becomes a help rather than a hindrance, as it serves to validate and strengthen faith. In this way both the subjective faith and the objective demonstration are perceived to compliment each other.

These three criticisms against Kierkegaard must therefore be accepted as being valid, as they apply to all stages of his polemic. It was found that his starting point was not subjective faith but reason (criticism number one). Thus Kierkegaard is internally inconsistent from the outset by postulating faith as the initial starting point, but not realizing that he failed in this task himself. Since the main body of his work is predominantly subjective, this leads to another problem, namely that there is no way to ascertain if his system is valid or not (criticism number two). With no objective criteria with which to test these views, one cannot know if subjectivity is the best approach to God. From these first two criticisms a third was deduced, that subjectivity is not solely the right approach to God, since we must start with reason and utilize some objective criteria to verify faith. Thus it was found that one possible approach would be to use history to investigate the Christian faith (and the resurrection in particular) to see if it offers a solid basis for faith.

Suffice it to say that the way has thus been opened for the historical examination of events such as the resurrection. If this occurrence is found to be historical, it could be used as a more rational basis for Christian faith.

Although Kierkegaard's exclusively subjective basis for his system fails, his emphasis on a faith-commitment for salvation still remains valid. This is especially so if historical (or other) evidence is found to verify such belief. This is because Kierkegaard is correct in establishing this as the central component of Christianity. The same conclusion was also reached in chapter 4 above, where it was found that even though reason was temporally first, faith was the most important and essential element. Therefore we should still accept this conclusion as authoritative, especially with an objective foundation. Kierkegaard's concept of the faith that leads to salvation and an authentic Christian life involves an individual's realizing that he is a sinner in need of repentance (a complete change of his life). This repentance is achieved by a complete surrender to God in faith, trusting the death of Jesus Christ on the cross to pay for all personal sins. The result is a total commitment of the individual to God for a life of obedience, based upon the death of the Son of God. This total transformation of the person, if genuine, leads to the joy of the Christian life. This is real faith.[58]

This definition of faith set forth by Kierkegaard, as presented here, is quite a well-stated view. It also accurately portrays the New Testament teachings on this subject. We agree with this scholar that the summary just presented is the most important part of the reason-faith relationship and as such it is essential for the Christian belief in salvation. These teachings must therefore remain in our concept of Christianity. But we also believe that there are reasonable evidences which help to validate these teachings.

---

58. For this definition of faith by Kierkegaard, see his *Attack Upon "Christendom," op. cit.*, pp. 149, 210, 213, 221, 280, 287, for instance. See especially Heinecken, "Søren Kierkegaard," in Marty and Peerman, *op. cit.*, pp. 131, 133, 134, 138 for the same summary.

CHAPTER VIII

Possibility Number Two:
Other Similar Views

A. KARL BARTH

We dealt above with some of the immense influence that Søren Kierkegaard's thought has had upon contemporary theology. His ideas were not very popular in his own day and did not become overly popular even in theological circles until the twentieth century. At this time his views were revived by Karl Barth in particular and by those who followed him (usually referred to as Barthians or neo-orthodox theologians).[1] Especially influential was Kierkegaard's emphasis on the subjective approach to God, which was discussed in the last chapter. Most of the neo-orthodox theologians agreed with him that God could not be approached by any rational means such as by proofs, historical demonstrations, or other means of verification. Many also accepted the belief that faith entailed an irrational "leap."[2]

It is in the works of Barth which one can probably see the strongest influence of Kierkegaard on this last point. Barth also believed that God must be approached by faith and not by objective means. In fact, his methodology revolves around the analogy of faith. This concept was perhaps developed most consistently in Barth's work *Anselm: Fides Quaerens Intellectum*,[3]

---

1. See the introduction to Kierkegaard in chapter 7 for many of these details. Cf. also Heinecken, "Søren Kierkegaard," in Marty and Peerman, *Ibid.*, p. 136.

2. Ramm, *A Handbook of Contemporary Theology, op. cit.*, pp. 74–76, 79–80, 89–92.

3. Karl Barth, *Anselm: Fides Quaerens Intellectum*, translated by Ian W. Robertson (Richmond: John Knox Press, 1960).

Possibility Number Two: Other Similar Views

where this theologian concluded that Anselm's ontological argument for the existence of God was not a philosophical proof formulated to induce faith, for Anselm needed no such impetus in order to believe.[4] It is argued that Anselm admitted that the existence of God was known by faith and not by such demonstrations of His existence. This is true, Barth asserts, because it is impossible to learn of God by any kind of proof. We believe in Him not because He is known to exist by various procedures of verification, but because He has revealed Himself to us, especially by faith.[5]

For this reason, Barth rejects the analogy of being, which attempts to argue to the existence of God by various demonstrations. This is an abortive attempt to gain knowledge of God apart from faith. Since faith is not primary in such a system, it must be replaced by the analogy of faith.[6]

Thus, for Barth (as for Kierkegaard), faith is primary. The proper approach to God is the acceptance of faith without trying to verify this belief by proofs.[7]

When one endeavors to examine Barth's view of the resurrection of Jesus, it is important to keep in mind his method, centering in the analogy of faith. Because of this methodology, Barth (again like Kierkegaard) therefore does not believe that it is possible either to demonstrate this event or to use it as the reason why we should believe in God. This is because God can only be approached by faith and not by demonstrations such as those from historical events.

It is especially in the early period of Barth's thought that the dialectical emphasis in neo-orthodox theology[8] played an important role. The approach taken to the resurrection is a good example of how this dialectic

---

4. Ibid., pp. 39–40, 101, 151.

5. Ibid., pp. 18–20, 80, 86, 128, 152.

6. See Hans Urs von Balthasar, The Theology of Karl Barth, translated by John Drury (New York: Holt, Rinehart and Winston, 1971), p. 148 and Herbert Hartwell, The Theology of Karl Barth (London: Gerald Duckworth and Company, 1964), pp. 49, 56, 184.

7. Barth, Anselm, op. cit., pp. 18–20, 128, 39–40; cf. von Balthasar, Ibid., p. 128.

8. Among other facets, neo-orthodox theology (also termed dialectical theology) affirms that there is a vast gulf between God and man. As a result, there exists a tension between the things of God and the things of man. An answer of both "Yes" and "No" is therefore given by these theologians to certain questions pertaining to this relationship. A possible example of such a seemingly contradictory position is that the Bible is both the Word of God and the word of man. Thus one might answer both "Yes" and "No" to the question of whether the Bible is the work of human writers. See Ramm, A Handbook of Contemporary Theology, op. cit., pp. 35–36.

might be applied to theology. Barth was, for instance, able to say "Yes" to
Jesus' resurrection being an actual event and "No" to its being a historical
fact like other occurrences which can be historically verified. This sounds
contradictory, but it is affirmed nonetheless:

> In the Resurrection the new world of the Holy Spirit touches the
> old world of the flesh, but touches it as a tangent touches a circle,
> that is, without touching it ... The Resurrection is therefore an
> occurrence in history ... But ... the Resurrection is not an event
> in history at all.[9]

We have here an illustration which presents quite a seeming contradiction in terms. In the example chosen by the author, one must hold
either that the tangent touches the circle or that it does not touch. But
Barth affirms both. This example serves to illustrate a point in his theology, because in a similar manner he also affirms that the resurrection
both is and is not an historical event. To the question of whether the resurrection is an actual event of history, we therefore receive both a "Yes"
and a "No" answer.

But how is this possible? Barth holds to the essential evil character of
the world, which is tainted by sin. As such, the world is opposed to God
and His purposes. If Christ was really to enter the actual history of the
world, then he would likewise participate in this evil.[10] For Barth, "if the
Resurrection be brought within the context of history, it must share in its
obscurity and error and essential questionableness."[11]

The only possible conclusion is that the resurrection occurred on "the
frontier of all visible human history."[12] It is a historical occurrence, but not
in the normal sense of the word "history." In fact, it may be considered
in some ways to be a nonhistorical occurrence.[13]

Barth continued a similar type of reasoning in other early works as
well. In 1920 he taught that the resurrection of Jesus was "not in time. It

---

9. Barth, *The Epistle to the Romans, op. cit.,* p. 30.
10. See the penetrating analysis by Daniel Fuller, *op. cit.,* pp. 82–84.
11. Barth, *The Epistle to the Romans, op. cit.,* p. 204.
12. *Ibid.,* p. 203.
13. *Ibid.,* cf. pp. 30, 195, 203.

is not one temporal thing among others."[14] An important distinction is made as follows:

> The resurrection of Christ ... is not a historical event ... though it is the only real happening *in* is not a real happening *of* history (Italics and wording are Barth's).[15]

Again we see the distinction between an event occurring and its being a part of history. The resurrection can really have occurred and yet not happen like other events for this scholar. Barth even goes as far as to say that we should not ask whether it is historical or not, for this event is a good example of the nonhistorical and the impossible.[16] Even though it is an actual event, it cannot be proven or demonstrated to have occurred.[17]

In 1924 Barth published his work *The Resurrection of the Dead*.[18] Herein is contained essentially the same view of the resurrection as was present in his earlier works.[19] This event is again presented as occurring on history's frontier (or boundary) in such a manner that it can only be understood as God's revelation and not proven or demonstrated by history.[20]

An additional opinion is further given and clarified in this work. Barth boldly asserts that alternate critical theories concerning the resurrection might even be true, for it makes no real difference if the tomb was closed or open that first resurrection morning. We accept Jesus' resurrection by faith and not because of any historical evidence. Thus this occurrence cannot be investigated or tested. It cannot be proven to have occurred.[21] Therefore, if there were news reporters present at the tomb of Christ on that first morning, they would not have been able to verify this event.

This last interpretation has been confirmed by American theologian Carl F. H. Henry, who questioned Barth on this very subject when he

---

14. Karl Barth, *The Word of God and the Word of Man*, translated by Douglas Horton (New York: Harper & Brothers, 1957), p. 89. The essays in this book are dated 1916–1923.

15. *Ibid.*, p. 90.

16. *Ibid.*, p. 91.

17. *Ibid.*, p. 92; cf. p. 120.

18. Karl Barth, *The Resurrection of the Dead*, translated by H. J. Stenning (New York: Fleming H. Revell Company, 1933).

19. Daniel Fuller, *op. cit.*, pp. 89–90.

20. Barth, *The Resurrection of the Dead, op. cit.*, pp. 134, 138, 139.

21. *Ibid.*, pp. 135–38.

visited America some years ago. When Henry asked if our news corre-
spondents could have reported the resurrection had they been there to
investigate it, Barth responded by saying that it was a private event for the
disciples alone. As the meeting broke up, one of the reporters remarked
to Henry that the other writers had clearly understood Barth's answer.
They knew that Barth was denying that they could have witnessed or
investigated this event.[22]

Thus we perceive the view of the early Barth on the resurrection of
Jesus. While this event is surely believed to have occurred, it is not an
event of real history that can be investigated and demonstrated like other
historical facts. Rather, it is an occurrence of superhistory.[23] Therefore
the resurrection also happened in a different kind of history than has
other events.[24]

Did Barth's position change substantially after his new emphasis on
the analogy of faith in his work on Anselm?[25] According to Daniel Fuller,
he did give more attention to the question of historicity, but he continued to reject the resurrection as an event which can be verified in any
way.[26] One does readily notice this change, however, as it appears that
more credence is given to the historical character of this occurrence. The
objectivity of the resurrection is even stressed more, especially the fact
that the disciples actually did see Jesus.[27] But Barth made it plain that he
still did not hold that the facts of the historical Jesus should be stressed.[28]

22. Carl F. H. Henry, editor, *Jesus of Nazareth: Saviour and Lord* (Grand Rapids: William B. Eerdman's Publishing Company, 1960), p. 11.

23. Karl Barth, *Theology and Church: Shorter Writings 1920–1928*, translated by Louise Pettibone Smith (New York: Harper & Row, 1962), p. 62.

24. See Montgomery, *Where Is History Going?*, *op. cit.*, pp. 111–12; cf. p. 115 and Charles C. Anderson, *The Historical Jesus: A Continuing Quest*, *op. cit.*, p. 157, footnote number 3 for instance. We will return later to Barth's conception of the resurrection as having occurred in a history different from that of other events.

25. Concerning Barth's earlier primary interest in dialectics and his later primary interest in the analogy of faith, see von Balthasar, *op. cit.*, pp. 78–80, 90, 92–93.

26. Daniel Fuller, *op. cit.*, pp. 147–48.

27. This greater emphasis on the reality of Jesus' resurrection is especially perceptible in Barth's *Church Dogmatics*, *op. cit.*, vol. 4, part 1, pp. 302, 309, 318, 336–37, 351–52, for instance. See also Barth's *Dogmatics in Outline*, translated by G. T. Thompson (New York: Harper & Row, 1959), pp. 122–23. Cf. Hartwell, *op. cit.*, pp. 122–23.

28. Karl Barth, *How I Changed My Mind* (Richmond: John Knox Press, 1966), see p. 69 for an example of his attitude.

In spite of this new emphasis, however, it is still obvious that Barth relegates the resurrection of Jesus to something other than the history in which other events happen. Sacred events like the resurrection cannot be subjected to an already existing view of history. Rather, God's revelation through such occurrences demands a particular type of history, a somewhat nonobjective, nondemonstrable variety. For Barth, there is such a definition of history which differs from the modern understanding of this word, and it is in this "metahistory" that Jesus is held to have risen from the dead. This event is judged to be nonhistorical by those who try to force the contemporary meaning of history upon it.[29]

In Barth's chief work, *Church Dogmatics*, we can plainly perceive the continuation of this stance. The resurrection is said to have occurred in a peculiar kind of history.[30] As "we pass from the story of the passion to the story of Easter we are led into a historical sphere of a different kind."[31] This is because the "death of Jesus can certainly be thought of as history in the modern sense, but not the resurrection ... the history of the resurrection is not history in this sense."[32]

Barth does give some vague indication as to the nature of the history in which he believes that the resurrection occurred. He relates several facts which serve in helping one to understand this peculiar mode of ascertaining certain incidents of the past. First, since this event is part of God's revelation (and thus an act of God), it is different from other occurrences from the very outset.[33] But this is not the only reason we are given as to why the resurrection is perceived to occupy a different kind of history. We are told, second, that this event is perhaps more properly viewed as being a "saga" or a "legend." As such it is termed "prehistory" because it cannot be understood historically in the modern sense of the word.[34] Here Barth identifies his concept more closely. There are also other differences between this prehistory and the modern concept of history. For instance,

29. Karl Barth, *The Faith of the Church*, edited by Jean-Louis Leuba, translated by Gabriel Vahanian (New York: Meridian Books, 1958), pp. 96–99.

30. Barth, *Church Dogmatics, op. cit.*, vol. 4, part 1, p. 335.

31. *Ibid.*, p. 334.

32. *Ibid.*, p. 336.

33. *Ibid.*, pp. 300–301.

34. *Ibid.*, p. 336; cf. Barth's *The Faith of the Church, op. cit.*, p. 99.

third (as we have remarked above), not only can the resurrection not be proven to have occured, but such a proof should not even be attempted.[35] It is thus unlike other events which can be verified by historical research. Fourth, Barth boldly announces that it makes no difference if Jesus' tomb was open or closed on the first resurrection morning, for faith can follow from it nevertheless. In this way he asserts that the historical character of this event provides no foundation for faith.[36]

Barth's understanding of the resurrection therefore appears to be quite an elusive concept to grasp. Not only the initial revelatory character of this event but even the event itself is prehistory or metahistory. It cannot be verified like other incidents and is construed in such a way that faith in it can remain even without various elements of the narratives. In spite of these characteristics which tend to point *away from* the historicity of this event and in spite of the insistence upon a different kind of history,[37] Barth still states that we cannot therefore say that Jesus did not rise, or that he did so only in a spiritual sense. We must understand that this scholar still believed that Jesus rose from the dead in time and space in an objective way. Jesus had a body and he could be seen, heard, and perceived to actually have risen from the dead.[38] While this conception of the resurrection appears quite contradictory,[39] it is another example of Barth's use of dialectic. He answers both "Yes" and "No" to the question of whether Jesus rose from the dead in actual human history.

We have seen that, whether we speak of the early or of the late Barth, we are dealing with a view of the resurrection that is essentially the same. Although a new stress is placed on the actual occurrence of this event in the later stages of this scholar's work, the belief that the resurrection is not history in the same sense as other events, and therefore not provable, still persists. It is noteworthy that Kierkegaard also accepted this occurrence as an enigma for history, a paradox that cannot be understood or

---

35. *Ibid.*, especially p. 335; see also pp. 300, 341.

36. Cf. Barth's work *The Resurrection of the Dead, op. cit.*, p. 135 with *Ibid.*, p. 335.

37. Indeed, in *The Faith of the Church*, Barth notes that he is utilizing a different definition of history when he affirms that events such as the resurrection occurred (*op. cit.*, pp. 98–99).

38. Barth, *Church Dogmatics, op. cit.*, vol. 4, part 1, pp. 336–37, 351–52.

39. More will be said about this criticism later.

demonstrated by historical research. It can only be embraced by faith and not by the intellect.[40]

Barth's view of the resurrection has been discussed in depth, with the emphasis being laid primarily upon his understanding of this event as a type of prehistory which is not the old liberal view of myth, but neither is it one of *complete* historical objectivity.[41] It has been our endeavor to be fair in this presentation, striving to deal adequately with both sides of this emphasis. It now remains for us to evaluate this approach.

Four major criticisms of Karl Barth's view of the resurrection will now be offered. The first, and one of the most comprehensive criticisms, involves the belief that the resurrection occupies a sort of parahistory which includes some aspects of objective history, while other facets of history are abandoned. Herein lies a main problem of Barth's interpretation.

An event must either be some kind of a myth which never literally occurred in actual human history, or it must have occurred in this same history. But Barth asserts that the resurrection is neither myth nor actual history in the modern sense. Rather, this event occurs in some sort of redemptive or religious history.[42] However, history simply knows nothing of such an inbetween ground, whether it is termed prehistory, saga, or legend, or referred to as the boundary or frontier of history.[43] As Wand so perceptively points out,

> History is concerned only with such events as happen within the space-time continuum. Events, real or imagined, which occur in an eternal or spiritual sphere are not the proper subject of history. The reason is that history has no tools by which it can deal with such events.[44]

In other words, history can only be concerned with events which occur in space and time in such a way that they can be investigated by

---

40. See especially Kierkegaard's *Concluding Unscientific Postscript, op. cit.,* pp. 188–90 and the discussion above on Kierkegaard. Cf. Brown, *op. cit.,* p. 59.

41. Cf. Barth's *The Word of God and the Word of Man, op. cit.,* p. 90.

42. Barth, *Church Dogmatics, op. cit.,* vol. 4, part 1, pp. 300–301, 334, 336.

43. Barth uses these descriptive words to refer to his concept of redemptive or spiritual history. See *Ibid.,* p. 336 and *The Resurrection of the Dead, op. cit.,* pp. 134, 139.

44. Wand, *op. cit.,* p. 23.

the tools of historical research. Since there are no means whereby events which occur in a spiritual in-between sphere can be so investigated, they are not actually within the scope of history. As Wand asserts, religious events which are perceived to have happened only in such an elusive realm cannot be properly regarded as history, whether these were real events or not. Historical facts must therefore be open to verification and research.

Admittedly, the resurrection (if it is found to have occurred) would have a different origin from other events because as such it would enter history as a direct act of God. The fact that Jesus' resurrection was not produced by any natural means, such as historical causation, should not be belittled. Barth is correct in asserting that it is possible for an event to have its cause in Divine action and still be a part of history. Thus the resurrection *would be* unique in the sense that this event would have to have originated with God.

But there is an immense difference between saying that this occurrence would be unique because of its being a direct result of God's revelation and saying that as such it cannot be investigated. This is where Barth's polemic fails quite noticeably. The point here is that once this occurrence enters the realm of history (even though the actual entering *is* unique), it must be open to historical investigation. To forego such verification means that it does not become normal history at all. Thus, removing such an event from investigation, as this scholar does, is not valid. One would have to also remove it from the scope of history in order to isolate it from such historical procedures.

Therefore, one cannot assert that certain events actually occurred and then add that we cannot speak historically about them or investigate them. Either the resurrection really happened in verifiable history or it did not happen in normal history at all. But let us not employ fancy theological verbiage to affirm its occurrence in an unverifiable, unobservable, contradictory realm of thought!

Pannenberg agrees in this criticism of Barth's view. He expressly states:

> If we would forgo the concept of a historical event here, then it is no longer possible at all to affirm that the resurrection of Jesus or that the appearances of the resurrected Jesus really happened at a definite time in our world. There is no justification for affirming

Jesus' resurrection as an event that really happened, if it is not to be affirmed as a historical event as such. Whether or not a particular event happened two thousand years ago is not made certain by faith but only by historical research, to the extent that certainty can be attained at all about questions of this kind. ... The only method of achieving at least approximate certainty with regard to the events of a past time is historical research.[45]

As pointed out here, it is impossible for a theologian like Barth to say that an event occurred but not in the same objective history as other events occur. As Pannenberg adeptly points out, it is incorrect to claim to be speaking of Jesus' resurrection as a historical event if, as such, it can only be known by faith and not by historical research. If one asserts that something is not even able to be investigated, neither can one say that the event still happened at a certain time in this world. We thus see that it is impossible for Barth to affirm that the resurrection really occurred while still having the understanding that this occurrence is not in objective, verifiable history. Such an event is not really history because no such concept of history exists. Therefore it is also impossible merely to claim that this event still happened just like other incidents in the past.

As a historian, Montgomery also objects to Barth's use of prehistory. The following illustration is introduced to demonstrate the folly of such a concept:

I wonder what you would say—what Barth would say—if I claimed that in my backyard there is a large green elephant eating a raspberry ice cream cone, but that there is no way by empirical investigation to determine that he is there. Nonetheless, I maintain, as a matter of fact, that it is there in every objective and factual sense. Now I have a feeling that you would either regard this as a claim that the elephant is there and is subject to empirical investigation, or contend that it isn't there by the very fact that there is no way of determining the fact. I wonder if this doesn't point up the problem.

45. Pannenberg, *Jesus—God and Man*, op. cit., p. 99.

To claim objectivity, but to remove any possibility of determining it, is by definition to destroy objectivity.[46]

Montgomery's criticism is well justified. A historical event must either be open to investigation or not claim to be history at all for the very reason that it cannot be investigated. We destroy the concept of historical objectivity when we endeavor to rule that this objectivity itself cannot be tested. Any claim to a historical "middle ground" of prehistory removed from such processes of verification is about as accurate and acceptable as the claim concerning the existence of the green elephant.[47] Montgomery thus agrees with others that the idea of parahistory is foreign both to history itself and even to the Biblical records.[48]

Other theologians have also noted Barth's tendency to rely on the concept of prehistory and the subsequent weaknesses in his approach to the resurrection which have resulted. They realize both that historians recognize no such realm of history and that the very assertion that such a realm exists with both historical and nonhistorical characteristics is itself contradictory.[49]

The second major criticism of Barth is quite similar to one of the main objections to Kierkegaard and will therefore not be labored overly much here. Even though Barth claims that the resurrection literally occurred, we have seen how he denies any possibility of verifying this event. In fact, such a procedure should not even be attempted.[50] Thus, in spite of his emphatic assertions that the resurrection occurred, his view also falls prey to the criticism that there is no way for one to ascertain if the Christian faith is valid or not. We have already seen that faith cannot stand alone and be its own criteria and proof for belief. These subjective, personal

---

46. Montgomery, *History and Christianity*, op. cit., pp. 87–88.

47. *Ibid.*, cf. also pp. 106–7.

48. Montgomery, *Where Is History Going?*, op. cit., pp. 111–12; cf. p. 115.

49. In addition to those listed above, see, for instance, Henry, op. cit., pp. 11–12 and Henry's own comments in the debate on the resurrection (he was a participant) recorded in the appendix of Montgomery's *History and Christianity*, op. cit., pp. 85, 96, 105. The contradictory aspect of Barth's concept was also confirmed by Clark Pinnock in personal correspondence with this writer, dated July 19, 1971. See also Daniel Fuller, op. cit., pp. 82–84; cf. pp. 69, 71. Charles Anderson, in *The Historical Jesus: A Continuing Quest*, op. cit., pp. 157–58, footnote number 3, and Ramm, in *A Handbook of Contemporary Theology*, op. cit., p. 90, also note Barth's position.

50. For example, see especially Barth's *Church Dogmatics*, op. cit., vol. 4, part 1, p. 335.

qualities provide no reason why someone else should believe this particular system or accept Christianity over alternative views. Faith simply is not a panacea for all theological problems because there is no reason to accept this faith if there are no grounds upon which its claims may be based. In spite of Barth's defense of faith as the only way (as opposed to any historical research or other rational approach), it still remains that this faith cannot verify itself or demonstrate its own validity. This can only mean that one cannot know if the grounds for belief are solid or not. There is no logical reason to accept such a faith.

In other words, to say that Jesus really rose from the dead but that this event can only be accepted by faith (without verification) is to leave one's entire faith open to question. Barth is of course not interested in verifying the grounds for Christianity. But without such objective criteria one can never know if one's faith is completely in vain or not.

Montgomery also realized the strength of such a criticism. Appropriating a fact by faith cannot make this belief factual. Simply by starting with faith we are not assured of arriving at a truthful, viable solution because the admonition to "have faith" cannot guarantee that one's beliefs are any more correct. Therefore, if faith does not have its starting point in objective, verifiable events, there is no way that one may ascertain if Christianity is the preferable faith-system in which to place one's trust.[51]

Therefore we perceive that which was stated earlier. Faith cannot create truth, no matter how intense it might be in the individual. Thus, faith cannot make itself valid by its intensity or by the fervency with which it is exercised. Because of this, it is important for the individual to know if his faith is valid, and objective criteria are best suited for this purpose.

The last two criticisms of Barth are internal critiques. The third major criticism concerns Barth's understanding of God's revelation in human events. It has been shown how this scholar contends that God reveals Himself in certain revelatory acts which occur in man's prehistory and not as an actual part of verifiable history.[52] But if revelation is not given objectively in historical facts which are open to historical research, then Jesus' death cannot be revelatory because even Barth believes that the

---

51. Montgomery, *History and Christianity, op. cit.*, pp. 99–101, 106–7.

52. Ramm, *A Handbook of Contemporary Theology, op. cit.*, p. 90.

crucifixion is history in the modern sense of the word.[53] But Barth also holds that the crucifixion is part of God's revelation, since Jesus died a substitutionary death to pay for the sins of those who surrender their life to God in faith.[54] Here we find an internal inconsistency. If one holds that the death of Jesus is part of God's revelation to man (as Barth is correct in doing), then one must abandon the previously held idea that God never acts meaningfully in this kind of history. And if we reject this, it also means that the resurrection could likewise be objective, verifiable history and still be a revelatory event as well.[55]

The fourth major criticism of Barth's treatment of the resurrection is that this theologian holds that the New Testament itself does not make any attempt to demonstrate or prove that the resurrection did occur. He holds, rather, that the earliest Christians were only interested in accepting this event by faith. Thus Paul, for example, was not trying to present a proof of this occurrence by citing the witnesses in 1 Corinthians 15.[56]

It has already been noted above that this portion makes it quite plain that although Paul is speaking of the faith of the first-century Christians, he is also explaining how this faith has its basis in objective, historical fact. The text clearly shows that Paul does intend to cite proof here, especially in verse six, where we are informed that most of the witnesses were still alive and could thus provide testimony concerning these events. This testimony would, in turn, provide historical eyewitness corroboration for Paul's claims.

Even Bultmann disagrees with Barth here, also noting that Paul *does* mean to use the list of the appearances of Jesus as proof for the resurrection.[57] Bultmann notes that there were two current proofs for this event, both of which are found in 1 Corinthians 15. There was the appeal

---

53. Barth, *Church Dogmatics, op. cit.*, vol. 4, part 1, p. 336; cf. p. 334.

54. *Ibid.*, pp. 248–54 for instance. See Ramm, *A Handbook of Contemporary Theology, op. cit.*, pp. 16, 108.

55. See Henry, *Jesus of Nazareth: Saviour and Lord, op. cit.*, p. 10 where this criticism is also developed.

56. This tendency to believe that the New Testament never intends to demonstrate that the resurrection really did happen is evident in both the early and in the late Barth. See his earlier work *The Resurrection of the Dead, op. cit.*, pp. 131–38 and his later opus *Church Dogmatics, op. cit.*, vol. 4, part 1, p. 335.

57. Bultmann, "New Testament and Mythology," in *Kerygma and Myth, op. cit.*, p. 39.

to eyewitness testimony, as we have perceived here (especially 15:5–8) and the appeal to the fulfillment of Old Testament prophecy (15:3–4).[58] Bultmann's testimony is valuable at this point mainly because it is apparent that Barth is desiring to use the Scripture to reinforce his polemic,[59] whereas Bultmann actually objects to Paul's using such a proof in spite of believing that he does just this.[60] This desire of course does not in itself mean that Barth is necessarily wrong. But it does appear that Bultmann is more accurate in ascertaining Paul's obvious motives here.

Reginald Fuller is somewhat close to Barth in his view on this question. He holds that Paul's primary intention was to identify his preaching of the resurrection with that of the earliest eyewitnesses. But he also believes that Paul intended to relate the eyewitness accounts in order to prove that Jesus actually appeared to his followers. He likewise agrees that 1 Corinthians 15:6 is the main pointer to the fact that Paul is establishing evidence to be used as proof for these appearances.[61]

But there are other portions of the New Testament which also establish the fact that other authors besides Paul endeavored both to prove the resurrection and to use this event as the basis for the establishing of other beliefs, contrary to Barth's view. It has been shown above how the gospels in particular sought to demonstrate the reality of Jesus' resurrection by stressing that he appeared to his disciples in bodily form. Although the new body had undergone some changes, it is reported that Jesus allowed his followers to examine and investigate this new body. We are even told that Jesus was touched and "held," thus demonstrating that he was alive. This emphasis is especially evident in passages like Luke 24:36–43,[62] where ample evidence of this attempt to prove that Jesus had risen is readily available.[63] We are even told in Acts 1:3 that Jesus "presented himself alive after his passion by many proofs" (RSV). In fact, the

---

58. Bultmann, Theology of the New Testament, vol. 1, p. 82.

59. See Barth's Church Dogmatics, vol. 4, part I, pp. 334–36.

60. Bultmann, "New Testament and Mythology," in Kerygma and Myth, op. cit., p. 39.

61. Reginald Fuller, op. cit., p. 29.

62. Besides this portion and 1 Corinthians 15:4–8, see such passages as Matthew 28:8–9; John 20:17 (in the Greek); 20:19–31; Acts 10:39–41.

63. Bultmann also believes that the Gospels and Paul endeavor to prove that Jesus had appeared to the apostles. He likewise recognizes that 1 Corinthians 15:3–8 and Luke 24:39–43 are good examples of this tendency. See "The New Testament and Mythology," in Kerygma and Myth, op. cit., p. 39.

Greek word used here for "proof" (*tekmeriois*) literally means a positive or certain proof.[64] Thus we see that it *was* the intention of several New Testament authors to prove that Jesus had risen.

In addition, it should be mentioned that the resurrection is also used in the New Testament as a proof for other Christian doctrines. For instance, Acts 17:30–31 shows that the earliest church believed that God verified Jesus' earthly teachings by raising him from the dead.[65] Acts 2:36 and Romans 1:4 are other examples which point to Jesus' being accepted as the Lord, Messiah, and the Son of God, based upon the resurrection.[66]

Thus we see that Barth also cannot rely on Scripture for support of his thesis. The claim that the New Testament does not seek to prove or demonstrate that the resurrection actually occurred is simply not supported by the facts.

For the reasons we have given above, it becomes evident that Barth's thesis fails. These four criticisms of his view on the resurrection point out the key weaknesses to which this view is most vulnerable. They also reveal the inadequacies of this approach.[67]

B. OTHER RELATED VIEWS

As Kierkegaard greatly influenced the views of Barth, so did Barth greatly influence the views of the many theologians who followed him. This is especially true on the question of Jesus' resurrection. Many prominent neo-orthodox theologians in particular accepted these views.

For instance, Swiss theologian Emil Brunner apparently affirms belief in the resurrection of Jesus as having actually occurred.[68] But like Barth, he concludes that this occurrence is not part of the realm of normal, verifiable history. He relates that the resurrection is not an event which can

---

64. See W. E. Vine, *An Expository Dictionary of New Testament Words*, four volumes in one (Old Tappan: Fleming H. Revell Company, 1966), vol. 3, pp. 220–21. See also Robertson, *op. cit.*, vol. 3, p. 6.

65. This is admitted by both Bultmann, "New Testament and Mythology," in *Kerygma and Myth*, *op. cit.*, p. 39 and by Marxsen, *op. cit.*, p. 169. Marxsen notes that the preaching of repentance and belief in the Lordship of Jesus are both based on the proof that Jesus rose from the dead, according to these verses.

66. See Bultmann, *Theology of the New Testament*, *op. cit.*, vol. 1, p. 27.

67. These four criticisms will be briefly summarized at the conclusion of the next section.

68. Emil Brunner, *The Christian Doctrine of Creation and Redemption*, vol. 2 of *Dogmatics*, translated by Olive Wyon, 3 vols. (Philadelphia: The Westminster Press, 1952) p. 366. See also Brunner's work *The Mediator*, translated by Olive Wyon (Philadelphia: The Westminster Press, p. 153.

be reported as is possible with other events.[69] In addition, we also learn that this occurrence cannot be the basis for the Christian faith.[70] Brunner is careful to stress his view that the Christian's belief in Jesus' resurrection is not based upon any records contained in the New Testament, including the testimony concerning the appearances. We cannot resort to historical or other means of verification of this event. Faith comes apart from any demonstrations or proofs that Jesus is alive. One simply accepts this by faith.[71]

Dietrich Bonhoeffer likewise relegates the resurrection to a realm other than normal history. He asserts,

> The historicity of Jesus Christ thus comes under the twofold aspect of history and faith. Both aspects are closely associated. The Jesus of history humbled himself; the Jesus who cannot be grasped by history is the subject of faith in the resurrection.[72]

We are therefore to understand that Jesus' resurrection is not an event which can be understood historically. It cannot be verified or proven, but only accepted in faith. Bonhoeffer thus believed that the resurrection really occurred, but that it had to be received by faith, apart from any historical research.[73]

Reinhold Niebuhr rejected the resurrection of Jesus as an event in his early years at Yale when he was still under the influence of liberal theology, and it appears that he never changed his mind. The physical resurrection of Jesus had to be abandoned as an actual occurrence.[74] Nevertheless, he treated it as parahistory. Speaking of the death and resurrection narratives concerning Jesus, he concludes,

69. Brunner, *The Mediator, Ibid.*, p. 573.

70. Brunner, *Dogmatics, op. cit.*, vol. 2, p. 369; cf. p. 153.

71. *Ibid.*, pp. 366–372; cf. Daniel Fuller, *op. cit.*, pp. 155–56.

72. Dietrich Bonhoeffer, *Christ the Center*, translated by John Bowden (New York: Harper & Row, 1966), p. 76.

73. *Ibid.*, pp. 74–77.

74. Ronald J. Stone, *Reinhold Niebuhr: Prophet to Politicians* (Nashville; Abingdon Press, 1972), pp. 22–23, 82.

The story of this triumph over death is thus shrouded in a mystery which places it in a different order of history than the story of the crucifixion.[75]

Once again we find the belief that the resurrection did not happen in history in the same way that the crucifixion did and therefore cannot be demonstrated to have occurred.

Barth's influence extended even further than the neo-orthodox theologians on the question of the resurrection. Günther Bornkamm sounds surprisingly like Barth in his belief that the resurrection is not open to historical verification. It can neither be proven or observed like other events. Yet it is said to have occurred. As such it can be understood properly only by faith.[76]

Reginald Fuller speaks of the resurrection as a metahistorical and eschatological event. Something occurred as revelation from God. However, this event cannot be verified or otherwise proven because it is comprehended only by faith, having taken place on the boundary between this world's history and the metahistory of the eschatological age that is coming.[77]

Hans Grass also follows a line of thought somewhat similar to Barth's. For Grass, the historical method provides no basis for investigating the resurrection. This occurrence cannot be approached by such methods of reason. But he differs from Barth in postulating that Jesus' appearances were spiritual and not physical at all.[78]

Jürgen Moltmann believes that the resurrection occurred, but that it cannot be historically demonstrated to have happened in the past. The theologian's object should not be to examine such past events, but to look to the future for the significance of them. Anyways, if we were to examine the resurrection by modern historical standards, it would be found to be historically impossible and meaningless.[79]

---

75. Reinhold Niebuhr, *Faith and History* (New York: Charles Scribner's Sons, 1949), p. 147.

76. Bornkamm, *op. cit.*, pp. 180, 183–84.

77. Reginald Fuller, *op. cit.*, pp. 23, 48, 81.

78. See Daniel Fuller's treatment of Grass' position for additional criticisms of it (*op. cit.*, pp. 150–56).

79. Jürgen Moltmann, *Theology of Hope*, translated by James W. Leitch (New York: Harper & Row, 1967), pp. 165–202. See especially pp. 165, 172, 174, 177, 188–89, 197. Cf. Nelson R. Chamberlain, "Jürgen Moltmann; Apostle of Christian Hope?," *Christianity Today* 18, no. 19 (June 21, 1974): 7, 8.

Moltmann's answer is to look for a new formulation of the concept of history. The resurrection is an eschatological event and as such it can be grasped historically only when it is viewed as to its future significance.[80] Thus, while Moltmann seemingly rejects the view of prehistory,[81] he still holds that the resurrection should be relegated to a different, eschatologically-oriented concept of history. He is quite specific in his belief that the resurrection was not observable and that this event cannot be verified at present.[82] Thus he also takes flight to a different sort of history in which past events such as the resurrection cannot be historically proven to have occurred apart from future vindication.[83]

We have already presented a critique of these theological attitudes while discussing Karl Barth's position. Almost the exact same criticisms also apply to the others (at least to the neo-orthodox theologians which we have discussed). Perhaps the main criticism involves placing the resurrection in prehistory or parahistory. While details as to what realm this is may differ somewhat (we have studied Barth's view in depth above), sociologist of religion Peter L. Berger's criticisms still apply. First, this category has no meaning for a scholar who desires to empirically investigate the data. One who supports such a view of parahistory has already chosen to leave the empirical realm of investigation. This concept is meaningless in this context. Second, this method is resigned to the few who feel that they have already attained the proper outlook with regard to theology.[84]

With a few variations, the following summary of criticisms applies at least to Barth and scholars like Brunner and Bonhoeffer. They are also more or less applicable to the others covered here, at least in part. First, history knows of no such concept as prehistory. It is not possible to measure or investigate such a realm. In addition, the inclusion of both

---

80. Moltmann, *Ibid.*, see especially pp. 178–82, 190, 202.

81. *Ibid.*, p. 178.

82. Jürgen Moltmann, *Religion, Revolution and the Future*, translated by M. Douglas Meeks (New York: Charles Scribner's Sons, 1969), especially pp. 50–51.

83. Moltmann, *Theology of Hope, op. cit.*, pp. 177–82, 190, 197. Cf. Robert J. Blaikie, *"Secular Christianity" and God Who Acts* (Grand Rapids: William B. Eerdman's Publishing Company, 1970), pp. 129–34. See the next chapter on Pannenberg for a critique of a position somewhat similar to Moltmann's, one which also gives the future the place of priority. Many of the criticisms offered in the next chapter also apply to Moltmann.

84. Berger, *op. cit.*, pp. 39–40.

historical and nonhistorical characteristics renders such a category contradictory. Real history can be investigated and examined to determine if
it is valid or not. One cannot make the claim that an event is real history
and then not subject it to investigation. Even if a metahistorical event
were possible, it must either be verifiable or not claim to be real history
at all. Therefore this concept must be rejected. Second, the stress on one's
affirming the resurrection by faith and the refusal to demonstrate this
event by any other method means that this view is not objective enough
to provide sufficient reason for one to know if the Christian faith is valid.
An intense belief cannot make this faith any more valid. With no such
methods of investigation we cannot know if such faith is simply in vain.

Third, neo-orthodox theology contends that God's revelation does not
primarily occur in actual history in the modern sense of the word.[85] Yet
Barth, for instance, bases the revelation in the death of Christ on what
he admits to be an actual historical fact, while refusing to do this in the
case of the resurrection. He is therefore internally inconsistent in holding that the resurrection *cannot* likewise be based on actual historical fact.
Fourth, at least Barth contends that the New Testament does not attempt
to prove the resurrection. The others at least agree that his event cannot
be demonstrated. But Barth's contention is not based on the available evidence. Contrary assertions in the New Testament invalidate these claims
and thus cannot be used to support this thesis.

For these reasons, it is our conclusion here that such an approach to
the resurrection is untenable. One cannot remove this event and, subse-
quently, the entire Christian faith, from the realm of investigation. There
are simply too many difficulties for one to hold to such a position. But
as with Kierkegaard's view, so Barth's emphasis on faith and its importance can remain. We have mentioned above how that Barth conceived
of the death of Christ as being a substitutionary death to pay for the sins
of those who surrender their life to God in faith.[86] This view of faith must
be retained. As it was concluded earlier in chapter 4, faith must remain
the most important element in a theological system. This is even shown
to be more true if there is an objective basis on which to rest this faith.

---

85. Ramm, A Handbook of Contemporary Theology, op. cit., pp. 90, 108.
86. Barth, Church Dogmatics, op. cit., vol. 4, part 1, pp. 248–54 for example.

CHAPTER IX

Possibility Number Three: That the Resurrection Did Occur and That It Can Be Demonstrated

A. WOLFHART PANNENBERG: AN INTRODUCTION

The third major possibility to be dealt with in this work is that Jesus' resurrection really did occur and that this occurrence can be demonstrated.[1] We will begin by examining the position of a very important scholar in contemporary theology today who holds this view. This theologian, Wolfhart Pannenberg (born 1928), is without much doubt the best-known representative of this viewpoint today.

Pannenberg has received much acclaim in recent years because of his defense of the historicity of the resurrection. In fact, he has been viewed by many as "the theologian of the resurrection."[2] It is this event which forms the basis for his polemic and which sets the stage for his theological system.[3] Now it is by no means unique either to defend the historicity of the

---

1. When it is asserted that this event can be demonstrated, reference is being made to probabilities. These scholars hold that this event can be demonstrated to a high probability by a reasonable approach to the Christian faith which includes a historical examination of the known facts.

2. See editor Richard John Neuhaus' introductory essay "Wolfhart Pannenberg: Profile of a Theologian," in Pannenberg's *Theology and the Kingdom of God*, (Philadelphia: The Westminster Press, 1969), pp. 9–50. See especially pp. 10–11 for this statement.

3. Pannenberg, *Revelation As History, op. cit.*, pp. 142–44 for instance.

resurrection or to use it as the basis for one's theological system.[4] But Pannenberg is probably the theologian who is best known for these tendencies. Therefore he becomes the logical choice as the primary scholar to be dealt with here.

Wolfhart Pannenberg is often connected with a new school of theology in Germany which is usually referred to as the "theology of hope." This generally optimistic understanding of theology was welcomed in the United States in the late 1960s by some of the leading newspapers and magazines. These publications seemed to be more than willing to report the demise of the pessimistic and short-lived reign of the "death of God theology" and greet instead its more hopeful and reassuring "successor."[5]

The motif of hope in many ways presented a novel approach to theology, being part of one of the first theological schools of thought that was not a development of the earlier dialectic theology of Karl Barth and those who followed him. Among others, those usually connected with the theology of hope are German theologians Pannenberg, Jürgen Moltmann, Johann Metz, and sometimes Karl Rahner.[6] However, it is actually difficult to be overly suggestive when speaking of those who favor this approach, and it is really only possible to speak rather generally of any group of "hope theologians."[7]

While Pannenberg was earning his doctorate at the University of Heidelberg in the early 1950s, a group of graduate students began meeting and exchanging ideas on the nature of Divine revelation. Apparently in opposition to Pannenberg's own wishes, this group began to be referred to as the "Pannenberg circle." The combined work of four of the members—Pannenberg, Rolf Rendtorff, Trutz Rendtorff, and Ulrich

---

4. See this proclivity in such scholars as Daniel Fuller, *op. cit.*, p. 144; Montgomery, *History and Christianity, op. cit.*, pp. 72–80; McNaugher, *op. cit.*, pp. 144–85 and Smith, *op. cit.*, pp. 187–228.

5. Editor Neuhaus in Pannenberg's *Theology and the Kingdom of God, op. cit.*, p. 9.

6. *Ibid.*, pp. 10, 17.

7. For instance, M. Douglas Meeks deals primarily with Moltmann in his work *Origins of the Theology of Hope* (Philadelphia: Fortress Press, 1974). See p. 2 for his conviction that others like Pannenberg and Metz cannot be connected completely with Moltmann.

Wilkens—produced the volume *Offenbarung als Geschichte*[8] in 1961. It represented years of study and discussion together.[9]

Although this work was not the first one of Pannenberg's to be translated into English, it was still significant in that it helped to bring this German scholar to the attention of other theologians. Perhaps Pannenberg's most significant work to date, *Jesus—God and Man*, was translated into English in 1968. It was his first major work to appear in an English translation. This Christology has been recognized by some theologians as one of the most significant to appear in many years.[10]

It soon became evident that Pannenberg's thesis was opposed to many aspects of Barth's and Bultmann's theology. For instance, Pannenberg was opposed to the subjectivism exercised by both of these theologians.[11] He also objected to Barth's concept of revelation, especially with regard to Barth's view that certain events such as the resurrection happened in a nondemonstrable, nonverifiable type of history. Pannenberg believed that such events both can and should be historically investigated, in opposition to Barth.[12] This, of course, also means that Pannenberg likewise objected to Bultmann's even more complete divorce of history from faith.[13]

With this introductory background, it is now advantageous to turn to Pannenberg's argument concerning the resurrection of Jesus. Both a presentation of these views and a critique of them will be given. It should be remarked that the following is not a presentation or discussion of the entire theology of hope, but only of Pannenberg's views on these subjects.

---

8. This work was edited by Pannenberg and published in English under the title *Revelation as History*, translated by David Granskou (New York: The Macmillan Company, 1968).

9. See editor Neuhaus in Pannenberg's *Theology and the Kingdom of God*, *op. cit.*, p. 16 and Daniel Fuller, *op. cit.*, p. 178.

10. Neuhaus, *Ibid.*, p. 11.

11. *Ibid.*, p. 15.

12. *Ibid.*, p. 30 See the treatment of Barth above, including Pannenberg's view. See also Pannehberg's *Jesus—God and Man*, *op. cit.*, p. 99; of. his *Revelation as History*, *op. cit.*, pp. 9–10. More will be said later concerning his views of the resurrection as a demonstrable event.

13. Neuhaus, *Ibid.*, p. 37 and Daniel Fuller, *op. cit.*, p. 178.

B. WOLFHART PANNENBERG'S
ARGUMENT AND A CRITIQUE

To put Pannenberg in proper perspective, it should be mentioned that the theology of hope stresses eschatological theology and the coming Kingdom of God in particular. The coming of the Kingdom has political and ethical repercussions, as well as theological ones. Also stressed is the death and resurrection of Jesus as historical events which set the stage for this eschatology, as will be perceived below.[14]

One of Pannenberg's chief aims is to restore to contemporary theology the concept of a functionally imminent Kingdom of God.[15] Most of contemporary theology is perceived to have failed in its approach to the Kingdom in that the eschatological centrality of this concept has been lost. But for Pannenberg, the teaching about the Kingdom must be the central message in Christian theology.[16]

The future Kingdom of God holds a special interest for Pannenberg with regard to God's existence. God is identified with the coming Kingdom in such a way that, in a certain sense, God does not exist as yet. It is only with the arrival of the future Kingdom that the existence of God is shown to be a definite reality.[17]

But this by no means signifies that God is not now present in this age or that He was not present in the past. The idea that God's existence is fully revealed in the future therefore does not disqualify Him from present existence. From His future existence God dominates both the past and the present.[18]

At first this concept of the existence of God appears contradictory. The key for understanding it lies in Pannenberg's ideas about the retroactive power of history and the ability of the future to reach backward into the past. God exists at present (and in antiquity) in the sense that

---

14. See Meeks, *op. cit.*, p. 10.

15. Brian O. McDermott, SJ, "Pannenberg's Resurrection Christology: A Critique," *Theological Studies* 35, no. 4 (December 1974): 711–21. See also Pannenberg, *Theology and the Kingdom of God, op. cit.*, p. 53.

16. Pannenberg, *Ibid.*, pp. 51–53, 73.

17. *Ibid.*, pp. 56, 62, 111–12.

18. *Ibid.*, pp. 62–63, 71.

His future is reaching back into the past. He thus exists at present as the partial arrival of the future.[19]

According to Pannenberg's concept of theology, it is God who will usher the Kingdom into human society. God thus works in the future as well as in the present. This Kingdom is not synonymous with the church, and neither will it arrive by man's power. He is quite emphatic that it will become part of history by the future actions of God Himself, even though there are present ramifications of the Kingdom as well.[20]

But it is not only the existence of God which reaches into the present from the future. In fact, all occurrences eventuate from the future.[21] As Neuhaus explains, we therefore cannot only refer to the future of an event simply as something which will happen, but rather as something which reaches back into the present and which is now in existence. Although one can perceive the final state of something only in the future, the affects are present.[22]

For instance, the authority of God was retroactively present in the teachings of Jesus.[23] This is shown to be the case especially by Jesus' resurrection from the dead.[24] In a similar way the Kingdom has also reached back into this present time, although it has not arrived in its fullness.[25] It is through such a stress on the fundamental importance and priority given to the future that Pannenberg can speak of the end time having participated in the life of Jesus.[26]

In *Revelation as History* Pannenberg wrote two key essays. In one, entitled "Dogmatic Thesis on the Doctrine of Revelation," he postulated seven theses which are crucial to the understanding of his thought. This essay sets forth much of the foundation of Pannenberg's theological system and expands on the points raised above. These theses are especially instrumental in pointing out the extremely important place that the resurrection of

---

19. *Ibid.*, pp. 68, 70–71.

20. *Ibid.*, pp. 76–77, 82.

21. *Ibid.*, p. 70.

22. Editor Neuhaus in Pannenberg, *Ibid.*, p. 42.

23. Pannenberg, *Ibid.*, pp. 133–35, 142–43; see McDermott, *op. cit.*, p. 714.

24. Pannenberg, *Revelation as History, op. cit.*, p. 127; see McDermott, *Ibid.*, p. 711; 715–17.

25. Editor Neuhaus in Pannenberg, *Ibid.*, p. 25; cf. p. 42.

26. See Pannenberg, *Revelation as History, op. cit.*, p. 139 for instance and *Theology and the Kingdom of God, Ibid.*, pp. 54, 63. Cf. Neuhaus, *Ibid.*, p. 41.

Jesus holds. Seeing this event in the context of Pannenberg's theological enterprise will allow for a much better understanding of this scholar and will also make the ensuing critique more accurate and meaningful. For these reasons the seven theses are presented below, with a short discussion of each included. Related key thoughts of Pannenberg's on Christology and eschatology will also be presented in the appropriate places.

Pannenberg's first thesis is that God's Self-revelation is not direct, but indirect, being effected by God's historical acts.[27] After a brief survey of some of the prominent views on Divine revelation, Pannenberg asserts that God did not reveal Himself to man by the announcement of His name to the Israelites, or by the inspiration of the Scriptures, or by the giving of the law on Mount Sinai or by any other direct means.[28] To the contrary, God revealed Himself indirectly through historical acts in both the Old and New Testament. He made Himself known by means of a revelation grounded in history.[29] The chief purpose of Pannenberg's essay is to explore this indirect revelation and to ascertain its value as God's chosen method of revealing Himself.[30]

An interesting aspect of this belief in the indirect self-manifestation of God in human history is that Pannenberg conceives of this revelation as permeating all of human history. God therefore does not simply reveal Himself in some small segments of history exclusive of other areas. Rather, the indirect revelation of God occurs in all of man's history. For this reason, Pannenberg relates that there can be no such thing as Supernatural events or miracles. Since God works in history *as a whole*, this means that we cannot speak of Supernatural history versus natural history. No such dichotomy exists. We are thus to perceive that God reveals Himself in all of human history, and since He works in *all* of history we are not to think of separate miracles or Supernatural events apart from the whole of

---

27. Pannenberg, *Revelation as History, Ibid.*, pp. 125–31.

28. *Ibid.*, pp. 3–13.

29. *Ibid.*, pp. 125–27; cf. Daniel Fuller, *op. cit.*, p. 182 and Blaikie, *op. cit.*, pp. 156, 162.

30. See Pannenberg, *Ibid.*, p. 19.

historical revelation.[31] Pannenberg realizes that this is not a new conception of revelation, as similar views were expressed in German idealism.[32]

The key to his thesis one is thus that God does not reveal Himself
directly. Any understanding of the concept of revelation that asserts otherwise is therefore not correct. God only allows Himself to be known
indirectly, and that is through His acts in the whole of human history.

Pannenberg's second thesis is that God's revelation is not known totally
at the beginning, but rather at the conclusion of revelatory history.[33] Since
God only reveals Himself indirectly, Pannenberg believes that it is therefore correct to link this revelation with the end of history.[34] Thus the early
events in the history of Israel whereby they learned of Yahweh were not
the final or the most important of God's acts. The most important revelation will occur only at the end of history.[35]

Some of the logic of this position has been presented above. It has
been stated that Pannenberg conceived of the end of history in such a way
that the future can have a retroactive affect upon both the past and the
present. As such, all occurrences eventuate from the future. According to
this understanding, God can be more or less identified with the coming
Kingdom and still have existed so as to have dominated the past and the
present. In a similar way, the resurrection is the sign that God's activity
was also retroactively present in the life of Jesus.[36]

Pannenberg thus accepts the priority of the future. Even at present the
future is more important. This is seen, for instance, by this scholar's belief
that all events reach into the past and the present from the future.[37] Since
these postulates are believed to be valid, one can therefore perceive
how Pannenberg further held that the final truth and result of an event

---

31. *Ibid.*, pp. 7, 16; cf. Blaikie, *op. cit.*, pp. 156–58, 162.

32. Pannenberg, *Ibid.*, pp. 16, 19. For instance, Schleiermacher's view is that all events, even the
most mundane ones, are miracles. It is not simply the strange or unexplained event alone which is
Supernatural. See the discussion of Schleiermacher's view of miracles above. See also Schleiermacher's
work *On Religion: Speeches to Its Cultured Despisers, op. cit.*, pp. 88–89, 113–14, explanation number
16 for instance.

33. Pannenberg, *Ibid.*, pp. 131–35.

34. The logic of this assertion will be challenged below.

35. Pannenberg, *Revelation as History, op. cit.*, pp. 132–34.

36. *Ibid.*, p. 127; see also Pannenberg's *Theology and the Kingdom of God, op. cit.*, pp. 62–63, 68,
70–71.

37. Pannenberg, *Theology and the Kingdom of God, Ibid.*, pp. 54, 63, 70.

is determined by the future of that event and not only by its present appearances.[38]

The natural outworking of this concept is that in the resurrection of Jesus the future already participated in the past. Through this event one can gain a preview of the future. Through this event the God of the coming Kingdom retroactively acted in the life of Jesus. It is an event such as this that illustrates the second thesis concerning how God's indirect revelation will be accomplished primarily at the end of revelatory history rather than at the beginning.[39] Another pointer to this second thesis is Pannenberg's belief that it is only with the arrival of the end of history that God will prove Himself to be a definite reality. Again revelation is perceived to be complete at the end of revelatory history.[40]

The third thesis which is presented by Pannenberg is that God's historical revelation is not restricted to special or private situations, but is open for all men to see. In this sense, revelation is universal.[41] Thus one is not to understand revelation as something secret or mysterious. It is not an entity known only to those who have been initiated into the life of faith. In fact, an individual need not even have faith first in order to see God's revelation. This is because one's faith is inspired by seeing the revelatory events. In other words, faith need not precede the perception of revelatory events, but arises after the recognition of them.[42]

As to the nature of the revelatory events in question, Pannenberg asserts that God has acted throughout the history of Israel all the way to Jesus' resurrection. These events communicate meaning to those who perceive and appropriate them. They are comprehended by reason and are open to the examination of all.[43]

By postulating that God's revelation is open for all to see and examine, Pannenberg is giving further explanation to this belief that Christianity is a rational faith. One is not required to make a leap of faith so that one might be able to believe in God. Such irrationality has no place in the

---

38. Neuhaus in Pannenberg, *Ibid.*, p. 42.

39. Pannenberg, *Revelation as History, op. cit.*, pp. 141–43. See McDermott, *op. cit.*, pp. 713–14.

40. Pannenberg, *Ibid.*, p. 134 and Pannenberg's *Theology and the Kingdom of God, op. cit.*, p. 62.

41. Pannenberg, *Revelation as History, Ibid.*, pp. 135–39.

42. *Ibid.*, pp. 135–37.

43. *Ibid.*, p. 137.

Christian faith. One believes because the facts are found to be reliable and trustworthy.[44]

Pannenberg realizes that there is a subjective factor involved when one speaks of a historical verification of one's faith and that one therefore cannot reach absolute results when studying history. Yet history is the proper method to use in examining the claims of Christian revelation, as it is capable of leading one to highly probable conclusions.[45] Therefore, historical examination of events such as the resurrection is needed to ascertain whether the reports are true or not.[46] One thing which Pannenberg insists upon in this research is that the investigator must be open to the results of the research and not have made up his mind in advance as to what did or did not happen.[47]

Pannenberg's fourth thesis is that God's universal revelation of His deity is not yet known in Israel's history. Rather, it was first revealed in Jesus' fate in that the end of history is already anticipated in this event.[48] Pannenberg is convicted that, in the ancient history of the Jews, God did not show Himself to be the God of all mankind. Rather, He was seen as the God of Israel.[49] But in the New Testament, God was shown to be the God of all of mankind by His act of raising Jesus from the dead. Through this act all men can look to the God of Israel as the only true God. Through the life and teachings of Jesus, the offer of the Kingdom is extended to all people.[50]

It is obvious that the resurrection holds a place of great importance in Pannenberg's theological enterprise. Indeed, this scholar's works reflect the Pauline conviction that if Christ had not risen, all faith would be in vain.[51] It is therefore important for one to know if this occurrence is a

---

44. *Ibid.*, pp. 138–39.

45. Cf. Pannenberg's *Jesus—God and Man, op. cit.*, p. 99 with editor Neuhaus in Pannenberg's *Theology and the Kingdom of God, op. cit.*, pp. 20, 38, 46.

46. See Neuhaus, *Ibid.*, pp. 20–21 and Daniel Fuller, *op. cit.*, pp. 180–81 for some of Pannenberg's techniques in investigating evidence.

47. Fuller, *Ibid.*, p. 180.

48. Pannenberg, *Revelation as History, op. cit.*, pp. 139–45.

49. *Ibid.*, pp. 139–41.

50. *Ibid.*, pp. 141–43. On the universal aspect of the offer of the Kingdom, see Pannenberg's *Theology and the Kingdom of God, op. cit.*, pp. 73, 76, 85, 88 for example.

51. Editor Neuhaus in Pannenberg's *Theology and the Kingdom of God, Ibid.*, p. 41; cf. p. 10. For the apostle Paul's stance, see 1 Corinthians 15:13–19.

historical fact which can be demonstrated. Pannenberg advocates examining the sources to see if any alternate explanations could account for the rise of the resurrection faith.[52] He entertains such hypotheses as the subjective vision theory,[53] the legend or myth theory,[54] and Barth's view of the resurrection happening in prehistory.[55] After a careful look at such theories, Pannenberg concludes that the resurrection of Jesus from the dead is the only adequate explanation for the subsequent faith of the disciples. Those who seek to deny the reality of this event must be prepared to provide a more adequate explanation. Pannenberg believes that the inevitable conclusion is that the resurrection can be verified as having occurred in human history.[56]

The fifth thesis which Pannenberg presents is that the deity of God is not revealed in the Christ event as an independent or isolated fact, but only as the event is part of Israel's history.[57] The Christ event cannot be separated from Israel's history because the God of Christ is also the God of the Old Testament. Jesus' mission and fate must therefore be understood from within the framework and context of Israel's history.[58] As such the resurrection remains the revelation of God whereby the end times have retroactively taken part in Jesus' fate.[59]

Pannenberg's sixth thesis is that the universality of God's eschatological participation in Jesus' fate found its actual expression in the Gentile Christian church's non-Jewish understanding of revelation.[60] The coming of the gospel to the Gentiles was a natural and necessary consequence of the eschatological significance of Christ. But Pannenberg asserts that there were differences between the Gentile and the Jewish conceptions of revelation. The influence of gnosticism is said to have brought some

---

52. Pannenberg, *Revelation as History, op. cit.*, p. 137; cf. Daniel Fuller, *op. cit.*, pp. 181–82.

53. Pannenberg, *Jesus—God and Man, op. cit.*, pp. 95–97.

54. *Ibid.*, pp. 90–91.

55. See *Ibid.*, p. 99 and Pannenberg's *Basic Questions in Theology, op. cit.*, vol. 1, pp. 15–16. Cf. editor Neuhaus in Pannenberg's *Theology and the Kingdom of God, op. cit.*, p. 30 and Blaikie, *op. cit.*, pp. 156, 206.

56. Pannenberg, *Ibid.*, pp. 145–48.

57. Pannenberg, *Ibid.*, pp. 145–48.

58. *Ibid.*, p. 145.

59. *Ibid.*, p. 146.

60. *Ibid.*, pp. 149–52.

non-Jewish elements into the Gentile understanding of God's revelation. For instance, gnosticism taught that revelation was direct and that it was imparted by means of secret initiation and knowledge, thus meaning that it was not available to the scrutiny of all men.[61] It has already been pointed out how Pannenberg conceived of Jewish revelation as being both indirect (by means of God's historical acts) and open for all to perceive.

Pannenberg believes that even though these important differences existed between the Jewish and Gentile ideas of revelation, the Christian conception of God's acting in Jesus in a final and universal manner still made its way extensively into the Gentile-gnostic concept of revelation. But one should not attempt to rule out portions of the New Testament which reveal a gnostically inclined view of revelation, for these portions still served to make God understandable to both Gentiles and to Jews. In other words, even though Pannenberg believes that gnosticism influenced portions of the New Testament teaching on the revelation of God in a way opposed to the Jewish concept, it must be realized that this still helped the Gentiles to know that God was the God of the Gentiles as well as of the Jews. God's actions in Jesus' fate therefore were shown to be universal in scope in that the Gentiles responded to this revelation and accepted it as having been extended to them as well.[62]

The seventh thesis presented by Pannenberg asserts that the imparting of God's word is related to revelation by its foretelling, forthtelling, and report.[63] Even though Pannenberg understands that any reference to the Biblical word of God as the direct revelation of God is influenced by gnosticism,[64] there is still a threefold relationship between these two concepts. First, the indirect revelation through historical acts confirms the promises which God had given *beforehand*. Here the word sets the stage for the revelatory actions by foretelling the promises of God which are then fulfilled in the revelatory future. Second, the words of God confirm His acts in history in the sense that they *follow* the revelation as forthtelling. In this sense, the actions of God establish the words that

61. *Ibid.*, pp. 149–50.

62. *Ibid.*, pp. 150–51.

63. *Ibid.*, pp. 152–55.

64. *Ibid.*, see pp. 10–12.

follow, such as with the Law or other commandments which were given to the people after they had seen God act. Third, emerging in the New Testament one finds that the kerygma acts as a report of what historical acts God has already performed. There can be no universal significance of God's revelation apart from some proclamation of these events. Thus this third relationship between word and revelation points to a spoken proclamation regarding the preceding revelation.[65]

None of these relationships between revelation and word give any revelatory nature to the word. The word of God, either spoken or written, is therefore conceived by Pannenberg as supplementing the actual revelation without being the revelation itself. The word may precede the indirect revelation in the form of a promise as to what God will do in the future (foretelling), or the word may follow the revelation, having been established by the acts of God (forthtelling). Yet again, the word may be a proclamation of the revelation (report). Thus the word may serve to explicate or proclaim revelation, or else the word may itself be expanded, verified, or established by the revelation. At any rate, the word is therefore related to the revelation without being the revelation itself.[66] From Pannenberg's presentation of these seven theses one can perceive how the past revelatory acts of God (both in Israel's history and the life of Jesus) and the future revelation of God are believed to be intricately interwoven. This scholar has indeed developed a theological system which seeks to explain the Biblical concept of God's indirect Self-revelation through His actions in history. However, Pannenberg fails noticeably in at least four key areas of his work, which will be investigated here.

The first major criticism of Pannenberg concerns his concept of God. This criticism is directed against the aforementioned understanding of God as reaching from a future existence into the past. Pannenberg believes that this view of God is confirmed by the Scriptures and especially by the preaching of Jesus. In the view of this scholar, Jesus conceived of God's claim to this world *exclusively* in futuristic terms. God is said to be in a process of coming to exist and so in a certain sense does not exist at present.[67]

---

65. Ibid., pp. 153–55.
66. Ibid.
67. Pannenberg, *Theology and the Kingdom of God, op. cit.*, pp. 56, 68.

In order to make the assertion that the New Testament also expounds this futuristic view of the existence of God, it appears that Pannenberg has to ride roughshod over the Scriptural evidence to the contrary. It is agreed that the main emphasis in Jesus' teaching is on the coming Kingdom of God and the resulting present faith-obedience to God.[68] But this is far from sufficient proof to require God's primary existence as issuing into the present from the future. In fact, Jesus seems to indicate the origin of God's existence as being different than what Pannenberg asserts.[69]

For instance, when Jesus refers to the eschatological judgment of the future, he likens it to the past judgment that God meted out both in the days of Lot and in the days of Noah (Luke 17:26–30, 32; cf. Matt 24:37–39). When on another occasion Jesus was asked for a sign, he did not point forward to any events in the future, but backward to the prophet Jonah, who was to be a sign of his resurrection form the dead (Matt 22:39; cf. Matt 16:4, Luke 11:29–30). Also, when questioned about divorce, Jesus informed the questioner that God has acted out of the *past* in making provision for marriage. Jesus refers his listeners to the mighty act of the creation of God for their answer concerning the seriousness of divorce (Mark 10:6–8; Matt 19:4–6).

Therefore it is obvious that Pannenberg is not correct in his statement that Jesus spoke *exclusively* of God in terms of His future rule.[70] To the contrary, several portions of the gospels indicate rather that Jesus also looked into the *past* for the unveiling of God's power. Jesus thus does not speak of God exclusively in futuristic terms, unless one has already *assumed* in advance that God works from the future into the past.

Now Pannenberg can admittedly explain these verses in which Jesus refers to God's power as also being demonstrated in the past. These were not supposed to be verses which he could not explain. They simply show that Jesus looked to the *past* as well as to the future in order to reveal the workings of God. There are admittedly many verses which do indeed

68. See *Ibid.*, pp. 50, 53, 73, 81, 133.

69. In the use of the New Testament Scriptures which are to follow, the issue is not to defend these words and argue if they were actually spoken by Jesus or not. Rather, we are primarily concerned at this point with what the Scriptures teach about the nature and existence of God, not about who said which words.

70. Pannenberg, *Theology and the Kingdom of God, op. cit.*, p. 56.

refer to future acts of God, but there are also ones dealing with His past actions. However, the significant point here is that Pannenberg can interpret the past actions of God according to his system only by utilizing the prior presupposition that God is already in the future, working into the remote past. His view that God reveals Himself only from the future is an unsupported assertion, and it is shown to be so simply by the fact that it must be assumed to be true before it can be accepted, as will be shown in the third criticism of Pannenberg below. He cannot point to these verses as ones which support his ideas, for they do not. He can only interpret them according to already existing assumptions.

But from whence does the actual idea that God exists primarily in the future arise? One might stress verses on the other end of the spectrum and build a case around the thesis that God exists primarily in the *past* and is revealed particularly through His creation. From this past existence He would then reveal Himself in the present and in the future. Verses pertaining to the future Kingdom of God would then be applied to the final and complete revelation of God. As clever as such systems can be made to sound, they appear to be based more upon philosophical speculation than upon theological revelation.

The point here is therefore not that Pannenberg cannot deal with these preceding verses, but rather that he must *assume* the primary importance of the future in order to do so. Both his thesis and the contrived one that perceives God to have acted mainly from the past through the creation event thus have the same problem. There is a lack of proof. Both views have inadequate reasoning to justify such a view of revelation. For instance, there is no support in the New Testament accounts of Jesus' teachings to justify the position that God does not yet exist, in whatever sense this may be taken. Neither does Jesus teach that God is in a process of coming into existence.[71] It is plain that in other similar ways as well, Pannenberg's overall conception of God appears to be based more upon philosophical speculation than upon revelation. There is a decided lack of evidence for his view.

---

71. For Pannenberg's connection of these ideas with Jesus' teachings, see *Ibid.*, p. 56. But he strangely gives no references for these assertions.

The second major criticism of Pannenberg concerns his hypothesis that God reveals Himself indirectly only through His actions in human history. For this scholar, God did not reveal Himself through any direct means, such as by the inspiration of the Scriptures, but only indirectly through the events of human history.[72]

Many theologians are of the persuasion that God acts in history and that this is one means of revelation.[73] But fewer are convinced that this is the only means of God's revelation. Certainly another shortcoming of Pannenberg's is in not recognizing the self-witness of the Scriptures as being another revelation of God, especially in portions which could not have been influenced by gnosticism.[74]

Pannenberg contends that the New Testament witness to the direct revelation of God in the Scriptures reflects the early influence of gnosticism, as already shown above. This direct Scriptural revelation is held to be contrary to the Jewish understanding of God's indirect revelation in history. To be sure, he does allow a close connection between the written words and this revelation.[75] But it appears that Pannenberg ignores the Old Testament witness to God's revelation in Scripture and through the prophets. This attestation would of course be removed from the influence of first century gnosticism.

A very clear reference to God's speaking through the Old Testament prophets is found in Numbers 12:6, 8. Here we are specifically told that God used this means *to make Himself known* to the Jewish nation. This is both an early and quite clear reference to the Jewish belief that God did reveal Himself to the Jews through the prophets. Statements such as this

---

72. For Pannenberg's assertions against the "direct" views of inspiration, see *Revelation as History, op. cit.*, pp. 9–13, 152. For his own view see pp. 125ff.

73. For example, see Ladd, *op. cit.*, pp. 17, 144; cf. Daniel Fuller, *op. cit.*, pp. 186, 230, 237; cf. p. 234. At this point, Pannenberg's contention of revelation in history is correct.

74. There is no attempt here to employ any kind of circular reasoning concerning the inspiration of Scripture by first asking what the self-witness of the Scriptures is and then assuming that this is true. This would not be a correct procedure. It is not our purpose here to even discuss whether this self-witness to inspiration is valid. Rather, the concern is that Pannenberg does not accept the New Testament's claim to revelation in the Scriptures because of what he feels is the influence of gnosticism (see *Revelation as History, op. cit.*, pp. 10–12, 152). It is this claim which must be examined, especially as regards the clearly non-gnostic portions of Scripture. This examination is very important, since Pannenberg is interested in developing an understanding of what the Jewish conception of revelation consisted. This will be our endeavor here as well.

75. *Ibid.*, pp. 152–55.

one in Numbers could be multiplied considerably.[76] In fact, hundreds of times in the Old Testament the phrase "thus said the Lord" serves to introduce a revelation of God for the people.[77]

The Jews were even responsible for distinguishing between the prophet who spoke the words of the Lord and one who did not. The sign that the prophet was relaying a revelation from God was that the prophecy would occur in history. Thus, the true prophet was one who correctly received revelation directly from the Lord and then proclaimed it to the people, with his word being confirmed by history (see Deut 18:20–22). The Old Testament therefore not only teaches that God's *indirect* revelation is manifested in *history*, in this instance by the fulfillment of prophecy, but also that God's *direct* revelation is given to the *prophets*, through whom God makes Himself known.[78]

However, the Old Testament witnesses report that God not only revealed Himself through the preaching of the prophets, but also through the written Scriptures. There is even a relationship between the revelation given to the prophets to speak and the recording of this revelation in written words, as the prophets were quite often required to record the words of their prophecies.[79] For instance, Moses[80] was commanded not only to speak the words of God, but also to write the words which had been revealed to him.[81] This means that God's revelation also comes through the written words of the Scriptures.[82]

Other prophets besides Moses are also commanded to write the revelation which was communicated to them by God. This is found to be the case with Isaiah (Isa 8:1; 30:8), Jeremiah (Jer 36:2), and Habakkuk

76. Cf. for example Numbers 22:38; 23:12, 16, 26: Jeremiah 1:6–9, 26:2; Ezekiel 3:10–11.

77. One such instance is Jeremiah 15:19–21.

78. See G. Ernest Wright's exegesis of "The Book of Numbers," in *The Interpreter's Bible*, edited by George Arthur Buttrick, *op. cit.*, vol. 2, pp. 450–51.

79. A general reference to the written words of the prophets occurs in Zechariah 7:12. The words here would probably be the written ones, since the reference is to prophets of former times whose writings were in existence.

80. Moses is referred to as a prophet in Deuteronomy 34:10.

81. See Exodus 17:24; 24:4; 34:27–28: Deuteronomy 31:9, 24–26.

82. As with the other Old Testament verses listed in this section, it is not our purpose here to debate who is the author of these words. It is rather our concern to ascertain what the Jewish view of revelation was, especially as spoken and written by chosen men of God. These verses are therefore very valuable in reflecting this belief.

(Hab 2:2). It is recorded that David also both spoke and wrote God's revelations to him.[83]

It is now plain from this preceding brief survey that Pannenberg's limitation of revelation to God's acts in human history is only presenting a part of the whole. In spite of this scholar's claim that his view faithfully represents that of ancient Judaism, it has been shown here that this is not the case.[84] The Jewish concept of revelation also includes at least the revelation given to prophets to speak the word of God and the revelation which is written in the form of the Scriptures. It is true that the Jews believed that God revealed Himself indirectly through historical acts. But it is also true that the Jews believed that God revealed Himself directly through the prophets and through the written word in the Scriptures. A proper view of Jewish revelation must include all of these factors and not just the first, as Pannenberg's does.

It is Pannenberg's opinion that only gnosticism teaches such direct revelation,[85] yet it has been shown that even in the earlier Old Testament writings this view is found. To claim the influence of gnosticism here is therefore clearly impossible. Rolf Rendtorff also asserts that God never revealed Himself in the prophetic word,[86] yet it has also been shown that several Old Testament passages teach the contrary view. Especially noteworthy here is Numbers 12:6:

> If there is a prophet among you, *I the LORD make myself known to him* in a vision, I speak with him in a dream. (Num 12:6, RSV, italics added)

---

83. Cf. Mark 12:36; Matthew 22:43–46; Luke 20:42 with 2 Samuel 23:2. One cannot object to the use of the New Testament verses here, because the Old Testament verse also confirms that the Lord spoke through David. Both express the direct revelation of God to him.

84. Rolf Rendtorff, in his essay, "The Concept of Revelation in Ancient Israel" (in Pannenberg's *Revelation as History, op. cit.*, pp. 46–47), also recognizes a close relationship between word and revelation. However, like Pannenberg, he insists that the word is not really revelation. His view likewise falls prey to the same criticisms raised here. For instance, in order for a prophet to foretell an act of God in history, he must have received such word from the Lord. This is the whole point of Deuteronomy 18:20–22. This word is God's revealing the future *through* the prophet *before* the event in history occurs. Pannenberg especially misses this point in his exposition of the similarities between word and revelation (*Ibid.*, 152–55). Without such revelation through the prophet there would be no foretelling of the event.

85. Pannenberg, *Ibid.*, p. 12; cf. p. 152.

86. Rendtorff in Pannenberg, *Ibid.*, p. 46.

As if to say that this Self-revelation of God was not direct enough in some instances, Numbers 12:8 adds concerning Moses,

> With him I speak mouth to mouth, clearly, and not in dark speech; and he beholds the form of the Lord (Num 12:8, RSV).

There can be no question about the intention of these two verses. God made Himself known to the prophets, but He revealed Himself even more directly to Moses. The Lord's making Himself known must necessarily involve Self-revelation. Other verses pointed out above also assert these beliefs. By making known His present admonitions for holy living by exhorting the Jews to keep the Law and by revealing the future by His prophets, it was believed that God was revealing Himself directly to the people. This was done by God's chosen messengers through both the spoken and the written word.[87]

Pannenberg's view of revelation therefore fails in its attempt to present the only revelation of God as being indirect by means of God's acts in human history. This is just a part of the Jewish concept, which also includes direct revelation through the oral proclamation and through the written word.

The third major criticism of Pannenberg is one which recurs throughout much of his work and is especially obvious in his presentation of his seven theses. Pannenberg's view of revelation in its relation to the future contains several inadequately supported statements. His theological system does include many intriguing and alluring points, some of which are certainly valid.[88] But the overall framework for this system, especially concerning God's revelation of Himself from the future, sometimes appears to be composed of assumptions which lack proper evidence. This has been perceived to some extent in the first objection above. Thus McDermott notes here that Pannenberg is sometimes guilty of inserting

---

87. Many scholars also believe that the Biblical witness provides written revelation of God. For this view see, for instance, Norwegian theologian Sigmund Mowinckel's work *The Old Testament as Word of God*, translated by Reidar B. Bjornard (Nashville: Abingdon Press, 1959), pp. 10–12, 23–26. See also Charles C. Anderson, *The Historical Jesus: A Continuing Quest, op. cit.*, pp. 9–51 and Bernard Ramm, *Protestant Christian Evidences, op. cit.*, pp. 224–49.

88. To be sure, there are some strong, carefully reasoned points in Pannenberg's work. The strongest part of his theology will be discussed later.

reality into a future which has obviously not yet arrived, and that he has done so without the proper clarification and evidence.[89]

Instances of this lack of evidence are readily available, and clearly affect the framework of Pannenberg's theological system. Pannenberg admits that his work rests upon two presuppositions, these being the reality of the future's power and the single future which exists for every event.[90] These two presuppositions are quite apparent in his seven theses, but strangely without supportive evidence in many cases.

For instance, the second thesis calls for a relationship between revelation and the end of all history. This relationship is said to be the result of the indirect nature of this aforementioned revelation. In fact, the connection of revelation with history's end is said to be the *direct* result of the indirectness of revelation.[91] But even if one were to grant the indirect nature of God's revelation in history,[92] how does this cause revelation to be known primarily at the end of history? Pannenberg never succeeds in demonstrating how indirect revelation automatically means that this revelation must be connected with the end of history. God could quite conceivably be acting *indirectly* in history from out of the *present*. In other words, Pannenberg has not shown why futurity must follow from indirect revelation. One must assume that his view of God is the definitive one to even begin to arrive at this conclusion, and we have already seen that this view is quite arbitrary and problematical as well.

Another example of Pannenberg's arbitrary theology occurs in the fourth thesis, where Jesus' fate is also connected with the end of history. Because of this formulation, Pannenberg asserts that there will be no further Self-revelation of God after the resurrection of Jesus.[93]

But this thesis also lacks conclusive evidence. Indeed, it raises several problems of its own. For instance, if revelation is mediated in *all* of history as Pannenberg claims, why should the indirect Self-revelation of

---

89. McDermott, *op. cit.*, p. 714.

90. Pannenberg, *Theology and the Kingdom of God, op. cit.*, p. 59.

91. Pannenberg, *Revelation as History, op. cit.*, p. 131.

92. As we have already noted, many would perhaps be more willing to grant that *one* of God's methods of revelation is His acting in history, *in addition* to other modes of revelation. See Ladd, *op. cit.*, pp. 17, 144; Daniel Fuller, *op. cit.*, pp. 186, 237.

93. Pannenberg, *Revelation as History, op. cit.*, pp. 142, 143.

God then end with the fate of Christ? Why should revelation not extend beyond this point? One could still hold that the supreme Self-revelation of God occurred in the Christ event, but that this revelation still progresses beyond this point. Is not Pannenberg's abrupt halt at the fate of Jesus a rather arbitrary termination of revelation? Indeed, it does appear to be simply a desired stopping point. But there is obviously a need for a logical reason to support such an abrupt halt. Pannenberg entertains this same objection at the end of his introductory essay, stating that he hopes this problem will be answered later.[94] But he never quite seems to come back to it with an appropriate answer.

Even if Pannenberg was successful in showing why revelation should end here, would it not then demand an adjustment in his previous concept of this revelation? It would appear that the previous notion that God's indirect Self-disclosure occurs in all of history—in everything that happens[95]—must be revised. How can one assert that everything which occurs is revelation and then later arbitrarily drop this notion after the Christ event becomes past history? Logically, according to Pannenberg's system, revelation should continue past this point.

A closely related problem with this fourth thesis is that if God's revelation occurs in all events of human history, why single out one strand, namely Jewish history, in which to concentrate almost all attention? To do so favors the Biblical witness, to be sure, but what is the rationale behind such an assertion if one begins with Pannenberg's presuppositions? As Daniel Fuller aptly points out, Pannenberg must deal with the problem of how God reveals Himself in all of history and yet all of the most important revelation occurs especially to a select group of Jews and Christians.[96]

Also, since God is said to act in all of history, how can one ascertain when He acts in a special way in just *one* event like the fate of Jesus? Some may look at an event and see God working, others may look at the same event and not notice this at all.[97] Perhaps these points indicate

94. *Ibid.*, pp. 17–19.
95. *Ibid.*, p. 16; cf. p. 7.
96. Daniel Fuller, *op. cit.*, pp. 184–86.
97. See Blaikie, *op. cit.*, p. 159.

that Pannenberg's view of revelation occurring in all of history needs adjustment.

It is therefore possible to perceive areas of Pannenberg's theological system which contain several inadequately supported assertions. These problems seem especially related to his view of the future and how it affects the present. Pannenberg's statements are not self-authenticating.[98] Yet he often fails to provide reasonable facts to back his claims. As a result, his theology remains quite problematical in that the logical demonstration in key areas is often lacking.

The fourth major criticism of Pannenberg concerns both his view of the nature of the resurrection appearances of Jesus and his treatment of the naturalistic alternative views. During a discussion of the historicity of this event, to which we will return briefly below, Pannenberg introduces his conception of the appearances of Jesus to the disciples and to Paul. For this scholar, the resurrection appearances involved several elements. Those who saw the resurrected Jesus saw a spiritual body, not a natural, earthly one. This appearance was accompanied by an audition and, at least in the case of Paul, a phenomenon of light. These were appearances from heaven and were recognized by all as the risen Lord.[99]

However, Pannenberg asserts that these appearances of Jesus were not very palpable ones. The nature of these occurrences was more similar to "objective visions," or visions which were not produced by the subjective consciousness of those perceiving the phenomena. In other words, the appearances of the resurrected Jesus were realities outside of the apostles in spite of a lack of corporeal qualities.[100] Pannenberg specifically opposes the subjective vision theory,[101] which makes the resurrection a concept in the minds of the disciples with no objective reality. His contentions against this view were presented above. The resurrection was rather an objective reality showing the disciples that Jesus was alive. As such it was an actual historical event.[102]

98. See editor Neuhaus in Pannenberg, *Theology and the Kingdom of God, op. cit.*, p. 42.
99. Pannenberg, *Jesus—God and Man, op. cit.*, pp. 92–93.
100. *Ibid.*, pp. 93–95.
101. *Ibid.*, pp. 95–97.
102. *Ibid.*, pp. 98–99, 105.

In spite of Pannenberg's more than adequate defense of the historicity of the resurrection, his stance against more objective appearances of Jesus is unwarranted. Pannenberg appears to feel that it is essential to choose between Paul and the gospels when discussing the nature of the resurrection body. Since he conceives of all the appearances being of a similar nature, Jesus must have always appeared as he did to Paul.[103]

It has been shown above that *both* the gospels and Paul maintain that Jesus' resurrected body was both similar to and different from his natural body. The emphasis in the gospels on the disciples' ability to touch Jesus' body and to otherwise verify his appearances to them has also been discussed above. This evidence in the gospels will therefore not be studied here again.[104] But the gospels also reveal the conviction that Jesus' body was somehow changed, having new qualities and powers.[105]

Paul's testimony is likewise that the resurrection body is a "spiritual body" different from one's physical body.[106] Nevertheless, it is the resurrection of a spiritual *body* and not simply the resuscitation of a spirit. This is recognized by most theologians today.[107] As William H. Johnson correctly contends, theological justice must be done to both words in the Pauline phrase "spiritual body." Neither word must be over-stressed at the expense of the other. Thus, Jesus did not rise as a spirit or in a physical body, but as a *spiritual body.*[108]

Yet, it is not recognized as often that Paul also gives some evidence for objective appearances of Jesus. Although he possessed a new body,

---

103. *Ibid.*, p. 92.

104. The key passages teaching the objective nature of Jesus' appearances include such portions as Matthew 28:9; Luke 24:36–43; John 20:17 (in the Greek); 20:20, 26–29; Acts 1:3.

105. For instance, the gospels assert that Jesus was already gone from the grave before the stone was rolled away, implying that he evacuated by means other than the doorway (Matt 28:2–6). It is also reported that Jesus left the graveclothes behind, undisturbed, showing that he passed through them rather than having to unravel them (John 20:6–9; cf. Luke 24:12). He was also able to appear and disappear at will, even into locked rooms (Luke 24:30–31, 36; John 20:19, 26). See Ladd, *op. cit.*, pp. 84–96, 126.

106. See especially 1 Corinthians 15:42–50.

107. For instance, see Pannenberg, *Jesus—God and Man, op. cit.*, p. 92; Ladd, *op. cit.*, pp. 111, 114–18; Brown, *The Virginal Conception and Bodily Resurrection of Jesus, op. cit.*, pp. 85–89 and Brown's "The Resurrection and Biblical Criticism," *op. cit.*, p. 236; Reginald Fuller, *op. cit.*, p. 179. See footnote number 113 below for others who also recognize this.

108. William Hallock Johnson, "The Keystone of the Arch," *Theology Today* 6, no. 1 (1949/1950): 20.

the Jesus who appeared to the disciples and Paul was the same Jesus who had died on the cross and was afterward buried.[109] Another indicator of the objectivity of Jesus' appearances was that he appeared to many on different occasions (see 1 Cor 15:5–8). It is especially Jesus' appearance to the 500 people at once (v. 6) which helps us to determine how objective these experiences were for the disciples. It is this appearance in particular which points to an objective manifestation. Paul's conception of Jesus' resurrection body was such that it could be seen by a group this size. It would therefore appear to require more than just a mystifying light and auditory phenomenon, along with an objective vision.[110]

Ladd also disagrees with Pannenberg's conception of "objective visions," which pattern all of Jesus' appearances after the one to Paul. The evidence shows that the gospels were written under the influence and control of various eyewitnesses of these events. There must be an underlying factual tradition behind these reports as well. Besides, once it is granted that Jesus actually rose from the dead, there is no reason why he could not have appeared various ways to various individuals.[111]

To reinforce this last statement, one must remember that, in the books of Luke-Acts, the author Luke does not seem to be aware of any contradiction in recording both the more objective appearances to the disciples and the more "spiritual" conversion appearance to Paul.[112] Similarly, many theologians also feel that the witness of the gospels is essentially compatible with that of Paul, in spite of the different stresses in each. The

---

109. See 1 Corinthians 15:3–4. For the reality of the empty tomb, see Pannenberg, *Jesus—God and Man*, *op. cit.*, pp. 100–104; Reginald Fuller, *op. cit.*, pp. 69–70, 179; Brown, *The Virginal Conception and Bodily Resurrection of Jesus*, *op. cit.*, p. 122, footnote number 204, and p. 126; see also Brown's article "The Resurrection and Biblical Criticism," *op. cit.*, p. 235. For the view that Paul also implied the empty tomb in 1 Corinthians 15:4, see Reginald Fuller, *Ibid.*, pp. 48–49, 69; Ramsey, *op. cit.*, p. 44. In addition, see Robert M. Grant, *A Historical Introduction to the New Testament*, *op. cit.*, p. 369 and Clark H. Pinnock, "On the Third Day," in Henry, *op. cit.*, p. 15

110. Cf. Ladd, *op. cit.*, p. 105; see also p. 138 and Brown, *The Virginal Conception and Bodily Resurrection of Jesus*, *op. cit.*, p. 91.

111. Ladd, *Ibid.*, pp. 126, 138–39.

112. Luke records the more objective appearances to the disciples (see Luke 24:36–43; Acts 1:3; 10:40–41) right along with the three passages which narrate Paul's conversion (Acts 9:1–9; 22:6–11; 26:12–18).

conclusion often is therefore that Jesus appeared in an objective way that could be verified, but in a new spiritual body.[113]

It is somewhat surprising that Pannenberg does not place even more stress than he does on the objectivity of Jesus' appearances. For the reasons just outlined here, it is therefore with good evidence that this fourth major criticism of Pannenberg remains valid. Eyewitness testimony witnessed to these objective appearances through such men as Luke (cf. Luke 1:1–4 with Luke 24:36–43; Acts 1:3). Such eyewitness testimony which has already been shown to exist behind the gospel traditions therefore reflects valid witness to the objectiveness of Jesus' appearances to the disciples. Even Paul refers to the original disciples' testimony of the resurrection appearances (1 Cor 15:11–15). The testimony of the Gospels is thus compatible with Paul.

The second part of this fourth criticism concerns Pannenberg's treatment of the naturalistic theories which have been proposed against the resurrection. Apart from his criticism of the subjective vision theory, his overall treatment of the other alternative theories is not entirely complete. He is still successful in refuting the other hypotheses, but he fails to disprove them as sufficiently as is possible. This is an important point, for since all of Christianity rests upon the validity of the resurrection, as was determined earlier, then refutations of rival views must be *as complete as possible* in order to more clearly ascertain if this event actually occurred. It is especially important to the validity of this third solution to the resurrection (that this event can be demonstrated) that there are no probable solutions other than Jesus' resurrection from the dead. This therefore points to the need for *as thorough an investigation and refutation* of the major naturalistic theories as is possible. In addition, it is true that the more thorough such a refutation of the alternate views is, the more convincing the resulting probability of the resurrection of Jesus is made.

Wolfhart Pannenberg has built a theological system which contains many intriguing and interesting ideas. However, his work has been shown to fall prey to four major criticisms. First, his view of God as being fully

113. See Ladd, *op. cit.*, pp. 126, 137–38; Brown, "The Resurrection and Biblical Criticism," *op. cit.*, p. 236; cf. Grant, *Miracles and Natural Law, op. cit.*, pp. 229–30; see also Charles C. Anderson, *The Historical Jesus: A Continuing Quest, op. cit.*, pp. 163–66; J. N. D. Anderson, *op. cit.*, p. 99; McNaugher, *op. cit.*, pp. 164–65; Smith, *op. cit.*, pp. 194–95.

revealed only in the future is an arbitrary one which lacks the proper evidence. The Scriptures, including Jesus, do not unanimously refer to God this way at all. Second, Pannenberg's view of God's indirect Self-revelation as occurring only in historical acts is only a part of the Biblical presentation of revelation. It was found that God also revealed Himself directly through the prophets and through the written word of God.

Third, the overall theological system of this scholar lacked conclusive evidence in several places. This is especially true with regard to Pannenberg's seven theses. There was a decided lack of evidence needed to demonstrate such items as the futurity of revelation and the end of all Self-revelation of God occurring in the Christ-event. Fourth, it was shown that Pannenberg's concept of the nature of the resurrection appearances was not objective enough and did not allow properly for the evidence for more objective manifestations of Jesus. In addition, his refutation of the naturalistic theories against the resurrection was not as complete as it should have been.[114]

It is easily perceived that the resurrection of Jesus is one of the central concepts in Pannenberg's theological system. The examination of the resurrection is also the strongest aspect of his theology. His treatment of this event has been dealt with above, but a few comments are in order here. Pannenberg logically investigates the resurrection with regard to its historicity. Rival theories which seek to explain this event naturalistically are entertained and dispelled, even though such procedures are not as complete as they should have been.[115] Anyone who disputes the claim that Jesus rose from the dead is welcome—in fact, required—to arrive at an alternative theory which is adequate enough to account for the facts.[116]

It is Pannenberg's conviction that when one conducts such an investigation of the facts, one arrives at the probability that the resurrection did, indeed, occur in actual human history. An examination of the facts

---

114. There are other substantial criticisms of Pannenberg's thought which have not been mentioned here. For instance, Neuhaus has pointed out that Pannenberg's concept of the Kingdom of God as a possibility to be worked for in human society is perilously close to some of the ideas of the social gospel movement of the nineteenth century. The view that the Kingdom of God could become established in the social order through the effort of men failed. See Neuhaus in Pannenberg's *Theology and the Kingdom of God, op. cit.*, pp. 31–33. Cf. Pannenberg, *Ibid.*, pp. 77, 79, 80, 84.

115. Pannenberg, *Jesus—God and Man, op. cit.*, pp. 88–106.

116. Pannenberg, *Revelation as History, op. cit.*, p. 147.

reveals the probable conclusion that Jesus did rise from the dead after the crucifixion. The resurrection is thus demonstrated to be an actual historical event.[117] In this conclusion Pannenberg is thorough and difficult to refute.[118] His own refutation of alternate views is valid and does indeed show that the resurrection is the most probable solution. Therefore, this conclusion appears to be quite valid.

---

117. Pannenberg, *Jesus—God and Man, op. cit.*, see this conclusion on p. 105.

118. Even those who do not accept Pannenberg's view of the resurrection find his defense of this event to be quite sophisticated. See for instance, Reginald Fuller, *op. cit.*, pp. 22–23.

CHAPTER X

Possibility Number Three: Other Similar Views

Other scholars besides Pannenberg also hold that Jesus rose literally from the dead and that this can be demonstrated to be the most probable conclusion in this issue.[1] This is surely not to affirm that these scholars followed Pannenberg in their conclusions, for most have not derived their inspiration from him, nor do they consider themselves part of the "theology of hope" school of thought. Therefore one finds that the techniques vary here, but the final result is similar.

One such theologian who believes that Jesus' literal resurrection from the dead can be demonstrated to be the most probable conclusion is Daniel Fuller. In his work *Easter Faith and History*, Fuller surveys most of the major theological approaches to the question of the relationship between faith and history. As the title of this work suggests, this question is surveyed particularly by examining the various views of the resurrection.

Beginning with Enlightenment rationalism and continuing through present contemporary theology, this scholar investigates most of the major theologians and their views of the historical and rational content of faith. After viewing the attempts of the major theological schools of thought down to the present, Fuller turns his attention to attempts to accept the resurrection as fact from three different standpoints. Attempts to hold belief in this

---

1. The word "demonstrated," once again, is not used here in the sense of absolute proof, but rather as it is related to probabilities. Thus, this section deals with the conviction that the factual evidence is such that the resurrection of Jesus is the most probable conclusion.

event *apart* from historical reasoning, by *partial* historical reasoning and *totally* by historical reasoning are then investigated. Fuller's conclusion is that none of these views are entirely acceptable, as each falls prey to various criticisms which he presents.[2] It should be noted that Fuller does agree with the principle of historical verification of the resurrection, as will be shown below. But he objects here to these methods by which such attempts are made.

Fuller's solution is to examine the first-century approach to the resurrection of Jesus which is taken by Luke in the New Testament work Luke-Acts.[3] After reviewing several key hypotheses concerning the theme of Luke-Acts,[4] Fuller sets forth what he believes is the major theme of these two books.[5]

The Lukan prologue (Luke 1:1–4) sets forth some key information concerning the intentions of the author. Here Luke claims that he received the information in this work from the original eyewitnesses (Luke 1:2). Fuller points out that while Luke was thus not himself an eyewitness of Jesus' ministry, he received the information from those who did originally participate in the events.[6] However, Luke did share first hand in the fulfillment of the resurrection event, namely, the mission of the Christian church to the Gentiles. Luke therefore experienced the *result* of the resurrection faith firsthand.[7]

Fuller finds that an important emphasis in Luke-Acts is Luke's writing so that his readers[8] could know the certainty of what had transpired in the life of Christ and especially in his resurrection. In fact, Luke's purpose in writing to these early believers was to inform them that they could be sure of what had been reported to them pertaining to the Christ event.

---

2. Daniel Fuller, *op. cit.* The examination of these various schools of thought and the subsequent evaluation of these three positions with regard to history is found on pp. 27–187.

3. Preliminary questions such as the authorship and date for Luke-Acts are discussed by Fuller, *Ibid.*, pp. 190–99.

4. *Ibid.*, pp. 199–208.

5. *Ibid.*, pp. 208–29.

6. *Ibid.*, pp. 188–90.

7. *Ibid.*, pp. 190–91, 220.

8. Luke-Acts is addressed to Theophilus in particular (Luke 1:3; Acts 1:1), but there may have been other indirect recipients as well.

This certainty which was available to each reader applied in particular to the surety that Jesus was raised from the dead (see Luke 1:4).[9]

Upon what was such certainty based? Fuller explains that for Luke, the early Christian mission to the Gentiles was the fulfillment of the resurrection of Jesus. Without the appearances to the disciples and the others and later to Paul, there could have been no such Gentile mission. In other words, the existence and continuance of the effort to evangelize the Gentiles depended upon the ministry of Paul and upon the authority and action of the other apostles. But Paul's involvement in such a work cannot be explained by anything other than the appearance of the risen Jesus to him, as recorded in Acts. Paul, the enemy and persecutor of the church in earlier years, would have no other impetus for such behavior. Likewise, the disciples were not very accustomed to the idea of taking the gospel to the Gentiles (at least in the form of a ministry) until they received just such a commission from the risen Lord who appeared to them after his death. Only such an appearance could account for their realizing that the offer of the Kingdom of God had also been extended to the Gentiles.[10]

In a sense, Luke taught that there were therefore two key points in the present which pointed backward to the resurrection. First, Paul's conversion could be explained no other way than his having seen the risen Jesus. No other conclusion is sufficient to account for this change in the life of a non-believing enemy of the early church.[11] Second, the outreach of the early Jews to the Gentiles, spearheaded by the disciples, pointed to a directive beyond the exclusivism of Judaism. Apart from the directives issued by the risen Jesus,[12] there is no other probable reason for the Jewish mission to the Gentiles, since the Jews considered themselves as the sole heirs of God's blessings.[13] Therefore, these two events point unequivocally to the historical resurrection of Jesus.[14]

For these reasons, Luke stood at a critical point in that he was both able to receive knowledge of the Christ event of the past via the eyewitnesses

---

9. Daniel Fuller, *op. cit.*, pp. 189–90, 223 for instance.

10. *Ibid.*, pp. 223–25, 229, 235.

11. *Ibid.*, see especially pp. 217, 219, 226.

12. Commands such as those recorded in Luke 24:47–48 and Acts 1:8.

13. Daniel Fuller, *op. cit.*, see, for example, pp. 223, 226–29, 246–47.

14. *Ibid.*, p. 220.

and also to participate in the present and future fulfillment of this event. From his vantage point he realized that the resurrection was the only logical explanation for occurrences such as the conversion of Paul and the Jewish outreach to the Gentiles with the gospel. Thus he encouraged Theophilus and his other readers to reason from these two events in the present to the resurrection of Jesus in the past, realizing that the present reality could only be explained by the factualness of the past event.[15]

After presenting Luke's position here, Fuller is careful to point out that the resurrection is the solution to these two present events *only if* the objections against the resurrection have been answered.[16] Earlier he entertained various alternate theories against the historical and verifiable nature of this event.[17] At this point, after a presentation of Luke's attempts to show that the resurrection was verifiable,[18] Fuller turns to the question of Paul's conversion. Alternate theories to explain this event are also investigated and refuted.[19]

Fuller's final investigation deals with Luke's arguments for the historicity of the resurrection. For Luke, history is viewed as having two sections, an "upper" and a "lower." In the first or lower section, all historical events are "natural" ones, as they originate from other historical events. But Supernatural events from the second, or higher section, do enter the first. These events could never be the results of occurrences in the first section, but do enter the first from the second "layer." Here they do not disturb other events, but also follow the patterns of history in the first section after they enter. Thus, for Luke, the resurrection can have a Supernatural origin and still be a historical event, known by historical reasoning.[20]

Luke's approach is found to be quite satisfying, according to Fuller. He agrees with Luke that the resurrection of Jesus can be verified. Given the

---

15. *Ibid.*, see especially pp. 190, 223, 235.

16. *Ibid.*, pp. 242, 245.

17. For instance, see Fuller's discussion and refutation of Paulus' swoon theory (*Ibid.*, pp. 38–39), Lessing's and Kierkegaard's attempts to remove this event from all verification (*Ibid.*, pp. 35, 255–56), and Barth's modification of this approach (*Ibid.*, pp. 83–84, 88–90, 155–56). Luke's proofs for the resurrection also serve as a refutation of Strauss' vision theory (*Ibid.*, cf. 45–49 with pp. 231–32).

18. *Ibid.*, pp. 231–32.

19. *Ibid.*, pp. 247–50.

20. *Ibid.*, pp. 252–61. See especially pp. 252–53.

possibility of believing in this event apart from historical reasoning or in holding that it is based upon evidences that can be historically verified, Fuller opts for the latter. The resurrection can be shown to be a historical event, both by the investigation of the original eyewitness testimony concerning the appearances and by viewing the fulfillment of this event in history in the conversion of Paul and in the Gentile mission. Belief in this event is thus based upon empirical claims.[21]

Fuller's approach to the resurrection sometimes appears to reach overly easy conclusions. This is most evident in his refutation of alternate views both with regard to Jesus' resurrection and in the appearance to Paul. Fuller desires to explore such theories[22] and does refute the major alternatives, as shown above. But the various refutations often appear irresolute and are generally, as with Pannenberg, not as thorough and strong as should be expected. As noted above, it is imperative that the alternative views are refuted as completely as possible in order to reveal if there is a probable naturalistic answer to the resurrection faith, which is rightly viewed as the central tenet of Christianity. It follows that the more thoroughly these alternative hypotheses are refuted, the more probable the resurrection becomes.

It is also possible that Fuller depends too much on the Gentile mission as demonstrating the resurrection, almost as if this conclusion could stand apart from any other investigation of the facts and alternate theories. It must be stressed once again that the Gentile mission can be a pointer to the resurrection only if other objections to this event are completely answered. Fuller does recognize this, but seems to neglect the conclusion that if a valid alternate theory to the resurrection is found, a valid alternate theory would also have to be applied to the Gentile mission. We once again perceive the need to refute alternative theories as completely as possible.

In spite of these criticisms, however, it is most difficult to annul Fuller's contention that the resurrection can be demonstrated. He does provide enough evidence to establish this event as probable. In so doing he avoids the pitfalls of Pannenberg's theological system and still succeeds

---

21. *Ibid.*, especially pp. 255–59. See also pp. 220, 231–32.

22. *Ibid.*, pp. 242, 245.

in showing how the literal resurrection of Jesus can be verified as a historical event.

Another theologian who likewise concludes that Jesus' resurrection is the best explanation for the facts is New Testament scholar George E. Ladd.[23] This scholar realizes that the modern concept of historical methodology argues for a reality in which God does not act in human history. Ever since the Enlightenment, the prevailing view has been that historical events must have origins which are grounded in history. Therefore, miracles with Supernatural origins are ruled out from the outset.[24]

In opposition to this view, Ladd proposes the use of the inductive method of historical inquiry, which allows for the conclusion which best fits the facts. Historical events which claim Supernatural intervention must be investigated to perceive if they are the best explanations for what is known to have occurred. Possible alternative theories must also be examined to see if these hypotheses are able to better account for the factual evidence.[25]

In the case of the resurrection of Jesus, Ladd points out that even if this occurrence were established as an actual event, it must still be counted as "nonhistorical" with regards to its origin. Since such an event would require a Supernatural origin, it could not be said to be historical in the sense that other events are, whose starting point is history itself.[26] Therefore, when judged by modern historical methodology, the resurrection is not a historical event. It is unlike other events in its unique entrance into history.[27]

However, looking at the resurrection only from the standpoint of its origin yields only a portion of the overall picture. For Ladd, historical inquiry cannot *prove* the resurrection, but it can establish it as the most probable explanation for what occurred. In fact, it is asserted that this event is the *only* explanation of the facts which adequately explains what is known to have happened.[28]

---

23. See Ladd's book, *I Believe in the Resurrection of Jesus, op. cit.*

24. *Ibid.*, pp. 12–13; cf. p. 23.

25. *Ibid.*, pp. 13–14. Concerning the need specifically to examine the resurrection, see pp. 27–28, 132–133.

26. *Ibid.*, pp. 21, 25.

27. *Ibid.*, pp. 25, 132.

28. *Ibid.*, cf. p. 27 with pp. 13, 27, 139–41. See footnote number 1 above.

The belief that this event can be demonstrated to be the only possible solution which accounts for all of the facts is based upon the idea that there must be an *adequate* explanation for any event occurring in history.[29] To this end, Ladd enumerates the core historical facts surrounding the resurrection which are known to be credible.[30] Later he investigates the major alternative theories which seek to account for these facts by naturalistic means. Each is examined and critiqued. Ladd concludes that each theory fails to explain these resurrection facts.[31]

It should briefly be noted however, that one of the same problems which appears in Pannenberg and Daniel Fuller is also apparent in Ladd with regard to the naturalistic theories of the resurrection. Although Ladd provides a good critique of the subjective and objective vision theories and generally does a better overall job here than Fuller, his treatment of the other theories is not developed thoroughly enough. In fact, the other theories are said to need very little refutation.[32] This lack of a more complete refutation is very important in that it must be ascertained as thoroughly as possible if the resurrection actually happened—if this Supernatural event is more probable than other explanations. The resurrection can be shown to be more probable when other alternate theories are more thoroughly shown to be less so.

As pointed out above, the explanation which best accounts for the historical facts is the one which is given the status of probability. Here Ladd arrives at the conclusion that Jesus' resurrection from the dead is the most probable explanation. It gives the most adequate explanation to the available facts. The only reason to reject this conclusion is that one has a closed mind to the occurrence of the Supernatural.[33]

Thus, while the resurrection differs from other occurrences in that it has a different origin into the historical processes, it is nevertheless an event in history. It therefore achieves the status of entering the historical

---

29. *Ibid.*, p. 20.

30. *Ibid.*, pp. 13, 91–94. Ladd does not simply enumerate facts just because they are recorded in the New Testament. Rather, he lists those which are *known* to be historically plausible.

31. *Ibid.*, see pp. 133–39, where Ladd discusses five major alternative theories concerning the resurrection.

32. *Ibid.*, see especially p. 136.

33. *Ibid.*, pp. 139–41.

process by means of a nonhistorical, Supernatural origin but still becoming a historical event.[34]

Ladd offers a logical approach to the resurrection which seeks to examine the most probable conclusion to this issue. However, he comes perilously close to making some of the same mistakes as Karl Barth.

It has been stated that Ladd explains the resurrection as being nonhistorical in that it enters history Supernaturally. Because of this origin, this event is not historical in the same sense as other events. Therefore, if evaluated in terms of the modern concept of history, the resurrection is not a historical fact.[35]

But Ladd moves even closer to Barth's position at other points. For instance, he concludes that even though the resurrection can be shown to be the best historical explanation for what occurred, it is still primarily perceptible to the "eye of faith." Thus, a historian looking at this event can only ascertain that something wonderful happened. The conclusion that Jesus was risen remains a tenet of faith. In fact, it is Ladd's opinion that even having actually seen the risen Jesus would still not prove the facticity of this event.[36] The appearances thus speak of the need for faith to approach this event.[37]

Admittedly, Ladd's position does differ from Barth's in other major facets. Unlike Barth, Ladd opts for investigating the historical evidence for the resurrection.[38] There is therefore an interaction between history and faith, as faith is logical and not simply a leap in the dark.[39] Also unlike Barth, Ladd admits that his faith would be seriously affected if an alternate

---

34. *Ibid.*, pp. 25, 58.

35. *Ibid.*, pp. 21, 25, 132.

36. *Ibid.*, pp. 101–2, 139–40.

37. *Ibid.*, p. 140. It must be noted here that the objection against Ladd is not due to his position that the resurrection is primarily known by faith, per se. It has already been pointed out above (chapter 4) that faith is more important than reason, and so it is with the resurrection. But to remove the resurrection to any type of metahistory is to begin to remove it from certain types of reasonable verification. This is to be guarded against. The problem is therefore in Ladd's tendencies to begin to remove the resurrection away from the grasp of history (see *Ibid.*, pp. 101–2, 139–40).

38. *Ibid.*, pp. 26–27, 29, 132–33.

39. *Ibid.*, pp. 12, 27, 140. It will be recalled that Barth opposed all such historical investigation of the resurrection and other modes of interaction between history and faith. As an example, see Barth's *Church Dogmatics, op. cit.*, vol. 4, part 1, pp. 335, 341.

theory were found to be plausible. Thus he takes considerable effort to refute the leading alternate theories against the resurrection.[40]

Probably the biggest difference with Barth is Ladd's contention that the resurrection can be demonstrated to be the most probable explanation for the facts. The only logical conclusion is that Jesus actually rose from the dead in history. Other naturalistic theories are found to be unacceptable. Here one finds that faith is reinforced by studying the evidences.[41] Barth opposed all such historical reasoning as an assistance to faith.[42]

In spite of the differences between these two theologians (especially Ladd's emphasis on the ability to demonstrate that the resurrection is the most probable conclusion), Ladd is still guilty of retreating to the concept of metahistory when confronted by modern historiography. In so doing, history is split into two divisions—the secular and the divine.[43] As mentioned with regards to Barth, history knows of no such differentiation and no such concept of prehistory. Montgomery points out that by making the resurrection a part of this questionable realm of history and by asserting that it can be known primarily by faith, Ladd makes this event only perceptible in any meaningful way to the believer. Thus the non-Christian is not able to benefit from the evidence in favor of this event.[44]

Ladd's concern with pointing out that the resurrection would require a Divine origin has been noted above. But one can recognize that the origin of this event is Supernatural and still not resort to the concept of metahistory. Daniel Fuller[45] and C. S. Lewis,[46] for instance, have both done credit-

---

40. Ladd, *Ibid.*, pp. 27, 132–42. As mentioned above, Barth asserts that it makes no significant difference if the tomb was opened or closed. In fact, sometimes a naturalistic theory is preferable to one's trying to treat the resurrection as actual, fully objective history. See Barth's *The Resurrection of the Dead, op. cit.*, pp. 135–38 and *The Word of God and the Word of Man, op. cit.*, p. 90.

41. Ladd, *Ibid.*, pp. 13, 27, 139–41. It is because of Ladd's emphasis on the ability of the resurrection to be demonstrated as the only adequate solution and because of the efforts to refute other alternate theories that he is included in this section and not with Barth in the former section. Ladd's entire emphasis on the ability of faith to be investigated and reinforced by positive findings was the deciding factor here.

42. See the discussion of Barth above. Compare his *Church Dogmatics, op. cit.*, vol. 4, part 1, p. 335.

43. This is Blaikie's criticism of Ladd's position, *op. cit.*, pp. 128–29, 134.

44. Montgomery, *Where Is History Going?, op. cit.*, pp. 114–16. However, Montgomery does not seem to be aware of Ladd's belief that investigation of the resurrection is still possible even if it can primarily be known only by faith.

45. Daniel Fuller, *op. cit.*, pp. 252–61 in particular.

46. Lewis, *Miracles, op. cit.*, see especially pp. 56–63.

able jobs in showing how an event can have a Supernatural origin and still be normally connected with history once it enters the historical process. Thus, the matter of Divine causation should not automatically determine that the event must be metahistorical and that it must be known only by the processes of faith. Once it enters history, this event could partake of the historical pattern without impeding other natural events. Therefore, in spite of the origin of a Supernatural miracle, it would become a historically verifiable event upon entering history.

To agree with Barth (and others) in holding that a Supernatural event remains metahistorical even after it enters the historical process is, once again, to divide history into the two component parts of the secular and the divine. But, as has been pointed out in the critique of Barth in chapter 8, this formulation is faulty. The criticisms directed against Barth will not be repeated here, as it has been sufficiently shown that such a concept is not valid.

To be sure, Ladd accepts critical examinations of the Christian faith. He believes that the inductive historical approach, which accepts the event which best fits the evidence, will demonstrate that the resurrection actually did occur.[47] Here he differs from Barth. But where Ladd does adopt Barth's metahistorical concept,[48] it must be agreed that he errs in committing some of the same mistakes as Barth. If the Supernatural is found to occur it must happen in *historically* verifiable history and not in metahistory. This is recognized by Pannenberg, Daniel Fuller, Lewis, and others.[49]

Ladd does not retreat completely into the realm of metahistory as does Barth. His emphasis on being able to demonstrate the resurrection is therefore, like the attempts of Pannenberg and Fuller, a positive aspect of his theology. All three theologians have succeeded in investigating the

---

47. Ladd, *op. cit.*, pp. 12–13, 27, 139–41.

48. It is actually difficult to ascertain how much Ladd does agree with Barth here. See indications of a partial acceptance of Barth's understanding of the resurrection in Ladd, *Ibid.*, pp. 21, 25, 101–2, 140. See also Montgomery, *Where Is History Going?*, *op. cit.*, p. 115.

49. By historically verifiable we are referring to the approach to history which accepts the event which best supports the known facts. To this Ladd, Pannenberg, Daniel Fuller, and C. S. Lewis all agree. In chapters 2 and 3 of this work this same conclusion of ascertaining historical events was also found to be the correct procedure. But we are also speaking here of the need to realize that God's raising Jesus from the dead is therefore a theological and historical explanation of a *historical* event. Thus we must not resort to any type of metahistory to explain the resurrection. With this Ladd seems to disagree (*Ibid.*, pp. 101–2, 139–40).

facts before arriving at a final solution and all three scholars have found the resurrection to be the most probable explanation of what occurred. These findings are further strengthened by the failure of any naturalistic theories to adequately account for what happened.

However, it is not only certain theologians who are convinced of this conclusion. Paul Maier is an ancient historian who also believes that the resurrection is the most probable answer for what occurred.[50] Although Maier is not the only historian to reach such conclusions,[51] his approach is probably the most thorough from the standpoint of historical studies.[52]

For Maier, the discipline of history is very valuable in helping to ascertain what occurred on the first Easter morning. While many ancient historical events are based upon only one source, and two sources often render an event "infallible," there are several ancient sources which point to the event of the resurrection of Jesus.[53] Even outside of the New Testament sources, there is important extra-biblical evidence especially for the empty tomb, and thus also for the resurrection.[54]

Maier points to such early historians as Tacitus and Josephus, who either infer or specifically mention the belief in the resurrection on the part of the disciples and the early church. Tacitus' reference to first century Christianity in Rome and to the "superstition" which broke out in Judea *after* the death of Jesus[55] is perceived to imply the Christian teaching of the resurrection of Jesus.[56] Maier also deals with the problem of a possible interpolation in Josephus' more specific reference to the resurrection of Jesus[57] and finds that there is very good reason to believe that Josephus did compose this statement concerning Christ minus a few of

50. Maier's chief work on the resurrection is his book *First Easter*, *op. cit.* See also "The Empty Tomb as History," in *Christianity Today*, *op. cit.*

51. We have discussed above the position of theologian and historian John Warwick Montgomery as well as ancient historian Edwin Yamauchi, both of whom also believe that the resurrection can be demonstrated to have occurred.

52. Montgomery, for instance, more often combines history and theology, being quite adept in both disciplines.

53. Maier, *First Easter*, *op. cit.*, p. 114.

54. *Ibid.*, and Maier's "The Empty Tomb as History," *op. cit.*, pp. 4, 5.

55. See Tacitus, *Annuals*, 15.44.

56. Maier, "The Empty Tomb as History," *op. cit.*, p. 4. J. N. D. Anderson concurs in this position, *op. cit.*, p. 19.

57. See Josephus, *Antiquities*, 18.3.

the more "Christianized" phrases. Thus we see that, in all probability, Josephus reported the early Christian *belief* in the resurrection and thereby acknowledged that the tomb was empty.[58]

The evidence presented by Josephus and implied by Tacitus is further corroborated by a few other sources. In the first century it was reported that the Jews spread the story that the disciples stole the body of Jesus in order to proclaim his resurrection from the dead. It is related that this story was still being voiced in the second half of the first century.[59] In formulating this totally inadequate view, the Jews not only did not succeed in offering a substantial objection to the resurrection, but in so doing they also admitted the empty tomb.

This Scriptural report is confirmed by second century scholar Justin Martyr, who reports in his *Dialogue with Trypho* (about 150 AD) that the Jews sent specially taught men across the Mediterranean Sea in order to

---

58. Maier, *First Easter, op. cit.*, p. 114. Other scholars also agree that Josephus did write this portion of Jesus (or at least one very similar to it), except for several "Christian" words. This position is held for at least three major reasons. First, there is no textual evidence against this section in spite of various readings in other places. Second, there is very good manuscript evidence for these statements about Jesus and it is therefore difficult to ignore it. Third, this portion is written in Josephus' own style of writing. It is thus a warranted conclusion that there are several good reasons for accepting at least that Josephus did write of Jesus, mentioning several facets of his career. It is also a justified conclusion to say that, in all probability, Josephus at least recorded the *belief* in the resurrection without actually acknowledging that he accepted such a fact. For these three reasons and the concluding facts given here, see, in addition to Maier, J. N. D. Anderson, *op. cit.*, p. 20. See especially F. F. Bruce's two works, *Jesus and Christian Origins Outside the New Testament* (Grand Rapids: William B. Eerdman's Publishing Company, 1974), pp. 32–41, especially pp. 36–41 and *The New Testament Documents: Are They Reliable?*, 5th ed. (Grand Rapids: William B. Eerdman's Publishing Company, 1967), pp. 102–112. Bruce, the Manchester scholar of Biblical criticism, has done much work on Josephus' reference to Jesus and comes to a conclusion quite similar to Maier's.

59. See Matthew 28:11–15 for this report. It has already been shown above that the theory of the stolen body (or other such fraud on the part of the disciples) fails miserably in its attempt to explain the resurrection of Jesus (see chapter 7, footnote numbers 163, 164, and the discussion corresponding to these remarks). Briefly, this theory ignores at least five key objections. First, men do not die willingly for what they know to be simply a falsehood. Second, the tremendous psychological transformation of the disciples from backward fishermen to bold preachers cannot be explained by any fraudulent action, or else there would not have been this change. Third and closely related, none of the disciples ever recanted even at the threat of losing his life, which would be the normal thing to do rather than die for a lie. This was totally opposed to their actions before the resurrection, such as in fleeing when Jesus was taken captive and by Peter's subsequent denials. Fourth, the quality of the ethical teachings promulgated by the disciples precludes such actions. Fifth, it is admitted by all that the disciples at least *believed* that Jesus had risen from the dead. They would of course not believed that this event had actually occurred if they were the ones who had perpetrated the fraud. For these reasons (see also footnote numbers 61 and 62 below), no reputable scholar holds this view today. There is little doubt that this is one of the weakest theories ever formulated against the resurrection, yet it was the one chosen by the early Jewish leaders.

counter the Christian claims of the resurrection. The explanation spread abroad by the Jews, once again, was that the disciples stole their dead Master's body. The Jews therefore continued to admit the empty tomb.[60]

As pointed out by Maier, the book of Acts gives further evidence that the tomb was empty on the first Easter morning. As the disciples and early Christians first began to proclaim the resurrection of Jesus from the dead, the Jewish authorities objected strenuously. But in several confrontations with the disciples, the Jewish elders never did what might have been most expected—they never led the disciples to the tomb for an investigation. Discovering the body of Jesus would of course have destroyed Christianity, as the Jewish leaders desired to do anyway. The obvious reason that they did not try to locate the body is because they knew that the tomb was empty. Maier asserts that even the impartial historian must admit this historical evidence for the empty tomb.[61] This implicit admission further pointed to the empty tomb mentioned by Josephus, Matthew, and Justin Martyr, and also implied by Tacitus.

Maier also utilizes circumstantial evidence of two kinds. First, Christianity could not have had its beginnings at Jerusalem, as it did, if Jesus' grave was still occupied just outside the gates of the city. This is the *last* place that the church could have begun if Jesus' body was still in the tomb. Here an investigation of the grave would have revealed the body and Christianity would have been destroyed before it really began. The birth of the church in Jerusalem can only be explained by the fact that Jesus' tomb was indeed empty.[62]

Second, the spread of Christianity around the Mediterranean region all the way to Rome itself by slightly after the first half of the first century is simply an astonishing feat to have been accomplished in so short a period of time. Approximately thirty years after the death of Jesus this amazing expansion had taken place. It is Maier's view that such expansion of any teaching or philosophy is unparalleled in ancient times. Could the

---

60. Maier, *op. cit.*, pp. 116–17.

61. *Ibid.*, pp. 114–15. In addition to the point made here by Maier, it should also be noted that the behavior of the Jewish leaders in Acts also constitutes another objection to the stolen body (fraud) theory. If the Jewish rulers really believed that the disciples stole the body, they would not simply have commanded the disciples not to preach about Jesus (such as Acts 4:18, 21; 5:28, 40), but they would have forced them to admit and recant of their actions.

62. Maier, "The Empty Tomb as History," *op. cit.*, p. 5.

preaching of and belief in the resurrection have provided the impetus for such growth, as the New Testament attests?[63]

Another piece of evidence has only a possible connection directly with Jesus' resurrection. A valuable archaeological discovery revealed a marble slab found in Nazareth which contained a warning from Caesar to all who were caught robbing graves in Palestine. Other such Roman edicts against grave robbing prescribed a fine against the offender, whereas this edict condemns the offender to capital punishment. Most scholars believed that the inscription was the command of emperor Tiberius or emperor Claudius. Why was the punishment to be so great in Palestine? Could this command have been prompted by the Jewish report of Jesus' stolen body or by the preaching of the resurrection?[64]

Theological evidence is also cited by Maier in his effort to deal historically with the resurrection. This historian points to at least three other factors which lead to the final conclusion. First, the aforementioned change in the disciples caused them to believe that Jesus had risen from the dead. Such a radical difference must be based upon some real experience and points to an actual encounter with the risen Lord, just as the New Testament claims. Second, the very existence of the Church points to some event which is worthy of such an enterprise. The New Testament claims this event was the resurrection. Third, there must have been a reason for the early church to have changed the day of meeting from Saturday, the Jewish Sabbath, to Sunday, the Lord's day. Again, the New Testament claims that the resurrection caused this change in order to commemorate the day on which Jesus had risen.[65]

The last type of evidence employed by Maier is of both a historical and theological nature. Maier entertains the objections raised by eight different naturalistic theories which are aimed at disproving the resurrection of Jesus. Each is then investigated and refuted by the available historical data. He finds that all of these naturalistic theories fail to provide a valid historical answer to what happened on the first Easter day. They must

---

63. Ibid., p. 4.

64. Maier, First Easter, op. cit., pp. 119–20.

65. Ibid., pp. 115, 121–22; "The Empty Tomb as History," op. cit., p. 5.

be rejected strictly on the basis of historical inquiry, as well as by theological reasoning.[66]

As for the question of discrepancies in the resurrection accounts, Maier
admits that they do exist, as in the rest of the gospels. However, he holds
that it is illogical to conclude that this event did not occur because of these
variations. Other historical reports also contain similar discrepancies and
there is no question about the events they report. For instance, the reports
of the great fire of Rome offer even greater conflicts than do the resurrection accounts. Some reports claim that the entire city was affected by the
burning flames while others claim that only three sectors of the city were
destroyed. There are also differences of opinion as to how the fire started.
In spite of these problems, the great fire of Rome is unquestionably a historical fact. In a similar way the resurrection of Jesus is also a historical
fact. The various sources simply point to the different traditions, all of
which provide evidence that Jesus actually rose from the dead.[67]

Maier concludes that the will not to believe has kept many from
accepting the historical evidence on the question of the resurrection.[68]
The empty tomb is found definitely to be a datum of history according
to the laws of historical research.[69] This conclusion is even strengthened
by the "hostile evidence" which has been presented here. The strongest
type of historical evidence is facts which are stated about an event by a
source which is hostile to that event. When such a source claims that an
event is factual when it is not advantageous to do so, this fact is in all probability a genuine one. The empty tomb is attested directly or indirectly
by Josephus, Tacitus, and by the witness of Matthew, Luke (Acts) and
Justin Martyr as to Jewish practice with regards to the resurrection. Such
Jewish and Roman evidence is hostile evidence, for it was not advantageous to either the Jews or to the Romans to acknowledge the empty tomb.
Other historical and theological evidence, circumstantial and otherwise,

---

66. Maier, *First Easter, Ibid.,* pp. 105–13, 122; cf. also pp. 77–80 and "The Empty Tomb as History,"
Ibid., p. 5.

67. Maier, *First Easter, Ibid.,* pp. 94, 96.

68. *Ibid.,* p. 105 and "The Empty Tomb as History," *op. cit.,* p. 5.

69. Maier, *First Easter, Ibid.,* this conclusion is stated on p. 120.

has also pointed to this fact. Therefore it can be asserted that the empty tomb is historical fact.[70]

From the empty tomb Maier then argues to the probability of the resurrection. Evidence such as that presented above (especially the threefold theological proof and the refutation of the naturalistic theories) points to the resurrection of Jesus. The historical evidence is not as strong as that for the empty tomb, but the evidence on the periphery of this event points to the probability that the event itself is historical.[71]

Maier has added a very valuable dimension to the study of the resurrection of Jesus in that he has pursued this subject from the standpoint of history. He thus approaches this question from the standpoint of the historian looking at theology. In his works, then, Maier certainly does not look at this question as one for theology only. Yet he arrives at the conclusion that the empty tomb and resurrection are historical events according to all probability.

Admittedly, his treatment of the naturalistic theories and refutation of them could have been developed more. It has already been shown above how important a complete refutation of alternative theories is in order to more fully determine how probable the resurrection is in actuality. Maier does a fairly creditable job in this respect, but still does not treat these naturalistic hypotheses as thoroughly as is possible.

Perhaps some will object that his treatment of the theological question did not deal with theology enough. Yet this letter criticism does not rightfully apply since his whole purpose is to approach this event as a historian and not as a theologian. Thus he cannot be judged for this second point.

Therefore, his overall effort has been a very successful one. He has logically and historically shown that naturalistic theories do not solve the historical needs on the one hand and that valid historical pointers to the resurrection do exist on the other hand.[72] This combination makes a strong case for the historicity of the resurrection.[73]

---

70. Maier, "The Empty Tomb as History," *op. cit.*, pp. 5–6.

71. *Ibid.*, pp. 4–5 and *First Easter, op. cit.*, pp. 120–22.

72. Maier, *First Easter, Ibid.*, especially pp. 105–13, 120–22.

73. For a very positive review of Maier's work *First Easter* and one which recognizes the excellent job done by Maier in his historical demonstration of Jesus' resurrection, see Lawrence E. Martin, "The Risen Christ," *Christian Century* 90, no. 20 (May 1973): 577.

After investigating the claims of three scholars who believe that the resurrection can be demonstrated, it must be concluded that the positions of Daniel Fuller, Ladd, and Maier are positive in their *overall* approaches and conclusions. We have found that these three also present some difficulties. However, a logical approach that is both historical and theological reveals that these positions are better supported by the evidence than the others which were discussed earlier. It yet remains for us to finally ascertain if this third possibility of demonstrating the resurrection is the one that best fits the facts.

PART 3

An Evaluation of
the Solutions to
the Question of the
Resurrection of Jesus

CHAPTER XI

An Evaluation of
Possibility Number One

C hapters 5 and 6 investigated the possibility that the resurrection of Jesus did not actually occur. In chapter 5 it was shown that the most influential position here was held by historian and philosopher David Hume. His essay "Of Miracles" set the stage for other views which also rejected the resurrection as an event, usually because it was held that such events were impossible from the outset because they contradicted the laws of nature.

It was apparent especially in chapter 6 that Protestant liberalism followed Hume in this position. In fact, John Herman Randall, Jr. explains that Protestant liberalism as a whole followed Hume in this line of reasoning. Hume's influence extended not only to the nineteenth-century liberals, but also on to this present day where men of this theological persuasion have often continued to reject the miraculous, based upon this essay.[1]

Other scholars also note that Hume's essay became the definitive stance for liberalism with regards to all miracles. Smith agrees with Randall in this assertion.[2] Montgomery likewise affirms the fact that both nineteenth- and twentieth-century theology derived its belief in the impossibility of miracles from Hume.[3]

It is interesting that these liberal theologians themselves also acknowledged that their views were based upon the stance taken by Hume. For

---

1. Randall, *op. cit.*, pp. 293, 553–54.

2. Smith, *op. cit.*, pp. 142–43.

3. Montgomery, *The Suicide of Christian Theology, op. cit.*, pp. 28, 37–38.

instance, in nineteenth-century liberalism, David Strauss was explicitly willing to acknowledge this dependence. For this scholar, Hume's essay had forever settled the question of the miraculous. Supernatural, nature-contradicting miracles simply do not occur.[4]

Other liberals also followed the position taken by Strauss in that they also favored Hume's position against miracles. Friedrich Schleiermacher, like Hume, asserted that miracles are found where there is little knowledge of the laws of nature. Miracles actually oppose nature and the idea of the miraculous must be abandoned.[5] Heinrich Paulus likewise followed Hume in believing that miracles are usually said to have occurred where there is a deficient knowledge of nature. Scripture is mistaken in claiming that miracles did occur and when the workings of nature are revealed, this mistake becomes even clearer.[6] Bruno Baur also affirmed that no events like miracles occur which break the laws of nature.[7] For Ernst Renan, Jesus believed that miracles were common, not because they actually were, but because he was unfamiliar with the uniformity of nature's laws.[8]

Later in the nineteenth and early twentieth centuries, liberal theologians were still following Hume and his reasons for rejecting miracles. Otto Pfleiderer held a notion that was very common, especially since Hume—that the events of nature follow an unchanging regularity and order.[9] Adolf von Harnack added his voice to the growing list of scholars who accepted, along with Hume, the belief that ancient peoples believed the miraculous because they did not understand the laws of nature. They did not realize that events which interrupt nature never occur. Thus, miracles cannot be believed.[10]

In the twentieth century, as mentioned above, liberal theologians continued to accept Hume's position on miracles as the definitive one. Rudolf Bultmann accepts the view that the modern conceptions of nature and

---

4. Strauss, *The New Life of Jesus, op. cit.*, vol. 1, pp. 199–201.

5. Schleiermacher, *The Christian Faith, op. cit.*, see especially vol. 1, pp. 179, 181, 183. Cf. also vol. 1, pp. 71, 178–84; vol. 2, pp. 448–49; and Schleiermacher's *On Religion: Speeches to Its Cultured Despisers, op. cit.*, pp. 88–89, 113–14, footnote number 16.

6. Schweitzer, *op. cit.*, pp. 51–53.

7. *Ibid.*, p. 154.

8. Renan, *Life of Jesus, op. cit.*, pp. 147–55.

9. Pfleiderer, *The Philosophy and Development of Religion, op. cit.*, vol. 1, pp. 5 6.

10. Harnack, *What is Christianity?, op. cit.*, pp. 25–31.

science do not allow for miracles. Because of the natural laws, the universe is closed to Supernatural workings. Thus miracles are no longer acceptable in today's world.[11] For Paul Tillich, no events such as miracles can break the laws of nature.[12] John A. T. Robinson holds that the Biblical miracles are myths because natural processes cannot be interrupted by God's intervention. The New Testament cosmology must therefore be abandoned.[13]

It is quite obvious from this foregoing survey that both nineteenth- and twentieth-century liberal theologians have followed Hume in rejecting all possibility for the miraculous. That Hume was the primary inspiration for this viewpoint is also plain.

Yet it has been shown above that Hume's thesis failed to provide an adequate prohibitive against the occurrence of miracles. Four major objections were raised against his view. Briefly, it was first discovered that Hume utilized a series of logical errors, especially circular reasoning and begging the question. This is especially noticeable in his definition of miracle and in his assumption of the negative value of all experience of miracles, when just such an investigation of this experience might demonstrate the probability of a miracle. Second, Hume arbitrarily rejects miracles even where he recognizes a high credibility for the Supernatural event described. Third, Hume rejects miracles because of a faulty view of the uniformity of nature which he himself had rejected in other works. This incorrect view of nature is the center of his polemic and must therefore be rejected. Fourth, in spite of Hume's agreements with modern thought in several aspects of his work, he reverted to a pre-modern stance with respect to his view of miracles. Although he rejected the then-popular view of a closed universe and opted for the use of probabilities, he inconsistently rejected miracles from the outset because they were believed to be impossible. He also ignored any probabilities for miracles and thus ruled them out in a way which is not consistent with the above modern concepts which he accepted. Here he is pre-modern and in error.[14]

---

11. Bultmann, "New Testament and Mythology," in *Kerygma and Myth, op. cit.*, pp. 4–5.

12. Tillich, *Systematic Theology, op. cit.*, vol. 1, pp. 115–17.

13. Robinson, *Honest to God, op. cit.*, pp. 11–18, 64–68.

14. This summary of the criticisms of Hume is necessarily a brief one and thus the logic for these four criticisms cannot be properly analyzed from this presentation. For a complete analysis of the reasoning behind these statements, see chapter 5.

All ten of the theologians just surveyed also agree in accepting the
view that the universe is closed to all occurrences of Supernatural miracles. These events are generally conceived of as being impossible because
they oppose the workings of nature. Ancient peoples who accepted such
reports as true were often said to have done so because they did not
understand nature properly.[15] It is therefore more possible to verify the
contention of Randall, Montgomery, and Smith given above that all of
liberalism as a whole followed Hume in these conclusions.[16] J. Gresham
Machen concurs with these scholars that liberalism did indeed agree in
abandoning belief in the miraculous.[17]

Because both nineteenth- and twentieth-century liberalism followed
Hume's reasoning in its rejection of the miraculous, it is thus possible to
ascertain that these theologians were, like Hume, also in error concerning
these views. For these reasons it is not surprising to find that almost the
same criticisms of Hume which were related in chapter 5 with regard to
the use of improper presuppositions and an incorrect methodology and
concerning the use of a faulty view of the uniformity of nature also apply
to these other scholars. As Hume was found to be in error in these concepts, so also is liberal theology likewise in error here. Miracles cannot
be ruled out by such an approach.

A second indication that the method employed by theological liberalism since Hume's time is in error concerns the naturalistic theories which
have been suggested in order to account for the resurrection of Jesus. Such
hypotheses were necessary in order to explain an event which had already
been rejected a la Hume. The major theories which have been formulated against the resurrection have been discussed above and refuted.[18] An
investigation of each demonstrated that they could not properly account

---

15. See the above references to these ten theologians for these beliefs (to varying extents) on the
part of each of them. In order to ascertain how similar the beliefs of these theologians are to Hume's
stance against miracles, compare chapter 5.

16. See footnote numbers 1–3 above and the corresponding discussion.

17. J. Gresham Machen, *Christianity and Liberalism* (Grand Rapids: William B. Eerdman's
Publishing Company, 1923), pp. 107–9.

18. The major theories advanced to explain the resurrection have been discussed earlier. It was
found that formulations based upon a swoon, subjective or objective visions (including the "telegram
theory" and ideas of the continuing spiritual presence of Jesus' personality in the minds of the disciples), the influence of other ancient myths, and the growth of legends or fraud (including the stolen
body theory) all failed to account for the known facts. See especially chapter 6 above.

for what is known to have occurred. Each can be adequately refuted historically, logically, and theologically.[19]

That none of the naturalistic theories adequately accounts for the resurrection of Jesus is indeed an extremely acute point against theological liberalism's stance on the resurrection. Our endeavor has been to find the historical conclusion which is most probable—the one which best accounts for what is known to have occurred. Yet, none of even the strongest alternative theories is even persuasive, let alone being probable. A more adequate solution is definitely needed here.

A third indication that the liberal theological position on the resurrection is incorrect is the fact that even those who formulated naturalistic theories against this event joined in the decimation of other "rival" theories. Thus it was shown earlier how Strauss and Renan (among others) were both strongly opposed to Paulus' swoon theory. In fact, it is usually believed that Strauss himself gave the final death blow to the theory, which destroyed it for good. However, Strauss' vision theory was opposed strenuously by such scholars as Schleiermacher, Paulus, and Keim. Once again it was a liberal theologian, Keim, who is generally considered to be the one whose logical arguments disposed of Strauss' theory.[20]

While such opposition by these of a similar theological stance surely does not automatically prove these theories to be wrong, the indications are that each felt that the other naturalistic theories were in error. This points to a real dissatisfaction with such theories on the part of these scholars. None could convince *even those of his own theological persuasion* that his view was the most probable one.[21]

There are thus three very important reasons for holding that the answer to the resurrection which is suggested by Hume and by all of theological liberalism fails to account adequately for what is known to have occurred.

---

19. See the conclusions against each of these theories, especially in chapter 6. Cf. for example, Maier, *First Easter, op. cit.*, p.113 and Ladd, *op. cit.*, pp. 139–41.

20. See the discussion of these facets in chapter 6 above.

21. Admittedly, no one is able to convince everyone that his view is right. However, if there was a naturalistic theory which was probable, one would think that those who otherwise objected to the facticity of the resurrection would be able to agree on that theory. However, the point being stressed here is not so much that the liberal scholars could not agree on any one theory, but rather that *the inherent weaknesses in each were pointed out*. In other words, these scholars provided adequate refutations of each of the theories and thus revealed that they were not capable of accounting for the facts.

First, much of the criticism directed against Hume in chapter 5 also applies to liberalism's approach to this event. Thus the entire methodology and the presuppositions which are used are invalid, as is the faulty view of the uniformity of nature. The resurrection and other miracles cannot properly be negated by these methods. This point alone is devastating to these positions. Second, the fact that no naturalistic theory adequately accounts for what occurred is an even stronger point against Hume and liberalism. That no probability can be established for any such alternative theory demonstrates that none of these hypotheses can be accepted as the probable solution. Third, not even those who reject the resurrection agree that any theory adequately accounts for the evidence. Rather, several scholars were content to destroy the arguments for theories which opposed their own, clearly revealing the inherent weaknesses of each.

It is popular in contemporary theology to deny Jesus' literal resurrection and at the same time to affirm that in some way he can still be said to be alive today. For instance, Bultmann contends that although Jesus did not actually rise from the dead,[22] he still meets us through the words of preaching as the risen Lord. Thus, while Jesus himself did not actually rise from the dead as the New Testament affirms, we can still encounter the risen Lord today by faith in the words which are preached. In fact it is only by this mode that the resurrection becomes present and it thereby becomes possible to meet the risen Jesus.[23]

Marxsen likewise accepts such a formulation. Although Jesus is dead, his offer of faith has not lost its validity[24] because Jesus lives today in the content of Christian preaching. Thus Jesus' activity continues beyond the grave. He shows himself to be alive because men still continue to respond to him in faith.[25] For Marxsen, Jesus' resurrection is thus not the raising of a dead man from the grave, but rather the crucified and dead Jesus still influencing men to believe even today.[26]

---

22. Bultmam, "New Testament and Mythology," in *Kerygma and Myth, op. cit.*, pp. 38, 42 for example.

23. *Ibid.*, pp. 41–43. R. Lofton Hudson reaches a similar conclusion concerning Jesus' being alive in the preaching of the church. See R. Lofton Hudson, "What One Easter Meant to Me," *Christian Century* 90, no. 16 (April 1973): 450–52, especially p. 451.

24. Marxsen, *op. cit.*, p. 147.

25. *Ibid.*, pp. 77, 110, 128, 141, 144.

26. *Ibid.*, cf. pp. 128–29 with p. 147.

The purpose behind such theological maneuvers is obvious. The desire is to be able to continue to teach that the Christian faith is still valid for modern man even though many are still inclined to reject the resurrection as an actual event in history. In this way traditional beliefs which in the New Testament are a result of the resurrection can be confirmed in a way that is more harmonious with modern thought.

However, this position is quite obviously laden with several incredibilities. There are at least two valid reasons for rejecting such a theological stance.

First, such an understanding of Jesus' resurrection, whereby he is said to be alive even though he did not literally rise from the dead, is contrary to the earliest Christian understanding of this event. The Jewish conception of resurrection involved the raising of the *body*. The first century Christians likewise believed in the resurrection of a *spiritual body* as clearly shown above, and Jesus was believed to have *literally* risen in this way. Therefore, to assert that this modern view is close to the New Testament is ridiculous.[27] For the earliest believers, Jesus was said to be alive at present, but *because he had literally risen from the dead*, not because his influence had simply continued beyond the grave in spite of being dead.

As asserted by Maier, the modern concept that the Christian faith would still be valid even if Jesus had never risen bodily would be nothing but nonsense to Paul and other first century Christians.[28] Brown agrees, adding that formulations such as Marxsen's are of little value if they do not do justice to the New Testament stance, which allows only one interpretation of the resurrection—a literal resuscitation.[29] Ladd states this well:

> The New Testament knows nothing about the persistence of Jesus' personality apart from the resurrection of the body. Neither does the New Testament know the 'resurrection of the spirit' to heaven. ... If his body is mouldering in a Palestinian tomb, he cannot be the exalted Lord.[30]

---

27. Marxsen does suggest just this (*op. cit.*, pp. 144–45).

28. Maier, "The Empty Tomb as History," *op. cit.*, p. 5 and Maier's *First Easter*, *op. cit.*, p. 115.

29. Brown, *The Virginal Conception and Bodily Resurrection of Jesus*, *op. cit.*, p. 75, footnote number 128.

30. Ladd, *op. cit.*, pp. 146–47.

Admittedly, the New Testament concept of Jesus' resurrection is not self-vindicating. But the point here is a crucial one. The testimony of Paul is that if Jesus did not rise literally in a spiritual body in such a way that he could appear to others, then he did not rise at all (1 Cor 15:1–19). This is the choice which is open to us. Either Jesus rose literally or he cannot be said to be alive in any other way than in a spiritual sense. To take a middle ground which claims that Jesus is alive but that he did not rise from the dead is not open to us. The earliest Christians in particular would not recognize such a compromising belief. If Jesus was dead, Christian theology could not be true at all. If Jesus is dead, neither can contemporary theology hold to the other affirmations and doctrines of the Christian faith. They all stand or fall together.

Second, logic alone dictates that this modern concept of the resurrection is invalid. As Ladd firmly states, if Jesus did not rise bodily from the tomb, then he is still dead.[31] It is plain that if a person is dead he cannot still be alive unless one is speaking of spiritual immortality or of the continuation of one's personality as he is remembered by others or some such understanding. Apart from just such a resurrection as the New Testament proclaims, Jesus cannot be said to be any more alive than anyone else who has ever died. Apart from a literal resurrection, he could still be influencing people today only in the sense of the continued affect of his life and teachings upon others. But to say that Jesus is risen because of such spiritual immortality or influence is plainly illogical and inaccurate. It also involves a gross misappropriation of words.

The early Christian belief in Jesus' resurrection could not have survived if Jesus' body was still rotting in the grave.[32] In fact, no part of the Christian faith could be considered true if Jesus had never risen from the dead. Ladd states this fact quite well:

> But if Jesus is dead,[33] his entire message is negated. If he is dead, he cannot come in his Kingdom. ... Furthermore Jesus' teaching about

---

31. *Ibid.*, pp. 152–53, footnote number 5.

32. Foremberg, *Jesus—God and Man, op. cit.*, especially p. 100.

33. At this point in the above quote, Ladd supplies a footnote in which he states his view that those who believe that Jesus is still alive but who insist that he did not rise bodily from the tomb are voicing all illogical opinion. Jesus either arose or he is dead (Ladd, *op. cit.*, pp. 152–53, footnote number 5).

the presence of the Kingdom and its blessings is also a delusion, for the presence of the Kingdom-blessings was but an anticipation of the eschatological Kingdom to be established by the heavenly Son of Man. ... If Jesus is dead, his entire message about the Kingdom of God is a delusion. If Jesus is dead, the heart of the New Testament Christology is also a delusion.[34]

For these reasons, the modern formulation[35] whereby it is held that Jesus is alive even though he did not literally rise from the dead cannot be valid. Such an interpretation does not coincide with the New Testament understanding of this event and thus cannot be understood as such. The New Testament presents a do-or-die attitude as regards the literal resurrection of Jesus. Only if it occurred literally can we hold Christian theology to be valid. Any other understanding of this event is therefore not possible if one still desires to embrace Christian doctrine.

In addition, this modern formulation is quite illogical. A dead man who did not rise from the dead is no more alive than any other dead individual. Such a man could only influence people by the inspiration of his *past* life and teachings. But such a person has not risen and is not alive any more than any other person. His present spiritual existence would therefore not be unique. Only by a literal resurrection can an individual be proclaimed as being risen.

Thus we must conclude that David Hume and theological liberalism as a whole (both nineteenth- and twentieth-century) do not offer a valid approach to the resurrection of Jesus. The methodology and presuppositions which are used have been shown to be in error, as is the incorrect conception of the uniformity of nature. Without these faulty premises the subsequent conclusions which were postulated against the resurrection most assuredly cannot be held. Also, the naturalistic theories which were proposed as alternate suggestions to account for the belief in the resurrection were shown to be inadequate to account for the known facts. These theories fall short historically, logically, and theologically. In addition,

---

34. *Ibid.*, pp. 145–46.

35. Machen notes that this interpretation was also prevalent in the older liberalism of the nineteenth and early twentieth centuries (*op. cit.*, pp. 108–9).

liberal theologians themselves showed that the alternate theories were not valid by demonstrating the inadequacies of each one.

It was likewise determined that the popular modern understanding of Jesus as being "risen" and "alive" today in spite of his having never risen from the dead is also a totally inadequate conception. It must be rejected, as shown above, in that it violates the earliest Christian understanding of this event and because it is quite illogical.

It is therefore necessary that the answer given by Hume and by contemporary liberal theology since his time be rejected as an inadequate solution to the question of the resurrection. None of the naturalistic theories are even historically plausible, let alone probable, and must therefore be abandoned. This theory that the resurrection did not occur thus fails at the crucial point of not being able to formulate a probable alternate theory or otherwise to properly rule out the resurrection. Any alternative theory such as these which have been examined and refuted here must therefore be rejected.[36]

The questions discussed in this chapter are very important ones. All of Christian theology relies on the validity of the resurrection and it is therefore imperative to understand if this event is an actual occurrence. To say that Jesus is risen or alive but that he did not literally rise from the dead just compounds the dilemma. It is inadequate as an answer to the question of whether Jesus really rose. It is our desire to evaluate the other possibilities in order to ascertain if they can come any closer to a probable answer.

---

36. Such theories would of course be rejected regardless of whether a theologian, historian, philosopher, or other such scholar formulated the hypotheses. The field of specialty makes no difference here, as the alternative theory would still be forced to answer the same objections as were raised above.

CHAPTER XII

An Evaluation of
Possibility Number Two

In chapters 7 and 8 the possibility was investigated that the resurrection of Jesus actually occurred, but that it cannot be demonstrated as such. It was shown in chapter 7 that the most influential position here was that of theologian and philosopher Søren Kierkegaard. It also became obvious, especially in chapter 8, that many others have followed him in this belief.

It has just been found that the conclusion that the resurrection did not occur fails in that it can neither provide a probable solution to the facts or otherwise properly negate this event. Thus an answer must be found elsewhere.

Kierkegaard popularized the conclusion that the resurrection (and other miracles) actually happened, but that this event cannot be proven to have occurred. It can only be accepted by faith. It is solely by faith and not by any type of demonstration whatsoever that we come to know God.

This position was further developed by Karl Barth, who clearly accepted the resurrection as a historical event which actually occurred. But, like Kierkegaard, this event cannot be proven to have occurred at all. However, Barth followed earlier theologians like Martin Kähler in relegating the resurrection to other than totally objective history. This event was believed to have occurred in a nonverifiable type of history removed from objective tests such as historical investigation.

245

Many theologians followed Barth in these views. Today it is quite popular to conceive of the resurrection as a real event, but one which is not verifiable.

The rationale behind such a theory is apparently to be able to affirm the resurrection as a real event for faith but at the same time to remove this event from the critical eye of modern historiography. Thus it appears that Barth's intention (and those who agree with him) is to remove the Christian faith from this realm of modern historical methodology and thus to keep Christianity from any possibility of being critically investigated.[1] Such methods of verification are viewed as being opposed to the New Testament presentation of faith.[2]

In spite of Barth's seeming desire to "preserve" Christianity from all such critical investigations, his formulation is still quite problematical. It has already been found in chapter 3 that history is required to investigate all possible facts surrounding an event in order to find the most probable conclusion. It was concluded that neither science or history can rule out the miraculous *a priori*. Rather, all of the facts must be thoroughly investigated with the conclusion which *best* supports the facts being viewed as the probable one. Therefore a miracle such as the resurrection might be found to be the probable conclusion and thus be viewed as an actual historical event. For this reason, Barth need not feel that the facts of Christianity must be preserved from historical or other types of investigation. If these facts are found to be probable they will thereby defend themselves. Otherwise such an event would not merit the faith which the New Testament asserts is dependent upon it. Barth is therefore in error in recommending such a procedure as being essential.

This last criticism of Barth's method is in addition to the other major problems which have been pointed out in chapters 7 and 8 with regards to both Kierkegaard's and Barth's position (and also concerning those scholars who follow them). Briefly, there were three major criticisms directed against Kierkegaard. First, even Kierkegaard himself is not successful in building a theological system that is not first built on some reasonable

1. See Blaikie, *op. cit.*, pp. 122–36 and Montgomery's *History and Christianity, op. cit.*, pp. 87–89 and *Where Is History Going?, op. cit.*, pp. 115–16.

2. Barth makes this claim, for instance, in his *Church Dogmatics, op. cit.*, vol. 4, part 1, pp. 335–36.

foundation. For instance, his polemic for faith and subjectivity is some-what rational, as he makes use of both logic and reason. Even his convic-tions were shown to be rationally-based. In fact, his entire system could not be formulated apart from reason. Thus it is shown to be impossible to have faith apart from some sort of rational basis. Second, since faith is construed as being temporally first and reason is given no real place by this scholar, it is not possible to know if such faith is valid. Since there would be no objective criteria by which to examine the Christian faith, we cannot know if it is correct in its beliefs or not. Faith must therefore be testable in order to determine if it is valid. Otherwise one never ascertains whether he was right in this faith and whether his belief was trustworthy and factual, or if it was simply spurious.[3]

From the first two criticisms of Kierkegaard it becomes apparent that (1) reason is temporally first and (2) faith needs an objective foundation so that it can be verified. A third criticism of Kierkegaard naturally fol-lows from these first two. Since some reasonable verification is there-fore needed upon which faith can be built, a historical examination of the claims of Christianity is the most likely procedure. At any rate, such a reasonable method could not be opposed since just such an objective basis is needed.[4]

From this treatment of Kierkegaard, some of the weaknesses of this proposed approach to the resurrection can be more clearly seen. There is definitely a need for a more objective approach to this event.

In addition to the one given above, four major criticisms were also presented concerning Barth's modification of this method.[5] Briefly, the first criticism concerns Barth's development of the idea that Jesus' res-urrection occurred in prehistory or parahistory. It involves a twofold critique. History knows of no such concept where events can occur on the boundary or outskirts of history. This realm cannot be measured by historical methods and is thus invalid. Additionally, Barth allows no verification for events in prehistory, but still insists that they are actually

---

3. For the reasoning for these first two criticisms, see chapter 4 above.

4. The logical steps for these three criticisms of Kierkegaard cannot be completely ascertained from this brief summary. See chapter 7 for an indepth study of this critique.

5. These four criticisms of Barth were later altered in chapter 8 so that they also applied to the scholars who followed him.

historical. However, actual history can be examined and investigated. If the resurrection occurred in history it must be open to such investigation or it cannot be referred to as objective history. Second, like Kierkegaard, Barth's method allows no means whereby the Christian faith can be examined. Thus, once again, it cannot be determined if this faith is valid or not. To remove Christianity from any investigation is to make it so subjective that no one could actually ascertain its trustworthiness. One could not be sure whether one's belief was factual.

Third, Barth accepts the death of Jesus as an event which occurred in real history in the modern sense of the word, while the resurrection is relegated to prehistory. Yet both events are believed to be revelatory. Barth is therefore illogical to declare that God does not reveal Himself in objective, verifiable events. Since He did so at the cross, He could also do so with the resurrection. Thus the resurrection could also logically be history in the modern verifiable, objective sense. The fourth criticism of Barth is that he has clearly been shown to be wrong in his belief that the New Testament does not ever try to demonstrate the resurrection. To the contrary, such a procedure occurs several times.[6] Thus he cannot claim Scriptural backing for his method.[7]

For the reasons stated here, this second possible solution to the resurrection also fails to account properly for the facts which are known to be true. Admittedly, it is laden with fewer problems that the first method discussed in the last chapter. For instance, this solution is not required to offer any naturalistic alternative views concerning the resurrection. But the approach taken by Kierkegaard, Barth, and others cannot adequately deal with all of the criticisms raised here and must therefore be rejected as an incorrect treatment of Jesus' resurrection.

As concluded in chapters 7 and 8, Kierkegaard and Barth both agree that faith in Christ is the most important element of Christianity. The same was also found to be true in this study in chapter 4 above, with faith as the more crucial element being built upon a reasonable look at the

---

6. For example, see 1 Corinthians 15:4–8, especially verse 6; Luke 24:36–43; John 20:24–28; Acts 1:3; 10:40–41. Christian doctrines are also said to be true because of the resurrection (see Acts 17:30–31; Romans 1:4).

7. As with Kierkegaard, the reasons for these four criticisms cannot be fully gleaned from this brief survey. See especially chapter 8 for the rationale here.

facts. Therefore, their conception of faith can remain valid even though the methodology by which they reach this conclusion is faulty. This is because the same conclusion, namely the importance of faith, can also be reached objectively.[8]

For both Kierkegaard and Barth, the center of Christianity is salvation by faith and commitment to Jesus as the Christ. Salvation is achieved when an individual is convicted that he is a sinner and experiences a complete change in his life by repentance. This spiritual experience consists of the individual trusting the death of Christ on the cross as a substitutionary death to pay for his sins and surrendering his life to God in faith as a result. Both of these theologians also stress the subsequent commitment and the changed life which will result from a genuine conversion.[9]

Because of the aforementioned study of the reason-faith relationship, these conclusions concerning the primary importance of faith must therefore be accepted as valid. They faithfully represent the New Testament position on this subject and will be found to be even more trustworthy if the resurrection is found to be an actual historical event because a firm, objective grounding will then have been given to this concept of faith.

---

8. This was the result of the logical study of faith and reason in chapter 4.

9. For Kierkegaard's view, see especially *Attack Upon "Christendom," op. cit.*, pp. 149, 210, 213, 280, 287; cf. Heinecken's "Søren Kierkegaard," in Marty and Peerman, *op. cit.*, pp. 131, 133, 134. For Barth's view, see in particular his *Church Dogmatics, op. cit.*, vol. 4, part 1, pp. 248–54.

CHAPTER XIII

An Evaluation of
Possibility Number Three

T he third possible solution to the resurrection of Jesus was investigated
in chapters 9 and 10, a solution which postulated that the resurrection
actually occurred and that it can be demonstrated to be a historical event. It
was determined in chapter 9 that Wolfhart Pannenberg is probably the best
known representative of this viewpoint. Several other scholars likewise hold
this view without following Pannenberg in these conclusions. In chapter 10
the views of three other key scholars who also believe that the resurrection
can be demonstrated to have occurred in history were also enumerated.

Generally speaking, each of these four scholars holds that history must
be investigated in order to ascertain if the resurrection occurred. All agree
that one must not be prejudiced concerning what is possible or impossible
in such an investigation. The only way to ascertain if a Supernatural event
such as the resurrection has actually occurred is to examine the facts and
then decide which conclusion best fits these facts. This conclusion is to be
accepted as the most probable one and is thus to be viewed as a historical
fact, even if it is a miracle.

After an examination of the available evidence, each of these four scholars arrives at the conclusion that the resurrection is the event that best
explains what happened. The method varies a little between each of these
men, but the primary result is the same. The facts are best explained by

the resurrection and as this is the most probable solution, it is regarded as historical fact.[1]

In spite of the logical approach taken by these scholars, some difficulties were detected in their work. This was especially true of Pannenberg's thesis. First, his concept of God was discovered to be quite arbitrary, lacking a sufficient amount of demonstration. Contrary to Pannenberg's belief, Jesus does not speak exclusively of God's working from the future. To hold such a position one must already have *assumed* that God works in this way in order to interpret all verses in light of this idea. This would be especially difficult with the verses which were shown to teach the opposite view. Second, in spite of Pannenberg's conception of the indirect Self-revelation of God, it was shown that the Jews also viewed revelation as occurring directly through both the spoken word of the prophets and the written word of Scripture. Thus it cannot be held that the indirect revelation of God in history was the *only* means of revelation accepted by the Jews.

Third, it was found that Pannenberg's overall system lacks proof at several crucial points. It is especially in the formulation of his seven theses that there is a decided lack of evidence for his views. This proclivity is perhaps best evidenced by the connection of both revelation and the fate of Jesus with the end of history. Several problems which arise as a result of these formulations were pointed out above. In fact, Pannenberg's theological framework as a whole, although interesting, sometimes lacks the demonstration needed to establish it beyond the realm of philosophical speculation. Fourth, Pannenberg's treatment of the resurrection fails in two respects. First, he firmly accepts this occurrence as a historical event, but rejects any strongly objective appearances of Jesus even when the evidence indicates otherwise. But it was shown that such conclusions are unwarranted and that the witness of the New Testament is to the contrary.

---

1. Ladd's conception of the resurrection occurring in history does differ somewhat from the others, and this has already been considered above. All four scholars agree that this event is the best explanation of the historical facts and thus they also agree in accepting it as the most probable conclusion.

Nevertheless, this scholar does indeed believe that Jesus actually did rise from the dead and appear to his disciples.

The second part of this fourth criticism concerns Pannenberg's treatment of the naturalistic theories which have been composed in opposition to the resurrection. With the exception of the subjective vision theory, his critique of these alternate theories is not as strong as it could have been. Yet it is imperative that these naturalistic views be refuted as conclusively as possible. Since the resurrection is the central element in the Christian faith, it is essential to ascertain if this event actually occurred. Therefore, a complete refutation of the naturalistic hypotheses would allow a more accurate decision on the probability of the resurrection. Also, the more thorough the refutation of these alternate views is, the easier it is both to conclude that there are no views which are more probable than Jesus' resurrection as a historical event and the more probable the resurrection is shown to be.

It was likewise found that Daniel Fuller, Ladd, and Maier also fell prey to this last criticism. Like Pannenberg, these three scholars were also successful in refuting the major alternative theories. But also like Pannenberg, seldom was a complete refutation given. Once again, a more thorough and entire negation of the rival views on the part of all four scholars would reveal even more positively if there were any probable solutions other than the literal resurrection of Jesus. The more complete this investigation and refutation is, the easier it is to verify that the resurrection is the most probable answer and the more probable this event itself becomes. Since all four scholars endeavor to establish the probability of this event, the object should of course be to do so as accurately and thoroughly as possible.[2]

In addition to this one common criticism made of all four of these scholars concerning their incomplete treatments of the alternate theories, other more individual criticisms were pointed out above. But in all cases, these critiques did not annul the defense of the resurrection which was presented by each of the four. In fact, it is quite difficult to annul these approaches when it is realized that to successfully abrogate them,

---

2. The significance of this criticism against all four of these scholars will be more fully explained in the last chapter.

one would have to propose a more probable naturalistic solution to the resurrection.[3]

Significantly, it was not only negative evidence (such as that which was presented against the alternate theories) which was ascertained to favor the resurrection as an actual even in history. It was also shown that there were positive facts and pointers which also indicate that this is the most probable explanation of the facts. For example, Daniel Fuller points to the conversion of Paul and the existence of the Gentile mission. Maier presented historical evidence of various types to corroborate his position.

It is for these reasons that the third possible approach to the resurrection, which proposes that this event actually occurred and that it can be demonstrated, presents itself as the best solution to the question of Jesus' resurrection. As will now be shown, the conclusion which best fits the facts is that the literal resurrection of Jesus from the dead can be demonstrated to have occurred as a historical event. The following discussion in the last chapter is not dependent upon the work of these four scholars discussed here, but still arrives at a similar conclusion.

---

3. See, for example, Pannenberg, *Revelation as History*, *op. cit.*, p. 147 and Maier, *First Easter*, *op. cit.*, p. 120.

CHAPTER XIV

A Concluding Demonstration

I t has been ascertained that the literal resurrection of Jesus from the dead is the historical event which best accounts for the known facts surrounding this occurrence. The objective in this chapter is to present one final demonstration by this writer that this event is the most probable. As explained earlier in this work, the word "demonstration" is used here not in the sense of "absolute proof," but rather as a reference to probabilities. Thus, it is asserted that the factual evidence is strong enough to warrant the conviction that the resurrection is the most probable conclusion for what occurred.

A. THE HISTORICAL METHOD

Modern historiography usually rules out the possibility of the miraculous *a priori*. According to this method, history is closed to the Supernatural workings of God in events such as miracles. In spite of the popularity of this procedure, it must be recognized that such a position is a historical presupposition.

This modern concept of history emerged from the intellectual environment beginning in the Enlightenment and continued on to nineteenth-century historical positivism. Miracles such as the resurrection were ruled out from the outset, often because of a supposed conflict with the concept of history. The result was an *a priori* rejection of all Supernatural intervention into history.[1]

---

1. See Montgomery, *History and Christianity, op. cit.*, pp. 88–89 and *Where Is History Going?, op. cit.*, pp. 115–16; Blaikie, *op. cit.*, p. 135; Daniel Fuller, *op. cit.*, p. 188; Ladd, *op. cit.*, pp. 12–13; Maier, "The Empty Tomb as History," *op. cit.*, p. 5.

One might wonder how historical this approach really is in actuality. In the case of a miracle-claim, the prevailing technique is to dismiss the possibility of it even before any investigation of the facts.

However, such was found to be an incorrect procedure in chapters 2 and 3 above. Science cannot rule out the miraculous *a priori* because the universe is no longer conceived of in terms of a closed system in which all events happen by means of a prescribed regularity. Science therefore cannot know beforehand that such miracles cannot occur. There can thus be no rejection of miracles such as the resurrection simply by referring to a modern world in which such Supernatural events do not occur.

In fact, modern science is quite limited as to what it can say about the resurrection. The scientific method is obviously concerned with measurable quantities. Concepts such as peace, freedom, or love cannot, of course, be measured in a test tube. Neither can a Geiger counter be used to verify the existence of Julius Caesar. In other words, empirical science has no instruments or other means whereby past history can be investigated. In addition, history is nonrepeatable, which is also required in order for science to make a proper judgment. Therefore, all that can be ascertained via empirical science is that the resurrection cannot be negated because of the scientific worldview. Rather, an impartial historical investigation of the facts is needed to see if this event actually occurred.

This is where the science of history emerges as the more proper method to be used in this instance. As with science, it was also shown that neither can history employ the scientific worldview to rule out miracles *a priori*. We are thus faced once again with the need *to historically investigate all of the facts to find the most probable solution.* Modern historiography cannot negate the resurrection as a historical event without such an examination. It is clearly impossible (as shown in chapters 2 and 3) to properly dismiss such a miracle-claim beforehand.

In this work, the historical method which is employed is therefore one which investigates the facts first before a decision is made as to what can or did occur. The status of probability is given to the event which is the *best explanation* for the known facts. Such an inductive approach is actually more scientific in its endeavor to base the final conclusion upon a thorough historical investigation of what is known to have occurred.

B. THE HISTORICAL FACTS

Throughout this work, many references have been made to the known historical facts and how the resurrection is the best explanation for these events. What are these facts? What are the events and circumstances which are known to have happened in conjunction with the belief that Jesus rose from the dead?

Surrounding the resurrection event are many facts which are usually recognized as being historical by most scholars who deal with this subject. It is known that Jesus actually died[2] and that he was buried. Also historical is the fact that, after the death of their Master, the disciples were extremely depressed and disillusioned. For them, Jesus' ministry had been ended prematurely by the Roman cross. It is unanimously agreed that they were thus quite discouraged and downcast. Afterward, as confounding as it was, the tomb in which Jesus was laid was later found to be empty.[3]

Very soon afterward, history relates that the disciples had several experiences which they believed were appearances of the risen Jesus. After these experiences there was a drastic change in their disposition—a transformation which made them bold preachers even in the very city where Jesus was crucified and buried. The result of this preaching was the birth of the Christian church, which began to meet on Sunday rather than on the Jewish Sabbath (Saturday). Lastly, it is an unquestionable historical fact that one of the most avid persecutors of the Christian church, Saul of Tarsus, was converted to Christianity by what he also believed was an appearance of the risen Jesus.[4]

From this summary, a *minimum* of ten historical facts can be gleaned which are held as being historical by the majority of theologians today: (1) Jesus actually died on the cross and (2) was buried in a tomb. (3) The disciples were extremely disillusioned and disconcerted by the death of Jesus, being bereft of all hope. (4) The same tomb in which Jesus was buried was found empty just a few days later, probably with the graveclothes still inside. (5) The disciples were the recipients of several experiences which

---

2. There are very few (if any) reputable theologians today who doubt that Jesus actually died on the cross.

3. Ladd adds here the historicity of the account of the graveclothes being found in the empty tomb (*op. cit.*, p. 94), since the description of them bears the marks of eyewitness testimony.

4. For similar lists, see Ladd, *Ibid.*, pp. 13, 91–94, 132–33.

they believed were resurrection appearances of Jesus. (6) Afterward, the disciples experienced a complete transformation, being willing to die for their new faith. (7) The resultant preaching often took place in Jerusalem, the exact place where Jesus was killed and buried. (8) This preaching led to the birth of the church, (9) featuring Sunday as the most important day of worship, instead of Saturday. (10) Later, Paul was converted to Christianity by means of an experience which he also believed was an appearance of the risen Jesus.

These, then, are the historical facts which must be dealt with and explained. The Gospels and New Testament as a whole agree with all ten of these either explicitly or implicitly. None of them is denied in any of the writings of the New Testament. In addition, as we have seen at various points in this work, the majority of theologians accept these as historical facts as well. It is therefore evident that the explanation which is given to the resurrection must also account for these events. The answer that is postulated in these early writings is that Jesus literally rose from the dead. Any alternate explanation must explain all of these facts adequately and still cross the hardest hurdle by proposing a probable naturalistic theory for the appearances to the disciples. Thus, one who would deny the resurrection must both adequately explain all of these facts *and* offer a *probable* alternate view to the appearances. But as we have seen, no such probable alternative views exist, as even the more popular naturalistic theories fail to properly account for the facts which occurred.[5]

The enumerating of these facts also makes it evident that there are *positive* historical facts which support a belief in the resurrection as well. This event therefore does not only depend upon what Ladd refers to as "anti-criticism,"[6] or the dismissal of all naturalistic theories which have been formulated against the resurrection. In other words, it is not only the evidence from the elimination of all alternate theories which makes the resurrection plausible, but there are actual "positive" facts which also demonstrate that this event is the most probable.

There are at least seven strong facts which indicate that Jesus actually rose from the dead. The first and by far the strongest fact is the positive

---

5. We will return to a final evaluation of these alternate theories later.

6. Ladd, *op. cit.*, pp. 27, 140–41, in reference to Helmut Thielicke's name for this evidence.

New Testament claim that the disciples did indeed see the risen Jesus. There is not only the eyewitness testimony of Paul to this fact, but the gospels are at least close to and include the eyewitness testimony of the disciples (see Luke 1:1–4 as an example), as discussed above. Paul also records the extremely important fact that the original disciples were also preaching about the appearances of the risen Jesus to them (1 Cor 15:11–15).

The power of this New Testament testimony is twofold. First, no alternative theory is sufficient enough to explain these appearances and the subsequent conviction of their reality. But it is not only the rejection of these theories that makes this claim so important. Second, the known facts surrounding this event tend to corroborate it and make the claim highly credible. For instance, the disciples came to believe firmly in the resurrection despite their overwhelming disillusionment and disbelief. Thus, *they came to believe in spite of themselves.* Other facts are also left unexplained apart from the literal resurrection of Jesus.

Other events in addition to the actual appearances are also positive evidence for Jesus' resurrection. Second, the incredible change in the lives of the disciples from dejected men who fled at the arrest of Jesus to bold preachers who asserted the teachings of the life, death, and resurrection of Jesus even in the face of their own death indicates unequivocally that these men firmly *believed* that Jesus had risen. Such elation is usually not the action of men who have been deceived by any kind of falsehood, either. Such undoubting belief even to the point of dying for their faith is not the mark of men who had even the faintest misgivings about this event. The transformation of the disciples is best accounted for by actual appearances of the risen Jesus.

Third, the evidence of the empty tomb, while not in itself providing proof of the resurrection, is a positive point in favor of those who accept this event as historical. At the same time it requires a probable explanation by those who reject this event.[7] Even more in favor of the resurrection is the discovery of the graveclothes inside the tomb, still unraveled with the body simply missing.

---

7. As was shown earlier, even those who do not accept overly objective appearances of Jesus often accept the belief in the empty tomb. See Reginald Fuller, *op. cit.,* pp. 48–49, 69–70, 179–80 and Pannenberg, *Jesus—God and Man, op. cit.,* pp. 100–104.

The attitude of the Jewish leaders in the book of Acts reveals a fourth set of historical circumstances strongly in favor of Jesus' literal resurrection. When the disciples were confronted by the Jewish elders on various occasions in the early chapters of this book (see especially Acts 4–5), these followers of Jesus were not charged with spreading false tales about Jesus' resurrection. Neither did the Jews go to Jesus' tomb, reveal his body, and thus crush the central belief of Christianity.[8]

Fifth, the very birth of the Christian church depends upon the message of Jesus' resurrection. This event forms the very center of Christianity and of the earliest Christian message. According to the earliest testimony, there would have been no church today apart from this event.[9]

A sixth fact pointing to the resurrection is the commemorating of this event in the Christian worship on Sunday instead of Saturday, the Jewish Sabbath. The first day of the week was referred to as "the Lord's day" because Jesus was believed to have risen on a Sunday (see Rev 1:10; cf. John 20:19, 26). Early Jewish Christians apparently still gathered at the local synagogue for worship on Saturday, but for the Christian believer, Sunday was the day for such important practices as partaking of the Lord's supper (Acts 20:7) and the gathering of one's offering (1 Cor 16:2). Soon Sunday became the day of pre-eminence for the Christians. But something must account for this day of worship since it was not the usual day. The New Testament witnesses that the change was due to Jesus' resurrection.

A seventh historical fact which makes the resurrection even more probable is the conversion of Paul. This enemy of the Christian church was suddenly converted to the faith which he had so avidly opposed. As Daniel Fuller shows, other naturalistic views which would account for this conversion are not convincing and must be rejected. Paul claimed his turnabout was due to an appearance of the risen Jesus and it is this view which still fits the facts best.[10]

These seven facts are therefore "positive" evidence for the resurrection of Jesus in addition to the "negative" evidence supplied by a refutation of

---

8. When speaking with an "agnostic" on the subject of Jesus' resurrection a few years ago, this writer was told that the stance taken by the Jewish leaders in the book of Acts was the strongest demonstration of the reality of this event.

9. See Acts 1:21, 22; 2:24, 32; 3:15, 26; 4:10; 5:30, etc.

10. Daniel Fuller, *op. cit.*, pp. 242–50.

the alternative views.[11] The appearances of the risen Jesus to his followers, the complete change in the disciples, the empty tomb, the attitude
of the Jewish leaders in Acts, the existence of the church, the Christian
worship day of Sunday, and Paul's conversion are strong facts in favor of
the resurrection. Earlier, other historical evidence was also given, such
as Daniel Fuller's thesis about the existence of the Gentile mission being
dependent on the resurrection[12] and Paul Maier's presentation of both
specific and circumstantial historical evidence for this event.[13]

However, contemporary theology has provided additional evidence for
the resurrection which reinforces each of these other points of evidence.
As explained in chapter 1, the application of form criticism to the gospel
records was thought to be helpful in ascertaining what the earliest church
believed about Jesus. One of the main expectations was to uncover how
the miraculous element was due to later additions and was not actually a
part of the life of Jesus. But such was not to be the case.

Contrary to what may have been expected if the origin of everything
miraculous in the New Testament was the faith of the early church rather
than a real part of Jesus' life, scholars cannot reach a form critical layer of
tradition in which the resurrection belief is not present. In other words,
form criticism has demonstrated that the resurrection belief is in the
earliest strata of Christian belief. As Carl Braaten explains these results:

> The form-critical study of the earliest Christian traditions has
> established beyond reasonable doubt that faith in the risen Christ
> is the point of departure and the essential content of the kerygma.
> Without the Easter faith there would have been no Christian
> church and the New Testament would not have been written. The
> belief that God raised Jesus from the dead on the third day is as
> old as the Christian faith and is now, as ever before, the article by
> which the church stands or falls ... it may be refreshing to know
> that even the more skeptical historians agree that for primitive

---

11. "Positive" evidence is a reference to events which point directly to the resurrection, while
"negative" evidence is that which is received from refuting the naturalistic theories. Of course, *both*
are positive as far as the reality of the resurrection is concerned.

12. Daniel Fuller, *op. cit.*, pp. 188–261.

13. Maier, *First Easter, op. cit.*, pp. 114–22 and "The Empty Tomb as History," *op. cit.*, pp. 4–6.

Christianity ... the resurrection of Jesus from the dead was a real event in history, the very foundation of faith, and not a mythical idea arising out of the creative imagination of believers.[14]

Other scholars likewise concur with Braaten in this view. Reginald Fuller agrees that there was no time in which the resurrection was not the center of Christian preaching.[15] Ramm asserts that the most important purpose served by form criticism has been to show that the miracles, and the resurrection in particular, have been embedded in Christian belief from the very beginning.[16] Wand notes that the further back that the texts are studied, the more clear it becomes that the risen Christ is the same as the Jesus of history.[17]

Thus form criticism only served to strengthen the belief that the resurrection is the historical basis of the Christian faith. It likewise confirmed the fact that this event occupied this very important position in theology since the very beginnings of Christianity.

In enumerating these historical facts surrounding the resurrection, it becomes apparent that this event is the best explanation for what has occurred. However, there is not only the evidence of these facts, but there is also the evidence from the refuted naturalistic theories. In addition, it was also found that there are at least seven major historical facts in favor of the resurrection besides those listed by such scholars as Maier and Daniel Fuller. These considerations therefore show that the literal resurrection of Jesus is the most probable conclusion to this historical question, especially when it is recognized that no alternate theories or other facts militate against this event.

C. THE THEOLOGICAL METHOD

It becomes especially apparent from the material presented in this chapter (as well as in the rest of this work) that the pivotal point in this discussion is the experiences of the earliest followers of Jesus. All admit that

---

14. Carl Braaten, *History and Hermeneutics*, vol. 2 of *New Directions in Theology Today*, edited by William Hordern, 7 vols. (Philadelphia: The Westminster Press, 1966) p. 78.

15. Reginald Fuller, *op. cit.*, p. 48.

16. Ramm, *Protestant Christian Evidences, op. cit.*, p. 194.

17. Wand, *op. cit.*, p. 122.

these witnesses really *believed* that Jesus actually rose from the dead.[18] But
the focal point here concerns whether these experiences were actually
appearances of the risen Jesus.

Naturalistic theories of these experiences have been proposed ever
since the earliest proclamation of these beliefs. Of the several alternative
views which were refuted here, there were three major hypotheses. These
were the swoon theory popularized by Heinrich Paulus, the subjective
vision theory formulated by David Strauss, and the legend or myth theory
taught by Otto Pfleiderer and others.[19]

It has been a very important emphasis in this work to provide a
detailed and complete refutation of each of the naturalistic theories, especially these three major ones. Although it may be thought that the tendency
was to overkill each of the theories by presenting more evidence than was
necessary to dispose of them, it must be strenuously objected that such
was the exact intention of this writer, and for good reason. The need for
a complete refutation of the alternative theories is too often overlooked
in the works of those who also opt for the belief that the resurrection can
be demonstrated. It is apparently not realized that *the more thorough such
a refutation is, the more probable the resurrection becomes.*

The reason for this assertion is acute. There are several very important facts which point to the facticity of the resurrection, the main one
being the appearances to the disciples. As long as a key alternate theory
remains unrefuted (in whole or in part), these facts which point to the
resurrection cannot be accorded the full impact which they warrant. But
the more the alternate theories are refuted, the more outstanding the
facts favoring the disciples' claims become, thus leaving the resurrection
as still even more probable. Then it follows that the more completely
such naturalistic theories are rejected, the higher the probability for the
resurrection becomes as the facts which demonstrate the reality of this
event are thereby shown to be valid. This is especially so when no other

---

18. Even critical theology accepts this belief on the part of the disciples. For instance, see
Bultmann, "New Testament and Mythology," in *Kerygma and Myth, op. cit.,* p. 42.

19. Other naturalistic theories refuted here in addition to these three include the objective vision
theory (including the telegram theory), the hypothesis of the continuing spiritual presence of Jesus'
personality in his disciples' minds, and the fraud theory (including the stolen body hypothesis). See
especially chapter 6 for these refutations.

alternate theories are shown to be probable. Therefore we perceive the importance of complete refutations of these other views.

In examining the approaches of Pannenberg, Daniel Fuller, Ladd, and Maier, it was found that each was not complete in his refutation of alternate views (to varying degrees). This is true in two different respects. First, many of the main reasons for rejecting each of the major theories were not presented. In other words, seldom was a theory rejected as thoroughly or strongly as it might have been.

Second, each of these scholars neglected completely (or almost so) one or more of the three major theories. In Pannenberg's section dealing with a defense of the resurrection against the alternate theories in his volume *Jesus—God and Man*, the swoon theory is neglected.[20] Fuller's treatise omits any specific refutation of Strauss' vision theory or of the legend or myth theory, although both are cited as alternate hypotheses. Also, the swoon theory is quickly passed over with very little disproof.[21] Ladd also ignores the legend or myth theory in his treatment of the naturalistic theories,[22] as does Maier.[23] Although it has been ascertained that these scholars were generally successful in their overall treatments of the resurrection, one cannot help but think that since it was their desire to demonstrate the probability of the resurrection, a more complete refutation would have been desirable.

Since a more adequate refutation of the alternate theories makes the resurrection more probable, the treatment of the three major theories and several lesser ones in this work has endeavored to be complete. In fact, the desire was specifically to present more evidence than was necessary in order to dismiss each one. The New Testament states that Jesus rose from the dead and demonstrated this by appearing to his followers. Other facts also corroborate this event. With these naturalistic theories thus shown to be quite inadequate to properly explain what occurred, the facts for the resurrection are shown to be highly probable. If one believes that it is still difficult to accept such a Supernatural event, it is even more

---

20. Pannenberg, *Jesus—God and Man*, op. cit., pp. 88–106.

21. Daniel Fuller, *op. cit.*, see pp. 38–39, 45–49, 67–68 for examples of this.

22. Ladd, *op. cit.*, pp. 132–42.

23. Maier, *First Easter*, op. cit., pp. 105–13.

difficult to formulate an alternative view which logically, historically, and theologically accounts for the known facts. The resurrection is the highly probable historical fact which best accounts for what occurred.

D. CONVINCED BY THE FACTS

One interesting point with regard to the facts of the resurrection is that, after an examination of the evidence, many scholars who had once rejected this event came to believe that it could be demonstrated to have occurred. They were convinced by the weight of the facts that this event was historical. This is not to say that no one who had been taught that the resurrection occurred has ever rejected such information later. But this writer knows of no instance where the resurrection was rejected *after an examination of the facts*, as was the case with these who accepted the reality of this event after just such an examination, against their former views.

Frank Morison, a lawyer, is surely one of the best examples of a scholar who became convinced against his earlier convictions after studying the evidence for the resurrection. As a young man, Morison began a serious study of the life of Jesus, being much influenced by the works of German liberal scholarship. He did not accept the miracles in Jesus' life and was determined to remove what he felt were mythical outgrowths.

Ten years after his first studies he received the opportunity to study the life of Jesus in depth. An examination of the last week of Jesus' life in particular brought him to a study of the resurrection. However, in endeavoring to write a book exposing these myths which he thought he would find, he was compelled by the factual evidence to write quite a different book in favor of the resurrection. This work, entitled *Who Moved the Stone?*, became a defense of the resurrection against the theological views formerly held by Morison himself. He explains that it was because of his investigation of the facts that he reversed his former views and that caused him to realize not only that the resurrection occurred, but that it could be demonstrated.[24]

---

24. See Morison's book *Who Moved the Stone?*, *op. cit.*, especially the Preface and pp. 9–12; cf. pp. 88–102 for instance. The first chapter appropriately tells of the original book that could not be written against the resurrection and life of Jesus because of the facts.

The late Simon Greenleaf, past Harvard professor of law and one of the greatest legal minds that America has ever produced, was a religious skeptic. Challenged by his students to apply the techniques of his legal masterpiece *A Treatise on the Law of Evidence* to the resurrection of Jesus, Greenleaf became a believer. He later wrote a book, the long title of which is *An Examination of the Testimony of the Four Evangelists by the Rules of Evidence Administered in the Courts of Justice.*[25] In this work he defends the resurrection and explains how, when judged by the laws of legal evidence, this event can be demonstrated to have actually occurred.[26]

Another scholar who was convinced by an examination of the evidence is medical doctor Viggo Olsen. He described himself as an agnostic who did not believe in the Supernatural elements of Christianity. But more than this, he constantly questioned the Christian faith and attempted to disprove it. Through the process of trying to expose these beliefs, he studied the resurrection and other evidences. Later he became convinced that God did exist and that there was more than a sufficient amount of demonstration for the resurrection. He realized that this event actually occurred and that as such it was the center of the Christian faith. It is noteworthy that Simon Greenleaf's book on the Christian evidences was a key influence on Olsen.[27]

Other scholars who have looked impartially at the facts have often likewise concluded that the evidence for the resurrection establishes it as a historical event. For instance, such was the conclusion of lawyer Sir Edward Clarke, KC, who also investigated the resurrection in terms of the evidential aspect. He remarked that this factual support was conclusive, as he had often secured a positive verdict in courts of law with less evidence.[28] McDowell lists numerous other instances where other scholars came to similar conclusions after an impartial examination of the facts.[29]

---

25. This work was reprinted in 1965 (Grand Rapids: Baker Book House).

26. See Josh McDowell, *Evidence that Demands A Verdict* (San Bernardino: Published by Campus Crusade for Christ International), especially pp. 199–200. See also the tape by McDowell distributed by this same organization, entitled "Resurrection: Fact or Fallacy?"

27. Viggo Olsen, *The Agnostic Who Dared to Search* (Chicago: Moody Press, 1974). For Olsen's discussion of the resurrection, see pp. 36–37, 39, 46–47 of this booklet.

28. Stott records a letter written by Clarke with the above affirmations. See John R. W. Stott, *Basic Christianity* (Chicago: InterVarsity Press, 1965), p. 46.

29. McDowell, *op. cit.*, pp. 196–202.

When speaking of such examples, the New Testament instances of similar results should not be ignored. It is known, for instance, that Jesus' brother James was almost assuredly not a believer before the resurrection (John 7:5; cf. Mark 3:21, 31–34). But after an appearance from Jesus he became a Christian and the leader of the Jerusalem church (1 Cor 15:7; cf. Gal 2:1–10). The example of Paul changing from a persecutor of the church (Acts 7:57–59; 9:1–2) to an ardent follower of Christ has already been mentioned above (see 1 Cor 15:8–9). Again it was an appearance of the risen Jesus that caused this change of heart. It is the opinion of contemporary theological scholarship that both of these men became Christians in spite of their former beliefs because of an appearance of the risen Lord.[30]

This brief presentation has shown that many have accepted the resurrection as a historical event after a careful investigation of the data, even when formerly opposed to this belief. Also extremely interesting is the stance taken by two "God-is-dead" or secular theologians, William Hamilton and John A. T. Robinson. In spite of the secular theological positions of these two men, they also recognize the strong evidence for the resurrection.

For Hamilton, the resurrection and empty tomb are highly probable. In fact, he believes that the resurrection may be affirmed as a regular historical event.[31] Robinson admits that the empty tomb is very difficult to dismiss because of the good evidence for this event.[32]

This survey of several scholars was presented in order to show how strong the evidence for the resurrection is for the one who looks impartially at the facts. Several scholars who were once opposed to this belief were convinced otherwise after an investigation of the evidence, as were others who studied the data in favor of this event. The New Testament also records two examples of men who were convinced by resurrection appearances of Jesus against their former views. Even two secular theologians were able to grant a high credibility to the resurrection, as one

---

30. See Reginald Fuller, *op. cit.*, pp. 37, 177–78; Raymond Brown, *The Virginal Conception and Bodily Resurrection of Jesus*, *op. cit.*, p. 94, footnote number 160, and p. 95; Ladd, *op. cit.*, pp. 104–6 for a few examples of this belief.

31. William Hamilton, *The New Essence of Christianity* (New York: Association Press, 1961), p. 116, note.

32. John A. T. Robinson, *Exploration Into God* (Stanford: Stanford University Press, 1967), p. 113.

accepted it as a historical event while the other admitted that it would be hard to reject the strong evidence in favor of it.

Such is the convincing evidence for the resurrection of Jesus Christ. As church historian Wand reminds us about this event,

> All the strictly historical evidence we have is in favor of it, and those scholars who reject it ought to recognize that they do so on some other ground than that of scientific history.[33]

This serves as a good reminder about our earlier conclusion to accept the answer to the question of the resurrection which best fits the facts. Wand notes that if naturalistic theories are unable to account for an event which claims that a miracle has taken place, then a Supernatural alternative must not be viewed as impossible. It is unscientific to begin with the presupposition that miraculous events cannot occur. Rather, a critical historian can only examine the facts involved in the situation before him and decide on the basis of this evidence. If the probable event is a Supernatural one, then it must be accepted as such, as with the resurrection. Modern science and history cannot refute this event, as we have seen.[34]

Therefore, in accordance with this historical principle, the literal resurrection of Jesus Christ from the dead must be accepted as an actual historical event according to its high degree of plausibility. Once again, those who find it difficult to accept this conclusion will have an even more difficult time endeavoring to formulate an alternative theory which is historically probable. It is not only possible to completely refute all of the naturalistic alternate theories which oppose a literal resurrection, as shown above, but there are several important facts in favor of this event. The most important of these facts is that, in all probability, Jesus appeared empirically to his followers after his death on the cross and no other thesis apart from the literal resurrection is capable of properly explaining these appearances. The resurrection of Jesus is thereby highly probable.

---

33. Wand, *op. cit.*, pp. 93–94.
34. *Ibid.*, pp. 30, 51–52, 70–71, 101.

E. THE CENTER OF CHRISTIANITY

It must be concluded that the knowledge that Jesus' resurrection is a historical fact is one of ultimate importance to the Christian faith. As was shown in chapter 11, one cannot hold that Jesus is dead and that he never rose from the tomb and still hold that Jesus is alive today in any unique sense. Neither can one hold that such doctrines as Christology and subsequent beliefs concerning salvation can have the same validity if the one around whom such beliefs revolve is dead, not even being able to conquer death himself. If such were the case, there would thus be no reason to suspect that Christians will receive such blessings either. As Paul asserts, apart from the resurrection there is no Christian faith at all (1 Cor 15:12–19). For this reason, the reality of the resurrection is absolutely essential for Christian faith.[35]

Therefore, the conclusion which asserts that Jesus actually rose from the dead is no meaningless assertion. It is not a matter of simply affirming the resurrection. To the contrary, it is very important to accept this event as historical, for in so doing the remainder of the Christian faith is demonstrated to be valid.

This is also why it was asserted earlier that the concept of faith as defined by Kierkegaard and Barth could remain valid in spite of the critiques of these two theologians. Each of these scholars agrees with the New Testament in recognizing that every individual man is a sinner in need of repentance, or a total change in one's life. A total surrender to God in faith, trusting Jesus' substitutionary death on the cross to forgive these sins, is needed for salvation. The result is a total change in one's life, a total commitment based upon the death of Jesus. In these principles, Kierkegaard and Barth both follow the New Testament definition of salvation. Jesus claimed to have come to this world chiefly to die a substitutionary death in order to procure such salvation for those who commit their lives in faith to God through His Son (see Mark 10:45; John 1:12–13; 1 Cor 15:1–4).

---

35. Even secular theologian William Hamilton opposes the contemporary view which gives existential importance to the concept that Jesus is alive but denies that he literally rose from the dead. Hamilton also asserts that without the historical event of the resurrection, Christian faith loses all meaning (*op. cit.*, p. 116, note). Here he perceives the case quite well.

Such teachings are often ignored today as outmoded products of ancient superstitions. But in light of our conclusions concerning Jesus' resurrection, such tendencies to dismiss the New Testament teaching on salvation are unwarranted. Since the resurrection is accepted as a Supernatural event, as shown here, then Jesus' ministry to mankind was for a reason. It would be illogical to accept the Supernatural demonstration of Jesus' mission and then reject the message which is corroborated by it. As the resurrection event cannot be denied, neither can the resurrection message of the subsequent availability of this salvation.

Bibliography

SOURCES IN INTRODUCTION

Bauckham, Richard. *Jesus and the Eyewitnesses: The Gospels as Eyewitness Testimony*. Grand Rapids, MI: Eerdmans, 2006.

Brown, Raymond E. *An Introduction to New Testament Christology*. New York: Paulist, 1994.

Bultmann, Rudolf. *Jesus Christ and Mythology*. New York: Charles Scribner's Sons, 1958.

———. "New Testament and Mythology." In *Kerygma and Myth: A Theological Debate*, edited by Hans Werner Bartsch, translation revised by Reginald H. Fuller. New York: Harper & Row, 1961.

———. *Theology of the New Testament*. Vol. 1, translated by Kendrick Grobel. New York: Charles Scribner's Sons, 1951, 1955.

Craig, William Lane. *Assessing the New Testament Evidence for the Historicity of the Resurrection of Jesus*. Lewiston, NY: Edwin Mellen, 1989.

Crossan, John Dominic. "Appendix: Bodily-Resurrection Faith." In *The Resurrection of Jesus: John Dominic Crossan and N. T. Wright in Dialogue*, edited by Robert B. Stewart. Minneapolis: Fortress, 2006.

———. "Opening Statement." In *The Resurrection of Jesus: John Dominic Crossan and N. T. Wright in Dialogue*, edited by Robert B. Stewart. Minneapolis: Fortress, 2006.

Cullmann, Oscar. *The Earliest Christian Confessions*. Edited by Gary R. Habermas and Benjamin Charles Shaw. London: Lutterworth, 1949; repr., Eugene, OR: Wipf and Stock, 2018.

Davies, W. D. *Paul and Rabbinic Judaism: Some Rabbinic Elements in Pauline Theology*. 4th ed. Philadelphia: Fortress, 1980.

Dodd, C. H. *The Apostolic Preaching and Its Developments*. London: Hodder and Stoughton, 1936; repr., Grand Rapids, MI: Baker, 1980.

Dunn, James D. G. *Beginning from Jerusalem*. Vol. 2. Grand Rapids, MI: Eerdmans, 2009.

———. *Christianity in the Making*. 3 vols. Grand Rapids, MI: Eerdmans, 2003–2015.

———. "Remembering Jesus: How the Quest of Jesus Lost its Way." In *The Historical Jesus: Five Views*, edited by James K. Beilby and Paul R. Eddy. Downers Grove, IL: IVP Academic, 2009.

Ehrman, Bart D. *Did Jesus Exist? The Historical Argument for Jesus of Nazareth*. New York: Harper Collins, 2012.

———. *How Jesus Became God: The Exaltation of a Jewish Preacher from Galilee*. New York: Harper Collins, 2014.

———. *The New Testament: A Historical Introduction to the Early Christian Writings*. 2nd ed. Oxford: Oxford University Press, 2000.

Fuller, Reginald H. "The Resurrection Narratives in Recent Study." In *Critical History and Biblical Faith: New Testament Perspectives*, edited by Thomas J. Ryan. Villanova: Villanova University Press, 1979.

Gundry, Robert H. *Sōma in Biblical Theology: With Emphasis on Pauline Anthropology*. Grand Rapids, MI: Zondervan Academic, 1987.

Habermas, Gary R. *Dealing with Doubt*. Chicago: Moody, 1990.

———. "Experiences of the Risen Jesus: The Foundational Issue in the Early Proclamation of the Resurrection." *Dialog: A Journal of Theology* 45 (Fall 2006): 292.

———. *Forever Loved: A Personal Account of Grief and Resurrection*. Joplin, MO: College Press, 1997.

———. "Mapping the Recent Trend toward the Bodily Resurrection Appearances of Jesus in Light of Other Prominent Critical Positions." In *The Resurrection of Jesus: John Dominic Crossan and N. T. Wright in Dialogue*, edited by Robert B. Stewart. Minneapolis: Fortress, 2006.

———. "Resurrection Research from 1975 to the Present: What are Critical Scholars Saying?" *Journal for the Study of the Historical Jesus* 3 (2005): 135–53.

———. "The Late Twentieth-Century Resurgence of Naturalistic Responses to Jesus' Resurrection." *Trinity Journal* 22 (Fall 2001): 179–96.

——. "The Minimal Facts Approach to the Resurrection of Jesus: The Role of Methodology as a Crucial Component in Establishing Historicity." *Southeastern Theological Review* 3 (Summer 2012): 15–26.

——. "The Resurrection Appearances of Jesus." In *Defense of Miracles: A Comprehensive Case for God's Action in History,* edited by Gary R. Habermas and R. Douglas Geivett. Downers Grove, IL: InterVarsity Academic, 1997.

——. *The Resurrection of Jesus: An Apologetic.* Grand Rapids, MI: Baker, 1980.

——. *The Risen Jesus and Future Hope.* Lanham, MD: Rowman and Littlefield, 2003.

——. *The Thomas Factor: Using Your Doubts to Grow Closer to God.* Nashville: Broadman & Holman, 1999.

——. *Why is God Ignoring Me? What to Do When It Feels Like He's Giving You the Silent Treatment.* Carol Stream, IL: Tyndale, 2010.

——, and Michael R. Licona. *The Case for the Resurrection of Jesus.* Grand Rapids, MI: Kregel, 2004.

Holladay, Carl H. *Theios Aner in Hellenistic Judaism: A Critique of the Use of the Category in New Testament Christology.* Society of Biblical Literature Dissertation Series 40. Edited by Howard C. Kee and Douglas A. Knight. Missoula, MT: Scholars Press for The Society of Biblical Literature, 1977.

Hurtado, Larry W. *How on Earth Did Jesus Become a God?* Grand Rapids, MI: Eerdmans, 2005.

——. "New Testament Christology: A Critique of Bousset's Influence." *Theological Studies* 40 (1979): 306–17.

Johnson, Luke Timothy. *The Real Jesus: The Misguided Quest for the Historical Jesus and the Truth of the Traditional Gospels.* New York: HarperSanFrancisco, 1996.

Licona, Michael R. *The Resurrection of Jesus: A New Historiographical Approach.* Downers Grove, IL: IVP Academic, 2010.

Lüdemann, Gerd. *The Resurrection of Jesus: History, Experience, Theology.* Translated by John Bowden. Minneapolis: Fortress, 1994.

McGrew, Lydia. *Hidden in Plain View: Undesigned Coincidences in the Gospels and Acts.* Chillicothe, OH: DeWard, 2017.

Meier, John P. *A Marginal Jew: Rethinking the Historical Jesus.* New Haven, CT: Yale University Press, 1991–2016.

Neufeld, Vernon H. *The Earliest Christian Confessions*. Edited by Bruce M. Metzger. New Testament Tools and Studies. Grand Rapids, MI: Eerdmans, 1963.

Perrin, Norman. *Rediscovering the Teaching of Jesus*. New York: Harper & Row, 1967.

Robinson, James M. *A New Quest of the Historical Jesus*. Studies in Biblical Theology 25. London: SCM, 1959.

Sanders, E. P. *Jesus and Judaism*. Philadelphia: Fortress, 1985.

Schweitzer, Albert. *The Quest of the Historical Jesus: A Critical Study of Its Progress from Reimarus to Wrede*. Translated by W. Montgomery. 1906; repr., New York: Macmillan, 1968.

Shaw, Benjamin C. F. "Philosophy of History, Historical Jesus Studies, and Miracles: Three Roadblocks to Resurrection Research." PhD diss., Liberty University, 2020.

Stein, Robert H. *Gospels and Tradition: Studies on Redaction Criticism of the Synoptic Gospels*. Grand Rapids: Baker, 1991.

Ware, James. "The Resurrection of Jesus in the Pre-Pauline Formula of 1 Cor 15.3–5." *New Testament Studies* 60 (October 2014): 475–98.

Waterman, Mark M. W. *The Empty Tomb Tradition of Mark: Text, History, and Theological Struggles*. Los Angeles: Agathos, 2006.

Wenham, David. *Paul: Follower of Jesus or Founder of Christianity?* Grand Rapids, MI: Eerdmans, 1995.

Wilcox, Max. *The Semitisms in Acts*. Oxford: Oxford University Press, 1965.

Witherington, Ben, III. *The Jesus Quest: The Third Search for the Jew of Nazareth*. Downers Grove, IL: InterVarsity Press, 1995.

Wright, N. T. *Christian Origins and the Question of God*. 4 vols. Minneapolis: Fortress, 1992–2013.

———. *Jesus and the Victory of God*. Vol. 2 of Christian Origins and the Question of God. Minneapolis: Fortress, 1996.

———. "Jesus, Israel and the Cross." In *SBL 1985 Seminar Papers*, edited by K. H. Richards, 75–95. Chico, CA: Scholars Press.

———. "Opening Statement." In *The Resurrection of Jesus: John Dominic Crossan and N. T. Wright in Dialogue*, edited by Robert B. Stewart. Minneapolis: Fortress, 2006.

———. *The Resurrection of the Son of God*. Vol. 3 of Christian Origins and the Question of God. Minneapolis: Fortress, 2003.

——. "Towards a Third 'Quest'? Jesus Then and Now." *ARC* 10, no. 1 (1982): 20–27.

——. *Surprised by Hope: Rethinking Heaven, the Resurrection, and the Mission of the Church.* New York: Harper Collins, 2008.

——, and Stephen Neill. *The Interpretation of the New Testament: 1861–1986.* 2nd ed. Oxford: Oxford University Press, 1988.

Yamauchi, Edwin M. *Pre-Christian Gnosticism: A Survey of the Proposed Evidences.* Grand Rapids, MI: Baker, 1983; repr., Eugene, OR: Wipf and Stock, 2003.

BOOKS

Anderson, Charles C. *Critical Quests of Jesus.* Grand Rapids: William B. Eerdman's Publishing Company, 1969.

——. *The Historical Jesus: A Continuing Quest.* Grand Rapids: William B. Eerdman's Publishing Company, 1972.

Anderson, J. N. D. *Christianity and Comparative Religion.* Downers Grove: InterVarsity Press, 1974.

——. *Christianity: The Witness of History.* London: Tyndale Press, 1969.

Barclay, William. *The Mind of Jesus.* New York: Harper & Row, 1961.

Barnes, Wesley. *The Philosophy and Literature of Existentialism.* Woodbury: Barron's Educational Series, 1968.

Barth, Karl. *Anselm: Fides Quarens Intellectum.* Translated by Ian W. Robertson. Richmond: John Knox Press, 1960.

——. *Dogmatics in Outline.* Translated by G. T. Thompson. New York: Harper & Row, 1959.

——. *How I Changed My Mind.* Richmond: John Knox Press, 1966.

——. *The Doctrine of Reconciliation.* Vol. 4, part 1 of *Church Dogmatics.* Edited by G. W. Bromily and T. F. Torrence. 13 vols. Edinburgh: T. & T. Clark, 1961.

——. *The Faith of the Church.* Edited by Jean-Louis Leuba. Translated by Gabriel Vahanian. New York: Meridian Books, 1958.

——. *Theology and Church: Shorter Writings 1920–1928.* Translated by Louise Pettibone Smith. New York: Harper & Row, 1962.

——. *The Resurrection of the Dead.* Translated by H. J. Stenning. New York: Fleming H. Revell Company, 1933.

——. *The Word of God and the Word of Man*. Translated by Douglas Horton. New York: Harper & Brothers, 1957.

Barth, Markus, and Verne H. Fletcher. *Acquittal by Resurrection*. New York: Holt, Rinehart and Winston, 1964.

Becker, Carl L. *The Heavenly City of the Eighteenth-Century Philosophers*. New Haven: Yale University Press, 1969.

Benoît, Pierre. *Jesus and the Gospel*. Translated by Benet Weatherhead. New York: Seabury, 1973.

——, and Roland Murphy. *Immortality and Resurrection*. New York: Herder and Herder, 1970.

Berger, Peter L. *A Rumor of Angels*. Garden City: Doubleday and Company, 1969.

Bishop, Jim. *The Day Christ Died*. New York: Harper & Row, 1965.

Blaikie, Robert J. *"Secular Christianity" and God Who Acts*. Grand Rapids: William B. Eerdman's Publishing Company, 1970.

Blüh, Otto, and Elder, Joseph Denison. *Principles and Applications of Physics*. New York: Interscience Publishers, 1955.

Bonhoeffer, Dietrich. *Christ the Center*. Translated by John Bowden. New York: Harper & Row, 1966.

Boring, Edwin G., Herbert S. Langfield, and Harry P. Weld, eds. *Foundations of Psychology*. New York: John Wiley and Sons, 1956.

Bornkamm, Günther. *Jesus of Nazareth*. Translated by Irene and Fraser McLuskey with James M. Robinson. New York: Harper & Row, 1960.

Braaten, Carl. *History and Hermeneutics*. Vol. 2 of *New Directions in Theology Today*. Edited by William Hordern. 7 vols. Philadelphia: The Westminster Press, 1966.

Bronowski, J. and Bruce Mazlish. *The Western Intellectual Tradition*. New York: Harper & Row, 1962.

Brown, Delwin, Ralph E. James, and Gene Reeves, eds. *Process Philosophy and Christian Thought*. Indianapolis: The Bobbs-Merrill Company, 1971.

Brown, James. *Kierkegaard, Heidegger, Buber and Barth*. New York: Collier Books, 1967.

Brown, Raymond E. *New Testament Essays*. Milwaukee: The Bruce Publishing Company, 1965.

——. *The Virginal Conception and Bodily Resurrection of Jesus*. New York: Paulist Press, 1973.

Bibliography

277

Bruce, F. F. *Jesus and Christian Origins Outside the New Testament*. Grand Rapids: William B. Eerdman's Publishing Company, 1974.

———. *The New Testament Documents: Are They Reliable?* 5th ed. Grand Rapids: William B. Eerdman's Publishing Company, 1967.

Brunner, Emil. *The Christian Doctrine of Creation and Redemption*. Vol. 2 of *Dogmatics*. Translated by Olive Wyon. 3 vols. Philadelphia: The Westminster Press, 1952.

———. *The Mediator*. Translated by Olive Wyon. Philadelphia: The Westminster Press, 1947.

Bulfinch, Thomas. *The Age of Fable*. Greenwich: Fawcett Publications, 1961.

Bultmann, Rudolf. *History and Eschatology*. New York: Harper & Row, 1962.

———. *Jesus Christ and Mythology*. New York: Charles Scribner's Sons, 1958.

———. *Theology of the New Testament*. Two volumes in one. Translated by Kendrick Grobel. New York: Charles Scribner's Sons, 1951.

Burtt, Edwin A. *Types of Religious Philosophy*. Rev. ed. New York: Harper & Row, 1939.

Cassels, Louis. *Christian Primer*. Garden City: Doubleday and Company, 1967.

———. *This Fellow Jesus*. New York: Pyramid Publications, 1973.

Cassirer, Ernst. *Determinism and Indeterminism in Modern Physics*. Translated by O. Theodor Benfrey. New Haven: Yale University Press, 1956.

Clough, Shepard B., Nina G. Garsoian, and David L. Hicks. *Ancient and Medieval*. Vol. 1 of *A History of the Ancient World*. 3 vols. Boston: D. C. Heath and Company, 1967.

Cullmann, Oscar, Harry A. Wolfson, Werner Jaeger, and Henry J. Cadbury. *Immortality and Resurrection*. New York: The Macmillan Company, 1965.

Cutten, George Barton. *Speaking with Tongues Historically and Psychologically Examined*. New Haven: Yale University Press, 1927.

Dobson, C. C. *The Empty Tomb and the Risen Lord*. 2nd ed. London: Marshall, Morgan and Scott, n.d.

Dray, William H., ed. *Philosophical Analysis and History*. New York: Harper & Row, 1966.

Earle, Edward M., ed. *Makers of Modern Strategy*. Princeton: Princeton University Press, 1943.

Eliade, Mircea. *Mephistopheles and the Androgyne: Studies in Religious Myth and Symbol*. Translated by J. M. Cohen. New York: Sheed and Ward, 1965.

——. *Myth and Reality*. Translated by William R. Task. New York: Harper & Row, 1963.

——. *The Quest: History and Meaning in Religion*. Chicago: The University of Chicago Press, 1969.

Evans, C. F. *Resurrection and the New Testament*. Vol. 12 of *Studies in Biblical Theology*, second series. Naperville: Alec R. Allenson, 1970.

Finley, M. I. *The World of Odysseus*. New York: The Viking Press, 1954.

Fuller, Daniel P. *Easter Faith and History*. Grand Rapids: William B. Eerdman's Publishing Company, 1965.

Fuller, Reginald. *The Formation of the Resurrection Narratives*. New York: The Macmillan Company, 1971.

Gaebelein, Frank E., ed. *Christianity Today*. Westwood: Fleming H. Revell Company, 1968.

Gilson, Etienne. *Reason and Revelation in the Middle Ages*. New York: Charles Scribner's Sons, 1966.

Grant, Robert M. *A Historical Introduction to the New Testament*. London: Collins, 1963.

——. *Miracle and Natural Law*. Amsterdam: North-Holland Publishing Company, 1952.

Hamilton, William. *The Modern Reader's Guide to John*. New York: Association Press, 1959.

——. *The New Essence of Chritianity*. New York: Association Press, 1961.

Harnack, Adolf. *What is Christianity?* Translated by Thomas Bailey Saunders. 3rd ed. London: Williams and Norgate, 1912.

Hartwell, Herbert. *The Theology of Karl Barth*. London: Gerald Duckworth and Company, 1964.

Heick, O. W. *History of Protestant Theology*. Vol. 2 of *A History of Christian Thought* by J. L. Neve. 2 vols. Philadelphia: The Muhlenberg Press, 1946.

Henry, Carl F. H., ed. *Jesus of Nazareth: Saviour and Lord*. Grand Rapids: William B. Eerdman's Publishing Company, 1966.

Hooke, S. H. *Middle Eastern Mythology*. Baltimore: Penguin Books, 1966.

Hordern, William. *A Layman's Guide to Protestant Theology*. New York: The Macmillan Company, 1956.

——. *Introduction*. Vol. 1 of *New Directions in Theology Today*. Edited by William Hordern. 7 vols. Philadelphia: The Westminster Press, 1966.

Hume, David. *An Abstract of a Treatise of Human Nature.* Cambridge: The University Press, 1938.

——. *A Treatise of Human Nature.* Edited by L. A. Selby-Bigge. Oxford: The Clarendon Press, 1964.

——. *Essays, Literary, Moral and Political.* London: Ward, Lock and Bowden, n.d.

——. *The Essential Works of David Hume.* Edited by Ralph Cohen. New York: Bantam Books, 1965.

——. *The History of England.* 6 vols. London: Gilbert and Revington, 1848.

Hunter, Archibald M. *Introducing the New Testament.* 2nd ed. Philadelphia: The Westminster Press, 1957.

James, William. *The Principles of Psychology.* 2 vols. New York: Dover Publications, 1950.

Jauncey, James. *Science Returns to God.* Grand Rapids: Zondervan, 1966.

Johnson, Howard A., and Niels Thulstrup, eds. *A Kierkegaard Critique.* Chicago: Henry Regnery Company, 1962.

Kant, Immanuel. *Religion Within the Limits of Reason Alone.* Translated by Theodore M. Greene and Hoyt H. Hudson. New York: Harper & Row, 1960.

Kaufman, Gordon. *Systematic Theology: A Historicist Perspective.* New York: Charles Scribner's Sons, 1968.

Kierkegaard, Søren. *Attack Upon "Christendom."* Translated by Walter Lowrie. Princeton: Princeton University Press, 1972.

——. *Concluding Unscientific Postscript.* Translated by David Swenson. Princeton: Princeton University Press, 1974.

——. *Philosophical Fragments.* Translated by David Swenson. Princeton: Princeton University Press, 1974.

——. *The Point of View for My Work as an Author.* Edited by Benjamin Nelson. Translated by Walter Lowrie. New York: Harper & Row, 1962.

King, Marie Gentert, ed. *Foxe's Book of Martyrs.* Westwood: Fleming H. Revell Company, 1968.

Kuhn, Thomas S. *The Structure of Scientific Revolutions.* Vol. 2, no. 2 of the *International Encyclopedia of Unified Science.* Edited by Otto Neurath, Rudolf Carnap, and Charles King. Chicago: The University of Chicago Press, 1971.

Ladd, George Eldon. *I Believe in the Resurrection of Jesus*. Grand Rapids: William B. Eerdman's Publishing Company, 1975.

Lessing, Gotthold E. *Lessing's Theological Writings*. Edited by Henry Chadwick. London: Adam and Charles Black, 1956.

Lewis, C. S. *God in the Dock*. Edited by Walter Hooper. Grand Rapids: William B. Eerdman's Publishing Company, 1973.

——. *Miracles*. New York: The Macmillan Company, 1965.

Lightfoot, J. B., ed. and trans. *The Apostolic Fathers*. Grand Rapids: Baker Book House, 1971.

Locke, John. *The Reasonableness of Christianity*. Edited by I. T. Ramsey. Stanford: Stanford University Press, 1958.

Machen, J. Gresham. *Christianity and Liberalism*. Grand Rapids: William B. Eerdman's Publishing Company, 1923.

Macquarrie, John. *An Existentialist Theology*. New York: Harper & Row, 1965.

Maier, Paul L. *First Easter*. New York: Harper & Row, 1973.

Marty, Martin C., and Dean G. Peerman. *A Handbook of Christian Theologians*. Cleveland: World Publishing Company, 1965.

Marxsen, Morris. *The Resurrection of Jesus of Nazareth*. Translated by Margret Kohl. Philadelphia: Fortress Press, 1970.

Mazlish, Bruce. *The Riddle of History: The Great Speculators from Vico to Freud*. New York: Harper & Row, 1966.

McDowell, Josh. *Evidence that Demands a Verdict*. San Bernadino: Campus Crusade for Christ International, n.d.

McKelway, Alexander J. *The Systematic Theology of Paul Tillich*. New York: Dell Publishing Company, 1964.

McLeman, James. *Resurrection Then and Now*. Philadelphia and New York: J. B. Lippincott Company, 1967.

McNaugher, John. *Jesus Christ the Same Yesterday, Today and Forever*. New York: Fleming H. Revell Company, 1947.

Meeks, M. Douglas. *Origins of the Theology of Hope*. Philadelphia: Fortress Press, 1974.

Miller, Laurence. *Jesus Christ Is Alive*. Boston: W. A. Wilde, 1949.

Moltmann, Jürgen. *Religion, Revolution and the Future*. Translated by M. Douglas Meeks. New York: Charles Scribner's Sons, 1969.

——. *Theology of Hope*. Translated by James W. Leitch. New York: Harper & Row, 1967.

Montgomery, John Warwick. *History and Christianity*. Downers Grove: InterVarsity Press, 1972.

———. *The Shape of the Past: An Introduction to Philosophical Historiography*. Ann Arbor: Edwards Brothers, 1962.

———. *The Suicide of Christian Theology*. Minneapolis: Bethany Fellowship, 1970.

———. *Where Is History Going?* Grand Rapids: Zondervan, 1969.

———, and Thomas J. J. Altizer. *The Altizer-Montgomery Dialogue*. Chicago: InterVarsity Press, 1967.

Moore, W. Edgar. *Creative and Critical Thinking*. Boston: Houghton Mifflin Company, 1967.

Morison, Frank. *Who Moved the Stone?* London: Faber and Faber, 1962.

Morris, Henry. *Many Infallible Proofs*. San Diego: Creation-Life Publishers, 1974.

Morris, William, ed. *The American Heritage Dictionary of the English Language*. New York: American Heritage Publishing Company, 1970.

Mowinckel, Sigmund. *The Old Testament as Word of God*. Translated by Reidar B. Bjornard. Nashville: Abingdon Press, 1959.

Niebuhr, Reinhold. *Faith and History*. New York: Charles Scribner's Sons, 1949.

Ogden, Schubert M. *Christ Without Myth*. New York: Harper & Row, 1961.

———. *The Reality of God and Other Essays*. New York: Harper & Row, 1966.

Olsen, Viggo. *The Agnostic Who Dared to Search*. Chicago: Moody Press, 1974.

Orr, James. *The Resurrection of Jesus*. Grand Rapids: Zondervan, 1965.

Pamphilus, Eusebius. *Ecclesiastical History*. Translated by Christian Frederick Cruse. Grand Rapids: Baker Book House, 1969.

Pannenberg, Wolfhart. *Basic Questions in Theology*. Translated by George H. Kehm. 2 vols. Philadelphia: Fortress Press, 1972.

———. *Jesus—God and Man*. Translated by Lewis L. Wilkens and Duane A. Priebe. Philadelphia: The Westminster Press, 1968.

———, ed. *Revelation as History*. Translated by David Granskou. New York: The Macmillan Company, 1968.

———. *Theology and the Kingdom of God*. Edited by Richard John Neuhaus. Philadelphia: The Westminster Press, 1969.

Perkins, Robert L. *Søren Kierkegaard*. Richmond: John Knox Press, 1969.

Perrin, Norman. *What is Redaction Criticism?* Edited by Daniel O. Via. Philadelphia: Fortress Press, 1971.

Pfleiderer, Otto. *Philosophy and Development of Religion.* 2 vols. Edinburgh: William Blackwood and Sons, 1894.

———. *Primitive Christianity.* Translated by W. Montgomery. 4 vols. Clifton: Reference Book Publishers, 1965.

———. *The Early Christian Conception of Christ.* London: Williams and Norgate, 1905.

Ramm, Bernard. *A Handbook of Contemporary Theology.* Grand Rapids: William B. Eerdman's Publishing Company, 1966.

———. *Protestant Christian Evidences.* Chicago: Moody Press, 1953.

Ramsey, A. M. *The Resurrection of Christ.* 2nd ed. London: Collins, 1965.

Randall, John Herman, Jr. *The Making of the Modern Mind.* Rev. ed. Boston: Houghton Mifflin Company, 1940.

Renan, Ernst. *Life of Jesus.* Vol. 1 of *The History of the Origins of Christianity.* No translator given. London: Mathieson and Company, n.d.

Revised Standard Version of the Bible. New York: Thomas Nelson & Sons, 1946, 1952.

Ricoeur, Paul. *History and Truth.* Translated by Charles A. Kelbley. Evanston: Northwestern University Press, 1965.

Robertson, Archibald T. *Word Pictures in the New Testament.* 6 vols. Nashville: Broadman Press, 1931.

Robinson, John A. T. *Exploration Into God.* Stanford: Stanford University Press, 1967.

———. *Honest to God.* Philadelphia: The Westminster Press, 1963.

Runes, Dagobert, ed. *Dictionary of Philosophy.* Totowa: Littlefield, Adams and Company, 1967.

Santoni, Ronald, ed. *Religious Language and the Problem of Religious Knowledge.* Bloomington: Indiana University Press, 1968.

Schaaffs, Werner. *Theology, Physics and Miracles.* Translated by Richard L. Renfield. Washington, DC: Canon Press, 1974.

Schaeffer, Francis. *Escape from Reason.* Downers Grove: InterVarsity Press, 1968.

———. *The Church Before the Watching World.* Downers Grove: InterVarsity Press, 1971.

———. *The God Who Is There.* Downers Grove: InterVarsity Press, 1968.

Schleiermacher, Friedrich. *On Religion: Speeches to Its Cultured Despisers.* Translated by John Oman. New York: Harper & Brothers, 1958.

——. *The Christian Faith*. Edited by H. R. Mackintosh and J. S. Stewart. 2 vols. New York: Harper & Row, 1963.

Schonfield, Hugh. *The Passover Plot*. New York: Bantam Books, 1967.

Schweitzer, Albert. *The Quest of the Historical Jesus*. Translated by W. Montgomery. New York: The Macmillan Company, 1971.

Shestov, Lev. *Athens and Jerusalem*. Translated by Bernard Martin. Ohio University Press, 1966.

Smith, Wilbur M. *The Supernaturalness of Christ*. Boston: W. A. Wilde, 1954.

Sparrow-Simpson, W. J. *The Resurrection and the Christian Faith*. Grand Rapids: Zondervan, 1965.

Spinoza, Benedict. *The Chief Works of Benedict de Spinoza*. Translated by R. H. M. Elwes. 2 vols. New York: Dover Publications, 1951.

Stagg, Frank, E. Glenn Hinton, and Wayne E. Oates. *Glossolalia: Tongue Speaking in Biblical, Historical, and Psychological Perspective*. Nashville: Abingdon Press, 1967.

Stone, Ronald J. *Reinhold Niebuhr: Prophet to Politicians*. Nashville: Abingdon Press, 1972.

Stott, John R. W. *Basic Christianity*. Chicago: InterVarsity Press, 1965.

——. *Your Mind Matters: The Place of the Mind in the Christian Life*. Downers Grove: InterVarsity Press, 1973.

Strauss, David Friedrich. *A New Life of Jesus*. No translator given. 2nd ed. 2 vols. London: Williams and Norgate, 1879.

——. *The Old Faith and the New*. Translated by Mathilde Blind. 2 vols. New York: Henry Holt and Company, 1874.

Swinburne, Richard. *The Concept of Miracle*. London: The Macmillan Company and St. Martin's Press, 1970.

Tenney, Merrill C. *The Reality of the Resurrection*. New York: Harper & Row, 1963.

Thomas, Owen C., ed. *Attitudes Toward Other Religions*. New York: Harper & Row, 1969.

Throckmorton, Burton H. *The New Testament and Mythology*. Philadelphia: The Westminster Press, 1959.

Tillich, Paul. *Systematic Theology*. 3 vols. Chicago: The University of Chicago Press, 1971.

Tomlin, E. W. F. *The Western Philosophers*. New York: Harper & Row, 1967.

Urs von Balthasar, Hans. *The Theology of Karl Barth.* Translated by John Drury.
        New York: Holt, Rinehart and Winston, 1971.

Van Buren, Paul M. *The Secular Meaning of the Gospel.* New York: The
        Macmillan Company, 1963.

Vine, W. E. *An Expository Dictionary of New Testament Words.* Four volumes in
        one. Old Tappan: Fleming H. Revell Company, 1966.

Walsh, W. H. *Philosophy of History.* New York: Harper & Brothers, 1960.

Wand, William. *Christianity: A Historical Religion?* Valley Forge: Judson Press,
        1972.

Weiss, Johannes. *Earliest Christianity: A History of the Period A.D. 30–150.*
        Edited by Frederick C. Grant. 2 vols. Magnolia: Peter Smith,
        Publishers, 1959.

Wells, H. G. *The Outline of History.* 2 vols. Garden City: Garden City Books,
        1949.

ARTICLES, BOOKLETS, AND ESSAYS

Anderson, J. N. D. *The Evidence for the Resurrection.* Downers Grove:
        InterVarsity Press, 1966.

Berlin, Sir Isaac. "The Concept of Scientific History." In *Philosophical Analysis
        and History*, edited by William H. Dray. New York: Harper & Row,
        1966.

Brauch, Manfred. "Head and Heart Go to Seminary." *Christianity Today* 19, no.
        19 (June 10, 1975): 11–12.

Brown, Raymond E. "The Resurrection and Biblical Criticism." *Commonweal*
        (November 24, 1967): 32–36.

Bultmann, Rudolf. "New Testament and Mythology." In *Kerygma and Myth*,
        edited by Hans Werner Bartsch and translated by Reginald H. Fuller.
        New York: Harper & Row, 1961.

———. "The Study of the Synoptic Gospels." In *Form Criticism*, translated by
        Frederick C. Grant. New York: Harper & Row, 1962.

Chamberlain, Nelson R. "Jürgen Moltmann: Apostle of Christian Hope?"
        Christianity Today 18, no. 19 (June 21, 1974): 6–10.

Clark, Gordon H. "Bultmann's Three-Storied Universe." In *Christianity Today*,
        edited by Frank E. Gaebelein. Westwood: Fleming H. Revell Company,
        1968.

Collins, James. "Faith and Reflection in Kierkegaard." In *A Kierkegaard Critique*, edited by Howard A. Johnson and Niels Thulstrup. Chicago: Henry Regnery Company, 1962.

Dodson, Daniel. "What is 'Myth'?" In *The Age of Fable* by Thomas Bulfinch. Greenwich: Fawcett Publications, 1961.

Feibleman, James K. "Myth." In *Dictionary of Philosophy*, edited by Dagobert Runes. Totowa: Littlefield, Adams and Company, 1967.

Ferm, Vergilius. "Deism." In *Dictionary of Philosophy*, edited by Dagobert Runes. Totowa: Littlefield, Adams and Company, 1967.

Fey, Harold E. "Apocalypse at Easter." *Christian Century* 90, no. 16 (April 1973): 453–54.

Gardiner, Patrick. "The Philosophy of History." Vol. 6 of *The International Encyclopedia of the Social Sciences*, edited by David L. Sills. The Macmillan Company and The Free Press, 1968.

Gilmour, S. MacLean. "Luke—Introduction." Vol. 8 of *The Interpreter's Bible*, edited by George Arthur Buttrick. 12 vols. Nashville: Abingdon-Cokesbury Press, 1951–1956.

Hamilton, Peter N. "Some Proposals for a Modern Christology." *Process Philosophy and Christian Thought*. Edited by Delwin Brown, Ralph E. James, Jr., and Gene Reeves. Indianapolis: The Bobbs-Merrill Company, 1971.

Heinecken, Martin J. "Søren Kierkegaard." In *A Handbook of Christian Theologians*, edited by Martin C. Marty and Dean G. Peerman. Cleveland: The World Publishing Company, 1965.

Hick, John. "Theology and Verification." In *Religious Language and the Problem of Religious Knowledge*, edited by Ronald E. Santoni. Bloomington: Indiana University Press, 1968.

Howard, Wilbert F. "John—Introduction." Vol. 8 of *The Interpreter's Bible*, edited by George Arthur Buttrick. 12 vols. Nashville: Abingdon-Cokesbury Press, 1951–1956.

Hudson, R. Lofton. "What One Easter Meant to Me." *Christian Century* 90, no. 16 (April 1973): 450–51.

Johnson, William Hallock. "The Keystone of the Arch." *Theology Today* 6, no. 1 (1949/1950): 12–24.

Johnson, Sherman E. "Matthew—Introduction." Vol. 7 of *The Interpreter's Bible*, edited by George Arthur Buttrick. 12 vols. Nashville: Abingdon-Cokesbury Press, 1951–1956.

Knapp, James F. "Myth in the Powerhouse of Change." *The Centennial Review* 20, no. 1 (Winter 1976): 56–74.

Loomer, Bernard M. "Christian Faith and Process Philosophy." In *Process Philosophy and Christian Thought*, edited by Delwin Brown, Ralph E. James, Jr., and Gene Reeves. Indianapolis: The Bobbs-Merrill Company, 1971.

Maier, Paul L. "The Empty Tomb as History." *Christianity Today* 19, no. 13 (March 28, 1975): 4–6.

———. "Who Was Responsible for the Trial and Death of Jesus?" *Christianity Today* 18, no. 14 (April 12, 1974): 8–11.

Martin, Lawrence E. "The Risen Christ." *Christian Century* 90, no. 20 (May 1973): 577.

McDermott, Brian O., SJ. "Pannenberg's Resurrection Christology: A Critique." *Theological Studies* 35, no. 4 (December 1974): 711–21.

Nagel, Ernest. "Determinism in History." In *Philosophical Analysis and History*, edited by William H. Dray. New York: Harper & Row, 1966.

Ogden, Schubert. "Toward a New Theism." In *Process Philosophy and Christian Thought*, edited by Delwin Brown, Ralph E. James, Jr., and Gene Reeves. Indianapolis: The Bobbs-Merrill Company, 1971.

Pinnock, Clark. "On the Third Day." In *Jesus of Nazareth: Saviour and Lord*, edited by Carl F. H. Henry. Grand Rapids: William B. Eerdman's Publishing Company, 1966.

Rendtorff, Rolf. "The Concept of Revelation in Ancient Israel." In *Revelation as History*, edited by Wolfhart Pannenberg. New York: The Macmillan Company, 1968.

Smith, Robert W. "Should the Christian Argue?" *Christianity Today* 18, no. 10 (February 15, 1974): 14–18.

Steiger, Lothar. "Revelation-History and Theological Reason: Critique of the Theology of Wolfhart Pannenberg." In *History and Hermeneutic*, vol. 4 of *Journal for Theology and the Church*, edited by Robert W. Funk and Gerhard Ebeling. New York: Harper & Row, 1967.

Turner, Victor. "Myth and Symbol." Vol. 10 of *The International Encyclopedia of the Social Sciences*, edited by David L. Sills. The Macmillan Company and The Free Press, 1968.

VanderMolen, Ronald. " 'Where Is History Going?' and Historical Scholarship: A Response." *Fides et Historia* 5, nos. 1–2 (1972/1973): 109–12.

Wright, G. Ernest. "The Book of Numbers." Vol. 2 of *The Interpreter's Bible*, edited by George Arthur Buttrick. 12 vols. Nashville: Abingdon-Cokesbury Press, 1951–1956.

Yamauchi, Edwin M. "Easter—Myth, Hallucination or History?" *Christianity Today* 18, no. 12 (March 15, 1974): 4–7; and 18, no. 12 (March 29, 1974): 12–16 (two parts).

Index of Subjects and Persons

Index of Scripture

Old Testament

New Testament

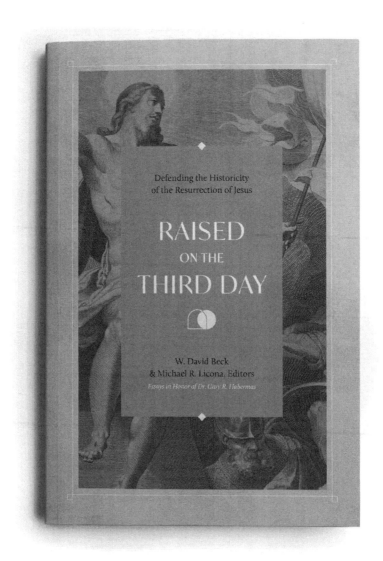

Defending the Historicity
of the Resurrection of Jesus

RAISED
ON THE
THIRD DAY

W. David Beck
& Michael R. Licona, Editors
Essays in Honor of Dr. Gary R. Habermas

ALSO AVAILABLE FROM LEXHAM PRESS

Raised on the Third Day: Defending the Historicity of the Resurrection of Jesus

—

Visit lexhampress.com to learn more